A PRAGMATIC APPROACH TO BUSINESS ETHICS

To
Ruth and Gord Kaufman, Don Ewing,
Peter Cameron, Don Kaufman, and Susan Neath,
who shared my dream of a compassionate community
and also shared the work required to
make the dream come true.

A PRAGMATIC
APPROACH
TO BUSINESS
ETHICS

ALEX C. MICHALOS

SAGE Publications
International Educational and Professional Publisher
Thousand Oaks   London   New Delhi

For information address:

SAGE Publications, Inc.
2455 Teller Road
Thousand Oaks, California 91320

SAGE Publications Ltd.
6 Bonhill Street
London EC2A 4PU
United Kingdom

SAGE Publications India Pvt. Ltd.
M-32 Market
Greater Kailash I
New Delhi 110 048 India

Printed in the United States of America

Library of Congress Cataloging-in-Publication Data

Michalos, Alex C.
    A pragmatic approach to business ethics / Alex C. Michalos
        p.   cm.
    Includes bibliographical references and index.
    ISBN 0-8039-7084-6 (alk. paper).—ISBN 0-8039-7085-4 (pbk.:
alk. paper)
    1. Business ethics.   I. Title.
HF5387.M52   1995
174'.4—dc20   94-45244

This book is printed on acid-free paper.

95 96 97 98 99 10 9 8 7 6 5 4 3 2 1

Sage Production Editor: Tricia K. Bennett
Sage Typesetter: Andrea D. Swanson

Contents

Introduction

The trouble with pragmatists is that they will get in bed with anyone. At least that has been the main complaint against them since the beginning of the 20th century. From a moral point of view, it is difficult to imagine a more devastating criticism. After all, although politics, prudence, or one's own self-interest narrowly defined might lead one to bunk down with strange bedfellows, human decency or morality requires considerably more. There must be some lines that a morally good person should not cross.

The defining characteristic of any sort of pragmatic philosophy is its emphasis on evaluating actions and beliefs on the basis of their consequences. But there is no generally accepted rule book to tell pragmatists which consequences are good and which are bad. So, pragmatism provides, at best, necessary but not sufficient guides to behavior. The bank robber, Willie Sutton, illustrated the moral bankruptcy of pragmatism when he said that he robbed banks because that is where we keep our money. The great American pragmatist, William James, would have been appalled by such a perversion of his philosophy. James was a relatively decent but apolitical human being who evaluated his actions and beliefs according to their contributions to sustaining other decent human beings. Some American pragmatists, like Sidney Hook, for example, leaned to the right or conservative side of the political spectrum. Some, like John Dewey, espoused relatively left of center or liberal political views. Still others, like myself and Deborah Poff, press pragmatism into the service of feminist and democratic socialist egalitarian ideals.

The trouble with business ethics is that many people think the phrase is an oxymoron. They hear it, giggle, and say things like, "You mean like military intelligence, eh?" In the chapters that follow, in a variety of ways, I will make it clear that the phrase is not an oxymoron. Here I will only say that the phrase refers to the application of ordinary ethical or moral principles of human action in businesses operating in a free or mixed market economy, such as Canada's. (I use the terms *ethical* and *moral* as synonyms.)

When I tell people that Deborah Poff and I have been editing the *Journal of Business Ethics* since 1980 and that for the past few years my introductory course in business ethics has averaged about 250 students per year, they often appear incredulous. What could one say about business ethics that would be useful, let alone believable? Besides, as one of my professors in Divinity School used to say, "Who cares about something that is good but not true?" It's easy to imagine a business student thinking it might be good to have such a course listed in his or her résumé, but it is more difficult to imagine such a student thinking that the content of the course might be true.

In light of these observations, the idea of a pragmatic approach to business ethics might seem both bizarre and dangerously plausible at the same time. It could be a marriage made in hell, a cross between the morally impaired and the logically impossible. One might suspect that the idea is likely neither good nor true.

Contrary to some appearances and perhaps to your own presently held convictions, by the time you reach the end of this book you should be convinced of the truth of my belief that the idea of a pragmatic approach to business ethics is a good one. I will not try to convince you that such an approach is the only one, the only reasonable one, or the best one in any sense at all. I do think that it is the best approach, all things considered. As I will explain in the first chapter following this introduction, however, it is practically impossible to consider all things. Indeed, it is far from clear exactly what these things might be. That is why I am only willing to make the relatively modest claim that the approach is good. If I can make a reasonable case for the truth of this claim, that will be enough to satisfy me. More important, insofar as such a case can be made, that will provide one good foundation for business ethics, and one is all anyone needs. This is the paramount reason for putting this set of essays together under one cover.

All but 3 of the 11 chapters in this book have been published somewhere in some form. In order to have seen all of them, one would have had to consult about eight different books and journals covering a period of about 15 years. Because it is highly improbable that anyone has done that, it is highly probable that much of what is contained in this book will be new to most people. This is the second reason for this collection. Although I do not suppose that what is contained here will be my last words on business ethics, they will be nearly my last words on most of the particular topics addressed. This is my final reason for the collection.

The chapters have been presented not in the order of their historical appearance but rather in something like a logical order. Chapter 2 provides a detailed account of my pragmatic model of moral decision making and shows that this model is identical to the sort of model most people have for rational decision making, except for one feature. A version of this chapter was presented as a keynote address to an annual convention of the Canadian Evaluation Society, which is our country's premier professional association for management consultants specializing in program evaluation. By displaying the similarities of models of moral and rational decision making, I hoped to prove that one could not reasonably take only one of the models seriously. In effect, the reasonableness of a consultant's business practice stands or falls with the reasonableness of a consultant's morality, from a pragmatic moral point of view.

Traditionally, the structure of a philosophical treatise was designed along the following lines. One would begin by stating some thesis to be proved. Then one would list every possible objection to one's thesis and show that each objection was defective for one reason or another. Following this attempt to give the other side its due, one would list every possible reason for believing one's thesis to be true, review every possible criticism of these supporting reasons, and finally show that all the possible criticisms are also defective. This is the structure of a kind of cost-benefit analysis or pragmatic defense of one's thesis. If one could successfully do everything called for in it, then one certainly would establish one's thesis.

Following this introduction, there are three chapters constituting a pragmatic defense of the thesis that businesspeople, in their roles as businesspeople, ought (morally and rationally) to support business ethics. The first two give the other side its due by presenting every argument I could find that might lead a businessperson either to merely fail to support or to openly oppose the application of ordinary moral principles in business. Fourteen distinct arguments are evaluated, and each one is shown to be defective. One of these, which I call the Loyal Agent's Argument, is singled out for a more intensive analysis in Chapter 4, an essay by the same name.

Chapter 5 has never been published, although I have been explaining its contents to students for more than a decade. It contains analyses of two arguments, one of which I think is the best and the other the worst argument in defense of the thesis that businesspeople ought to support business ethics. I show first that the best argument I can think of still leaves something to be desired, which, unfortunately, I am unable to provide. Then I show that the most frequently used argument in defense of business ethics actually dangerously undermines the whole idea. Briefly, this is the argument that a businessperson ought to support business ethics because it is good business, that is, because it is profitable.

Because of their generality and relative timelessness, Chapters 2 through 5 may be regarded as providing the basic building blocks or foundation for a pragmatic approach to business ethics. The remaining seven chapters deal with fairly specific issues in considerable detail. In a better world these chapters would be much more time-dependent than they probably are in this world. In this world it is likely that most of the issues examined in these chapters will be live issues for the foreseeable future. If the chapters hit their mark, they should demonstrate collectively and individually that the approach recommended here has significant merit. Although the chapters on commercial polling, wealth taxation, tobacco promotion, and the arms trade arose out of perceived problems in Canada and offer solutions that are or hopefully could be useful to Canadians, virtually every industrial democracy has such problems and might find my proposed solutions useful.

Chapter 6 arose as a result of reading several papers in the research literature on these three areas (business, international security, and quality of life) all showing the same thing, namely, that most people do not trust most people and, what is even more interesting, that most people's lack of trust in others is not warranted by the evidence. My chapter provides an overview of the relevant literature, draws out some of its implications, and suggests some plausible explanatory hypotheses based on my pragmatic approach.

This is followed by Chapter 7, which deals with ethical considerations in commercial public opinion polling. Public opinion polls are an apparently permanent feature of Western democracies, becoming especially salient during election campaigns. They represent a public voice filtered through the special interests of some private enterprise. Elected officials, their supporters, and virtually anyone who pays any attention to news media cannot avoid paying attention to published polls. When they do, many important questions arise. How much attention should be paid to them and exactly how should one do it? Do they provide a scientific view of the General Will or merely a highly selective and crafted view of what some polling firm would like us to take as the

General Will? Should they be regulated or not regulated in the interests of strengthening democracy? My chapter provides a brief overview of some of the difficulties of getting reliable and valid poll data, evaluates a variety of arguments for and against banning the publication of commercial polls during election campaigns, and finally supports those who reject banning but insist on more stringent disclosure standards regarding particular features of published poll results.

Chapter 8 involves a discussion of three fairly distinct topics related to advertising, namely, subliminal ads, government ads for lotteries, and some arguments advertisers often use to defend their particular interests and role in a market economy. I think the most important part of this chapter is the part condemning the Canadian and provincial governments' practice of selling lottery tickets without publishing their estimated expected value. There is considerable and increasing evidence indicating that relatively poor and uneducated people are disproportionately represented among lottery ticket purchasers and, more important, that a high percentage of such people would not buy lottery tickets if they were fully informed of the estimated expected value of a ticket. Because Canadian provincial and federal government officials are certainly aware of this evidence, one can only assume that they are immoral parasites or that they have never taken the time to evaluate all of the consequences of their advertising. In either case, they continue to deserve our moral condemnation.

Chapter 9 arose initially as a result of a controversy in the city of Guelph over whether or not the city council should accept an offer of $700,000 from Imperial Tobacco Ltd. to help build a proposed civic center. Along with many other citizens, I offered the council my opinion in writing and did not expect to use the material again. However, shortly after I decided to put this collection of articles together, representatives of R. J. Reynolds Tobacco, Co. and Philip Morris International, Inc. informed the Canadian House of Commons Standing Committee on Health that "the Canadian government would be left to face huge compensation claims" to these companies if the government carried out its proposed plan to require plain packaging of all brands of cigarettes. Because the plain packaging plan seemed imminently reasonable to me and the threat from the tobacco manufacturers seemed outrageously presumptuous and offensive, I decided to include my views on the promotion of tobacco products.

Chapter 10 cuts to the very core of a market economy or the sort of democratic capitalism that characterizes Canada and other Western democracies. So far as business is concerned, the name of the economic game in these countries is increased accumulation and concentration of wealth, with all of its implied benefits for those who win the game. Unfortunately, where there are great concentrations of wealth supporting special privileges for a few people, there are usually also great numbers of underprivileged poor people. What is worse, such economic and political disparities undermine the institutions of democracy today and reduce the chances of developing a strong and free democracy in the future. My chapter reviews all the arguments for and against net wealth taxation, and shows that a strong case can be made for it. The fact that many businesspeople regard such taxation as an assault on the viability of market economies even though such industrial giants as Japan and Germany have had such taxation for many years indicates that a more pragmatic and less ideological approach to this issue must be taken.

Chapter 11 on the North American Free Trade Agreement (NAFTA) has not been published before. This agreement, like its predecessor, the Canada-United States Free Trade Agreement (CUSTA), was strongly advocated by the business communities in North America and strongly opposed by most labor, environmental, church, and women's organizations. Although the business communities had their way on both occasions, the last words on these deals have not been written. A variety of ethical, political, economic, and environmental issues were raised, and the consequences of implementing the deals will be felt for years to come. My chapter reviews some of the evidence regarding the predicted and actual consequences of CUSTA approximately 5 years after its implementation, and presents some of the arguments against the implementation of NAFTA. From a pragmatic moral point of view, these particular deals appear to be seriously defective and counterproductive for the sort of world in which most North Americans want to live. Hence, it is important for critics of the deals to remain vigilant, to continue to monitor the effects of the deals, and to press for significant changes or outright abrogation as the evidence mounts against them.

Chapter 12, the final chapter, is a detailed analysis of the case for reducing the production and export of military arms. Again, in a better world, such a case would not have to be made and remade over and over again. In this world, it does. Although Canada is a relatively minor player in the international arms market, it is not for lack of trying to be a major player. The Canadian government continues to aid our producers of military goods in selling them abroad, even to Third World governments who can ill afford them, and to profit from such commercial ventures. My chapter is an attempt to show that a full and fair assessment of all the benefits and costs of such ventures leads one to press for immediate and sustained reductions. It seems to me that if a pragmatic approach to business ethics failed to reach such a conclusion, it would prove that the approach was fatally flawed.

Finally, then, as I reflect on the chapters presented here, it is clear to me and I hope it will be clear to others who read these chapters, that many of the ethical problems arising in our mixed market economies are the result of some people's determination to make money no matter what it costs other people. Reasoned arguments may be relatively poor weapons to use in the fight against such evil, but they are the very least we should expect from proponents of business ethics. We cannot help beginning our lives in a world made by others, but with some effort and good luck, we might make it better than we found it. From a moral point of view, the effort is required from each of us and all our communities.

2

Ethical Considerations in Evaluation

The aim of this chapter is to explain one way of viewing the nature of and relationships among morality, rationality, politics, and evaluation. To tie these things together, I provide brief accounts of social indicators, knowledge, and objectivity. Obviously, some corners must be cut to cover all this ground in a short time, but the world is full of good things without corners.

The structure of the chapter is as follows. In section two the ideas of a moral point of view and moral or ethical actions are explained. Section three provides an account of social indicators of the quality of life, which are necessary ingredients in the definition of moral action. In section four, the Canadian Evaluation Society's sketch of the nature of evaluation is reviewed in order to have a generally acceptable and clear concept to connect to moral and rational action. On the basis of this sketch, in section five rational action is explained, followed in section six by explanations of rational and ethical evaluation. Section seven reveals a fundamental limitation of the analysis, and possibly of anyone's analysis of morality. Finally, I offer brief conclusions.

A MORAL POINT OF VIEW

The terms *ethics* and *morals* are used here as synonyms. What is morally good or evil is ethically good or evil, and vice versa. If something

AUTHOR'S NOTE: Adapted from "Ethical Considerations in Evaluation" by A. C. Michalos (1992). In *Canadian Journal of Program Evaluation*, 7, pp. 61-75. Used with permission from University of Calgary Press.

is morally or ethically good or evil, it is good or evil from a moral point of view. In the view adopted here, the institution of morality, and the ideas of moral goodness and evil, are human artifacts designed by human beings to serve a variety of purposes. One important purpose is the resolution of conflicts of interest without resort to civil or criminal law. Insofar as people are willing and able to perceive, judge, and act in accordance with a moral point of view, morality exists. If people stop caring, morality will cease to exist.

Because morality rests on the adoption of a moral point of view, the latter must be defined. Such a definition would be tantamount to the articulation of a principle or principles that may be used as a foundation for morality. Generally speaking, moral philosophers may be divided into two groups, depending on which of the following two principles they regard as the fundamental basis of morality.

1. *Principle of Beneficence:* One ought to act so that one's actions tend to impartially improve the quality of life.
2. *No-Harm Principle:* One ought to act so that one's actions tend not to harm anyone.

The principles are not exclusive, and there are other ways to express them. For example, what is here called the Principle of Beneficence might be expressed in terms of the impartial maximization of utility, happiness, satisfaction, or well-being. Theological ethicists might capture much of what is in this principle with their insistence on loving one's neighbor, and contemporary feminist ethicists' emphasis on care and nurturing might capture it from a slightly different point of view. Instead of a single No-Harm Principle, one might capture the same idea with a list of duties, freedoms, or rights. This is the moral significance of the United Nations Declaration of Human Rights and Freedoms and Canada's own Charter of Rights and Freedoms. For example, when nations or individuals grant that everyone has a right to life, they are implying that everyone else has a duty or a moral obligation to refrain from taking people's lives for the fun of it. They are creating moral codes as an immediate implication of their declarations. Although everything important about duties, rights, respect for persons, and so on, may not be captured in these two general principles, enough can be captured for present purposes.

As the principles are formulated, they refer to acts rather than to mere intentions to act in certain ways. Because people live in a complex world of interactive and interdependent things, they seldom, if ever, have complete control over what they do. The German philosopher Immanuel

TABLE 2.1 Possible States of Affairs

	Intention	Behavior	Consequences
1.	to improve	to improve	improves (the quality of life)
2.	to improve	to improve	destroys
3.	to improve	to destroy	improves
4.	to improve	to destroy	destroys
5.	to destroy	to improve	improves
6.	to destroy	to improve	destroys
7.	to destroy	to destroy	improves
8.	to destroy	to destroy	destroys

Kant was so impressed by people's inability to control external events that he occasionally (not always) claimed that only people's wills or intentions could be subject to moral appraisal. The Greek philosopher Aristotle was a bit more expansive. He recognized that every human action is usually characterizable in terms of an intention or motive, some physical behavior or content, and some consequences. For example, the writing of this chapter required the formulation of an intention to do so, some hours spent typing out the thoughts, and culminated in the product before you, for better or worse.

Assuming that each of the three aspects of an action might tend to improve or destroy the quality of life, every action implies one of eight possible states of affairs, as shown in Table 2.1.

Whether one agrees with Kant or not, the first and last of these eight cases leave no doubt about the moral praiseworthiness or blameworthiness of one's action. In the first case, one intends to do something to improve the quality of life, does something that might be expected to have such a result (gives bread to a starving person), and precisely such a result occurs. In the last case, one intends to do something to destroy the quality of life, does something that might be expected to have such a result (gives a stone to a starving person), and precisely such a result occurs. All (three) things considered, the first actor is clearly morally praiseworthy and the second is morally blameworthy.

Unfortunately, the other six cases are unclear. Depending on how creative one is and how one describes the intentions, behavior, and consequences, a particular actor and action might be morally good or bad. Although Kant might have said that a person acting in accordance with Cases 1 to 4 must be morally praiseworthy because in every case his or her intention is good, others might be skeptical. For example, people would be skeptical about someone if, although that person always reported having good intentions, he or she always behaved in ways that practically everyone could see would be counterproductive and, sure enough, always had disastrous results (Case 4). Some people would say this is a fair description of the actions of our former federal finance minister, Michael Wilson.

At any rate, the point of the previous three paragraphs was to indicate how complicated the statement of my fundamental moral principles might be, and to emphasize that the word *act* that appears in the statement is used to designate a fairly robust idea. Morality requires more than merely having good intentions. (Even more complications inherent in these principles are revealed below.)

There is probably no absolutely irrefutable argument leading to the conclusion that one or the other of these principles must be taken as fundamental. People operating primarily on the Principle of Beneficence will try to do as much good as possible. People operating primarily on the No-Harm Principle will try to do as little harm as possible. Personally, my preference is for universal beneficence because moral goodness ought to require more of people than a life of anxious inactivity mixed with pious hopes for our common future. Obviously, one cannot be expected to behave ideally all or even most of the time, with respect to morality or anything else. But that is not a serious objection to any ideal. If one has a choice about what sort of moral ideal one ought primarily to be guided by, what sort one ought to recommend to family, friends, and the rest of the human race, it is wise to aim high rather than low. So, universal beneficence is here regarded as more fundamental than the mere avoidance of intentional harm.

Contrary to the view of morality just sketched, there is the view that some questions, issues, or actions are not only inherently moral or ethical, but inherently morally or ethically good or evil. When Brian Mulroney talked about giving his caucus a free vote on the government's new abortion bill, he usually mentioned that he thought such a vote was appropriate because abortion was "a moral issue." Similarly, some people would say that telling the truth and keeping promises are also inherently morally good things to do or inherently morally right. A good example of an act that might be regarded as inherently morally evil is that of killing someone for the fun of it.

Those who hold the view that some things (actions, issues, etc.) have an inherent moral status and some things do not have such a status seem to have an easier moral road to walk. In principle, at least, they could prepare a list of moral prohibitions and prescriptions, and if some particular action or issue was not on the list, it would have no moral relevance. Regarding issues not on the list, morally speaking, anything goes. Some years ago, the British philosopher Bertrand Russell complained about the ethical views of the American philosopher John Dewey precisely because, as Russell said, Dewey left people with no moral holidays. Russell's assessment was absolutely accurate. According to the view adopted here, which follows that of Dewey, ethical or moral principles are constructs or artifacts designed by humans in the interest of building a good life, and everything is subject to appraisal in the light of such principles. So, there are no moral holidays.

Although there are no moral holidays, one's moral burdens are lighter on some days than on others as a result of the great variety of things that occupy people. For example, most of the itches that one scratches do not entail any significant alterations in the quality of anyone's life but one's own, though it is easy to imagine cases in which scratching some of one's itches in some ways, at certain times and places, could be highly significant from a moral point of view. It is even easier to imagine morally significant cases in which someone scratches someone else's itches or someone else scratches one's own itches, or cases in which people give each other an itch and engage in mutual scratching.

SOCIAL INDICATORS

Assuming that one is going to try to conduct one's human relations from a moral point of view as expressed in the Principle of Beneficence, there are, again broadly speaking, two ways to go. One can:

1. Try to improve relatively objective circumstances that are measured by things like full employment, cleaner and safer workplaces, equitable distributions of wealth and income, longer lives free of disability and disease, elimination of poverty and homelessness, and the reduction of crime.
2. Try to improve relatively subjective circumstances that are measured by people's reported peace of mind, contentment, happiness, and satisfaction.

Clearly, if one's relatively objective and subjective circumstances are improved, then the quality of one's life is improved. Since the fifth century B.C., people have haggled about what is objective, what is subjective, and which is more important. But it is evidently trivially true that if one's total circumstances are improved, one is better off and the quality of one's life has improved.

Social indicators are statistics that are supposed to have some significance for the quality of life. Statistical measures of relatively objective things, such as death rates, are referred to as *objective indicators* or indicators of objective well-being. Measures of relatively subjective states of affairs, such as personal satisfaction and happiness, are referred to as *subjective indicators* or indicators of subjective well-being. Thus, social indicators are measures of objective and subjective well-being. Speaking generally, they are the instruments, means, or technological software constructed in the interests of measuring the degrees to which we are realizing our various desired ends. Speaking specifically, they are one of the means by which one might hope to be able to identify and fulfill moral obligations.

Evaluation indicators, as the Treasury Board of Canada (1981) uses the term, are a subclass of social indicators. They might be regarded as social indicators used in evaluation studies.

EVALUATION

According to the Canadian Evaluation Society's (CES) (1989) pamphlet, *The Value in Evaluation,*

> Evaluation is a form of analysis undertaken to help managers make decisions about current or future projects, programs or initiatives. Evaluation helps managers determine how well projects are working and to identify reasons for success or failure . . . uses accepted research techniques in a systematic way to compile, organize and analyze information about the impact and effects of activities . . . [and] differs from other forms of analysis in that it concentrates on the links between an organization's mandate and the results achieved through its activities, rather than on financial or administrative systems and controls. (p. 2)

In response to the question, What constitutes good evaluation? the pamphlet says,

> Each evaluation calls on different skills and expertise, but several features distinguish quality in any evaluation research design: . . . skilled evaluators consult managers at every step, from planning to formulating recommendations, ensuring that evaluations address real concerns and managers are not surprised by results; . . . ethical research—respect for anonymity and confidentiality of data is paramount; . . . the evaluation is planned to supply information when needed and is completed on time; information is useful in both managing and decision making; . . . management receives balanced, independent assessments from evaluators with no direct stake in decisions resulting from evaluation findings. (p. 7)

This is a thought-provoking paragraph in many respects. No particular sort of goodness or point of view is mentioned in the question, What constitutes good evaluation? What is being asked for is the CES's view of what makes a good evaluation. But what sort of good is at stake? Presumably the question is not about what makes a morally good evaluation, or an economically or politically good evaluation. Is it sensible to suppose the question is about the nature of an evaluatively good evaluation, that is, an evaluation that is good from an evaluator's point of view, whatever that is? If so, the answer is roughly that an evaluatively good evaluation is one in which managers are frequently consulted, anonymity is protected, balanced assessments are made, and so on.

This seems to be the sort of thing that the authors of the pamphlet had in mind. In this paragraph and the rest of the pamphlet, evaluation is conceived along the lines of a logical positivist's view of autonomous science. A less sympathetic reader might say it is conceived along the lines of macho science. The phrase *evaluation science* never occurs in the text, but it is probably coming. The words that are most frequently used to characterize evaluators and evaluation are *objective, independent, rational, credible,* and *reliable.* The word *valid* belongs to this vocabulary, but is never used. The word *ethical* is used only once, in the fairly narrow context of protecting anonymity.

No doubt different members of the CES would have different views about just how objective, independent, rational, and so on, evaluators and evaluations can be. Here it is assumed that any claims to objectivity, independence, rationality, and moral goodness must be made with considerable caution. Strictly speaking, one can only approach objectivity, independence, and so on, as a limit, and one probably can't approach the limits very closely at that. At any rate, most of the rest of this chapter is connected to this claim.

To begin with, then, what turns mere opinion or belief into knowledge is that the latter is supported by good reasons or good arguments. Because good reasons and arguments are not self-identifying and self-certifying, to have such things there must be some sort of a community with the authority and wisdom required to establish the rules.

In science, what counts as a good reason or a good argument depends on what a relevant research community collectively negotiates and decides. Similarly, outside of science, what counts as a good reason or argument depends on what a broader community collectively agrees to count as such. Because there is no rule book to turn to in order to decide how people should write their rule books regarding the warranting or certification of knowledge claims, all that people can do is negotiate some agreements about how to proceed and then muddle through. Thus, the total corpus of the most sophisticated scientific knowledge is contingent on and relative to some set of negotiated agreements among a community of mere mortals. Therefore, what is confidently called "objective," "credible," and so forth, can at best only mean "relatively objective, given a certain set of assumptions," or "relative to some assumptions, objective."

If the argument in the previous paragraph is sound, then it is fair to say that all knowledge, including all scientific knowledge, rests on politics. At least it is fair to say this if one thinks of politics as the art and practice of reaching agreements through negotiation. Insofar as one thinks of evaluation along the lines indicated in the CES pamphlet, that is, as similar to science, it would also be fair to say that all evaluation rests on politics. Then, insofar as one undertakes an evaluation or engages in politics to impartially improve the quality of life, one is doing what one ought to do from a moral point of view. In other words, one is undertaking a morally good evaluation and engaging in morally good political action.

RATIONALITY

So far, definitions have been constructed for the terms *morality, ethics, moral point of view, social indicators, evaluation indicators, evaluation, politics,* and *morally good evaluation.* It has also been explained why claims to objectivity should be made with caution and modesty. Now the term *rationality* will be defined, and it will be explained why claims to rational evaluations should also be made with caution. More important, once these things have been explained, it will be possible to construct a lucid and useful connection between the ideas of rational and ethical evaluations.

Roughly speaking, an action is rational insofar as it produces benefits that are at least as great as its costs. On the contrary, an action is irrational insofar as its costs outweigh its benefits. In roughly other words, rational actions are at least self-sustaining or self-enhancing, whereas irrational actions are self-destroying. Briefly, rational actions have benefit-to-cost ratios equal to or greater than unity ($B/C \geq 1$), and irrational actions have benefit-to-cost ratios less than unity ($B/C < 1$).

These ideas will be recognized as similar to economic definitions of efficient and inefficient actions, with perhaps one immediately notable difference—that economists often reserve the term *efficient* as an honorific title of the single relevant action with the maximum benefit-to-cost ratio. In Michalos (1978), arguments were constructed against policies of maximization on the one hand and Herbert Simon's satisficing on the other, on the grounds that the former demanded too much and the latter demanded too little. There is no need to repeat those arguments here.

If these rough definitions sound plausible as far as they go, then the rest of this section should be worthwhile. If your understanding of rationality is radically different from that outlined above, then from here on things are going to get worse.

The rough definitions of rational and irrational actions that were just sketched must be polished to be useful for measurement. In particular, one must specify the following.

1. *Recipient Populations:* Exactly whose benefits and costs must be counted? Broadly speaking, one's options run from a single actor or client, through some selected subsets of individuals more or less likely to be affected by one's actions, to everyone likely to be affected by one's actions.

2. *Temporal Coordinates:* Within what time frame should one count? How far back in the past should one look, how far forward in the future, and what duration of time counts as the present?

3. *Spatial Coordinates:* Within what spatial frame should one count? Should one focus attention on one's own house, one's firm, town, city, province, region, country, the western hemisphere, or the whole world?

4. *Benefit and Cost Composition:* Which particular benefits and costs should one count? Should one focus on economics, money, inflation rates, unemployment rates, politics, victory in elections, social welfare, the environment, energy conservation, health, aesthetics, art, tourism, intellectual or educational achievement, poverty, peace of mind, happiness, satisfaction, trust, transportation, or indigenous research and development? All things considered, is there a single best choice of types of benefits and costs to calculate in order to judge rationality?

5. *Measures:* Which particular measures of benefits and costs should one count? Supposing one could pick out the appropriate set of types of benefits and costs, one is still left with the task of constructing appropriate measures. Should one prefer ordinal scales or cardinal scales, relatively objective or subjective measures, single-item measures or multiple-item indexes?

6. *Confidence Levels:* What levels of confidence should one have before one accepts any information or claim as true? Does rationality require a 99% confidence level, more or less, and if so, on what grounds? When survey research is employed, what error margins should be posited for sampling and nonsampling errors? Because there are no generally accepted estimating functions for nonsampling errors, where should one begin to choose an appropriate function? How will one identify a rational choice here?

7. *Research Procedures:* What research procedures should be used to obtain measurements? This discussion reveals a bias in favor of quantitative

research, but such research is frequently shallow, narrow, and deceptively oversimplifying. Some qualitative procedures are always necessary. Conceptual analysis prior to counting is necessary to make sure the right things are counted, counted once, and counted accurately. But careful observation of one or a few cases by a keen observer might yield more accurate information than the relatively brief, if not careless, observation of many cases by uninformed data collectors.

8. *Research Personnel:* Who is going to be given the task of carrying out the research required to get accurate measurements? Prior to that, who is going to be trusted to test the theories one might want to employ? Who is going to train the researchers using what teaching methods? Who is going to be admitted to training and for how long? How should one decide who does not belong in one's schools or on one's research teams? Have the requirements of rationality been satisfied if one leaves such questions undecided or decided by others?

9. *Aggregation Functions:* What mathematical functions should one use to calculate total from individual benefits and costs? Traditionally, philosophers have distinguished monistic from pluralistic value theories. Roughly speaking, monistic value theorists think that different types of valuable things, like health, money, and love, have more or less of some single value or valuable thing. For example, they might say that health, money, and love are valuable things insofar as they produce more or less satisfaction in people. Satisfaction, then, is intrinsically valuable, whereas health and so on are merely instrumentally valuable as means for getting satisfaction. Pluralistic value theorists think that different types of valuable things also have different types of values inherent in them. For example, just as health is different from love, the value of health is different from the value of love. The assumption that there is always an appropriate aggregation function to combine any types of benefits and costs is tantamount to the assumption of monism. Finally, that is, it is assumed that everything is comparable to everything else using some common currency, which might be very subjective, such as personal satisfaction. What does rationality require here?

10. *Discount Rates:* What discount rates should be used? The question is not merely about what rates should be used to put appropriate expected values on things clearly understood but obtainable only at some future point in time. The question also applies to things that are not and may not ever be clearly understood. For example, one might say that although it is easy to understand what it means to have trees disappear in the future, it is not so easy to understand how people will feel when the trees disappear.

By now, the main point to be grasped about rationality and rational evaluation is probably obvious. Those who think of rational action in terms of a favorable benefit-to-cost ratio must admit that the precise definition of such action is fraught with loose ends requiring judgments about which there are no rules. Given enough time, effort, good will, and luck, many groups of people could reach agreements about appropriate judgments regarding the 10 specific features mentioned. That is to say, given enough time and patience, many groups could perform the politically necessary tasks required to achieve some sort of consensus about what and who is rational. Such groups could even take the extra step of agreeing that their judgments were objective. Nevertheless, the most that they could legitimately claim from their political success is just that—political success. The more groups there are with different negotiated agreements about the various 10 features, the less their political success will matter and the more discord there will be. Granting this, one ought to remain cautious about one's claims to rationality in general and to rational evaluations in particular.

RATIONAL AND ETHICAL EVALUATIONS

Given the proposed accounts of moral action and rational action, it is fairly easy to tie the two together. A moral action is just a rational action in which the recipient population is regarded as everyone affected by the action. Actions that tend to impartially improve the quality of life will either sustain or enhance it. Actions that do not tend to sustain or enhance the quality of life will undermine or destroy it. The only way to determine the overall impact of one's actions is to measure the benefits and costs that they generate. So, the determination of moral praiseworthiness and blameworthiness is finally as complicated as the determination of rationality and irrationality. With the possible exception of the size of one's recipient population, the models are the same.

The word *possible* was slipped into the previous sentence because, as indicated above, there is no rule book about the size of the recipient population required for rational action. There is a long tradition extending back at least to Aristotle that asserts that prudence, or practical reason, requires merely that one use oneself as an appropriate recipient population. This view has prevailed right up to today in microeconomics, choice and decision theory, bargaining and games theory, and more generally in exchange theory. In these fields of research, it is usually assumed that rational action generally focuses on a recipient population consisting of an individual actor or perhaps some suitable extension of such an actor, for example, an actor's own family, friends, or firm.

In contrast to this older minimalist view of the recipient population required for rational action, Michalos (1978) argued for a broader view, primarily to close the gap between morality and rationality. The view was called "consensual rationality," and the older view was called "egoistic rationality." Needless to say, the idea of consensual rationality never caught on. More important, for present purposes, the fact that it never caught on means that it remains possible for there to be a difference between what a consultant and a client might regard as morally required and what they might regard as rationally required concerning an appropriate recipient population.

In the above quotations from the CES pamphlet, it is assumed that one of an evaluator's main functions is to help a client arrive at whatever goal the latter aspires to. Evaluators find out what their client's mandate is and then try to help him or her carry it out. In other words, consultants assume that the appropriate recipient population for an evaluation is the client or the target population specified in the client's mandate. That seems to follow as a result of being loyal agents of one's client and of clients being interested in pursuing their own goals. Of course, agency law stipulates that no one can be obliged to do anything immoral or illegal in the interest of a client, and Michalos (1991) argued that, in any case, loyal agency cannot be regarded as a supreme moral principle. Still, the fact is that there may be a difference between what is morally required and what is rationally required in the interest of a satisfied client. The question is, then, What should one do about such problems?

The answer to this question is clear and unequivocal. As indicated above, the Principle of Beneficence is here regarded as the supreme moral principle, the absolute tiebreaker. In case of prima facie conflicts, morally speaking, one ought to act in accordance with that principle above any others.

Of course, if one raises the significantly different question about what one is most likely to do, the answer can only be: "It depends on who the 'one' is, what the circumstances are, and so on." Presumably, most evaluators are like most other people, and deal with such conflicts in the same way. The preferred first strategy is to ignore the problem, the second is to deny that it exists, and the third is to try even harder to make the first or second strategy work. If all of these fail, then the typical fourth strategy is to minimize or appear to minimize the difference between what one supposes would be morally correct and what is required to keep one's job. Occasionally, one's luck simply runs out, and one must do what is morally required even at some severe personal expense. Sometimes one receives the moral praise merited by such heroism, but one can't count on that. Sometimes all one gets for one's efforts is a clear conscience or, better still, the feeling that when push came to shove, morally speaking, one had the right stuff. Clearly, different people feel differently about the value of having such stuff.

A KIERKEGAARDIAN CAVEAT

Some time ago, the Danish philosopher Søren Kierkegaard uttered the paradoxical proposition that "Sin presupposes itself." It was paradoxical to all those Christians and Jews who thought that God made a thoroughly good world that, nevertheless, allowed evil to flourish as a result of someone's bad behavior. One would have thought that an all-knowing, all-good, and all-powerful deity would have closed such loopholes. Anyhow, because the problem (i.e., the inclination to sin) couldn't be laid at God's feet, the evil inclination must have been there before the evil deed was there. But because the evil inclination was also sinful, some sin preceded the original sin, and it's best not to ask where the earlier one came from.

All of this is directly related to what is here regarded as the fundamental moral obligation to act to improve the quality of life. One way to find out what would improve the quality of someone's life is to ask that person. To fail to do so would be to risk paternalism at best and genuine harm at worst. One might just help someone get what they most want to avoid or to miss what they most want to have. So, do-gooders in general and evaluators in particular must consult with their clients to be genuinely helpful. In the previous section I concluded that morality might require one to abandon one's client or perhaps even to resist openly what the latter was trying to do. Here there is a paradoxical point to be made about doing what is required according to the moral point of view. The assumption is that people are basically decent. So, usually people have morally good aims in view, and helping them realize such aims is morally praiseworthy. If, on the other hand, people have indecent aims in view, then helping them realize their aims is not morally praiseworthy. In a sense, then, moral goodness as it is construed here presupposes itself. That's a pity, to say the least.

On the other hand, if one must bear such bad news, there is probably no better place to bear it than at a meeting of the Canadian Evaluation Society (CES). After all, according to the CES's official propaganda, evaluators are in the business of helping managers fulfill their mandates. If consultants did not believe that managers' mandates are usually morally decent, they would be in a pretty sick business. Consultants would be little better than white-collar hit men and hit women. Presumably, most evaluators will agree that their business is no sicker than the average. But will most evaluators agree that the average is not sick? One would hope so, but that has not been proven here.

CONCLUSION

In conclusion, then, the aim of this chapter has been to present one view of the nature and relations among morality or ethics, rationality, evaluation, and politics. Hopefully, most of what has been presented is believable. On John Dewey's 92nd birthday he admitted that it was only in the last few years that he had come to understand what he had been saying most of his life. Some people suspected he still didn't know what he was talking about, but that is not the point of the story. The point is merely that it takes some time for one to appreciate all the implications of one's views. Throughout this chapter, caution and modesty have been recommended, and right now this sounds like excellent advice. If this chapter serves to open some fruitful lines of thinking and discussion, then it has been worth the effort of writing it.

REFERENCES

Canadian Evaluation Society. (1989). *The value in evaluation*. Ottawa: Canadian Evaluation Society.

Michalos, A. C. (1978). *Foundations of decision-making*. Ottawa: Canadian Library of Philosophy.

Michalos, A. C. (1991). The loyal agent's argument. In D. C. Poff & W. J. Waluchow (Eds.), *Business ethics in Canada* (2nd ed., pp. 236-241). Scarborough, ON: Prentice Hall Canada.

Treasury Board of Canada. (1981). *Principles for the evaluation of programs by federal departments and agencies*. Ottawa: Minister of Supply and Services.

Moral Responsibility in Business
or
Fourteen Unsuccessful Ways to Pass the Buck

In the Middle Ages, philosophical essays had a standard format. An author would begin by stating a thesis to be proved. Then arguments opposed to that thesis would be presented and systematically demolished. Following the demolition, the author would present arguments in favor of the thesis. If all went according to plan, nothing further could be done. There would be no good reasons left supporting the other side, and only good reasons left supporting the author's thesis. It's a tedious process to be sure, but effective. By the time one reaches the end, one is pretty sure of one's conclusion.

This is not the Middle Ages, so I am not going to provide that sort of analysis. Instead, I am going to undertake the first half only. My thesis is that businesspeople should be morally responsible agents *as* businesspeople. In other words, my thesis is that businesspeople ought to be morally responsible agents not merely in their role as citizens of a moral community, but in their role as people engaged in competitive enterprise. My strategy of defense will be to present apparently plausible arguments opposed to my thesis and to show that these arguments are defective. If I

AUTHOR'S NOTE: Adapted from "Moral Responsibility in Business" by A. C. Michalos (1991). In *Business Ethics in Canada* (2nd ed., pp. 58-71), edited by D. C. Poff & W. J. Waluchow. Scarborough, ON: Prentice Hall Canada. Used with permission of the publisher.

am successful, you will be persuaded that, so far as we know, there are no good reasons to deny or reject my thesis. I leave it to another occasion to persuade you that there are, in addition, good reasons to accept it.

Before I get to those defective arguments, however, let me clarify some terminology.

Complementary Versus Contrary Terms

The words *moral* and *ethical* in English are ambiguous insofar as they may be used merely to designate classifications or to designate evaluations. So it will be useful to eliminate this ambiguity. First, it is necessary to distinguish complementary from contrary terms. *Complementary terms* are used to divide the world, the whole world, into two mutually exclusive and exhaustive classes. For example, everything in the world is a competitor or a noncompetitor, a horse or a nonhorse, a banana or a nonbanana. Quite generally, take any word at all and then put a *non* in front of it, and you have a pair of complementary terms. Thus, whatever *moral* and *ethical* mean, one may divide the whole world into things that are moral and nonmoral, or ethical and nonethical. To say that actions are moral or nonmoral, when these words are used as complementary terms, is not necessarily to make a moral appraisal of those actions; it is, or may be, merely to classify the actions prior to a moral evaluation. To perform the latter task, one would make use of contrary terms.

Contrary terms are used to divide only a part of the world into mutually exclusive and exhaustive classes. For example, within the subset of the world known as competitors, there are winners and losers. All competitors are winners or losers. Similarly, within the subset of actions appraised from a moral point of view, there are morally good and morally bad (evil) actions. Unfortunately, in English one may use the words *moral* and *ethical* alone as abbreviations of "morally good" and "ethically good," respectively. In such cases, the words are used as contrary terms and their opposites are "morally bad" and "ethically bad," respectively, or simply "bad." Thus, in the next section when social are distinguished from moral responsibilities, it is the complementary or classificatory sense of the word *moral* that is intended. The distinction is not between morally good and bad responsibilities, but between moral responsibilities and nonmoral responsibilities.

Social Versus Moral Responsibilities

In most of the literature on business ethics, people refer to social responsibilities and contrast them with other kinds of responsibilities.

In virtually all cases, the phrase *social responsibilities* is used to designate what are really "moral responsibilities," roughly as these will be defined shortly. The issues typically discussed under the rubric of "social responsibilities" are usually not merely matters of good manners or etiquette, but of something much more serious. So, it will be useful to clarify this distinction.

Roughly speaking, one may say that human action is socially responsible insofar as it does not violate any rules of etiquette, good manners, good taste, or generally accepted social practice. Examples of socially responsible behavior include such things as thanking people for gifts received, arriving at and leaving parties at suitable times, answering letters or other messages requesting acknowledgment, and so on. Socially responsible action is necessary for human community, and in one way or another appropriate criteria of evaluation and sanctions for irresponsible action are routinely developed in all societies.

There are at least two ways to identify morally responsible action, a narrow way and a broad way. Narrowly speaking, one may say that human action is morally responsible, or simply moral, insofar as it does not violate any generally accepted moral maxims. Examples of moral maxims include such things as "One should not steal," "One should always tell the truth," and "One should avoid harming innocent people." Broadly speaking, one may say that human action is morally responsible or moral insofar as it is reasonably intended to impartially maximize human well-being. Because the actual consequences of action often involve unexpected, unintended, and uncontrollable elements, one cannot require the actual maximization of well-being with every action of every agent every moment of every day. Instead, one requires a reasonable amount of attention to the likely consequences of one's action, a reasonable amount of care with one's performance, and a relatively clear intention to act so as to produce a fairly specific sort of result. In particular, one should intend and try to act so that everyone affected by one's action is affected in an evenhanded, unbiased, impartial, or a similar way unless there are good reasons for affecting some people in different ways.

Perhaps the easiest and most morally neutral way to understand the terms *impartial, evenhanded,* and *unbiased* in the preceding sentence is probabilistically. That is, these terms should be understood as indicating that one is intending and trying to act such that every person affected by one's action has the same probability or chance of being affected in roughly the same way. More precisely, one is trying to give every affected person both an equal probability and as high a probability as possible (consistent with the former) to maximize their well-being.

Because there is a generally accepted formal principle of justice that demands that similar people and similar actions should be treated in similar ways unless there are good reasons for treating them in different ways, the broad criterion of morally responsible action includes a condition of justice. Thus, on this broad account of moral action, one who acts morally must also act justly to some extent. It is not clear (to me at least) that morality and justice are entirely coextensive domains, but there is some overlap.

Clearly, what I have called the narrow and broad ways to identify morally responsible action might not define exactly the same set of actions. What's more, this might not be merely the result of a semantic disagreement or the fact that people have just never gotten around to articulating all the moral maxims they implicitly accept. On the contrary, the narrow and broad ways to identify morally responsible action might be based on significantly different views of what is required for such action. In particular, some people might believe that no one is ever morally required to try to maximize anyone's well-being. They might say that morality is essentially concerned with trying to prevent certain kinds of harm from certain kinds of people, and that although universal beneficence is praiseworthy, it cannot be morally required. In short, they might say such beneficence is appropriate for saints or those who aspire to sainthood, but it has no essential role to play in the morality of ordinary people.

There is no rule book to consult now to decide whether a reasonable and morally good person should adopt the narrow or broad way to identify morally responsible action. In fact, I prefer the broad way because I think a world populated by people holding such a view would be a better place to live in than a world populated by people holding the other view, all things considered. In other words, I think a world populated by people motivated by universal beneficence would be better than one populated by people motivated merely by a desire to prevent certain harms. Moreover, because morality is to some extent always a matter of aspiration rather than achievement and the latter may easily be constrained by limitations in the former, I think wisdom is on the side of taking a broad view of morally responsible action.

Moral Maxims Versus Moral Theories

It will be worthwhile to draw one other fundamental distinction before proceeding to the main part of my story. I have already referred to moral maxims such as "One should tell the truth," "One should not steal," and so on. In all countries around the world maxims of this kind are recommended. Students are sometimes shocked by this assertion, for they often have the mistaken belief that in some far-off places radically different maxims are accepted. Of course there are *some* contradictory moral maxims recommended in different countries, for example, that women should or should not have to cover their faces, or that men should or should not be allowed to have more than one wife. That is, however, entirely consistent with my claim that there are some universally accepted maxims. To take the simplest example just to prove my point: Around the world it is universally accepted that it is morally wrong to kill innocent babies for pleasure. Such actions, including the particular motive mentioned, are always condemned. Furthermore, there are no societies in which a contradictory maxim would be recommended. That is, there are no societies (and I would be willing to bet there never have been any) in which the following maxim is part of their moral codes: "It is morally right to kill innocent babies for pleasure" or, briefly, "One ought to kill innocent babies for pleasure."

Although there is universal agreement about some moral maxims, there is no such agreement about the justification, reason, or warrant for accepting these maxims. Much of moral philosophy is concerned with questions of justification. We want to explain why it is reasonable to accept some maxims and not others. As rational beings, we want to have good reasons, warrants, or justifications for accepting some maxims and rejecting others. In other words, we want our moral judgments to be well grounded or well supported rather than capricious, unprincipled, or ad hoc. In short, we want to have our moral maxims derivable from moral theories. Just as any scientist wants to have generally acceptable theories to account for observable facts and law-like regularities, moral philosophers want to have generally acceptable moral theories to account for moral claims and maxims.

Moreover, just as all scientific theories are fallible and limited, so are all moral theories. In truth there are few, if any, scientific theories that can claim the longevity of some moral theories, which also surprises some people. In particular, for better or worse, no scientific theory has lasted as long as the theory that moral maxims ought to be accepted because they are legislated by God. But longevity is beside the point here. The main point is that although there is some universal agreement about some moral maxims, there is no universal agreement about moral theories. Thus, it is obvious that whenever one is engaged in any moral controversy, it is a wise strategy to try to resolve issues at the level of moral maxims. If that is impossible and one must resort to higher level moral theories, one is bound to encounter more problems. Again, as rational beings, we must have theories, and occasionally theoretical agreement is precisely what is required to solve some lower level problems. But, to paraphrase a remark made by Martin Luther King, Jr., concerning violence, when you resort to theories, the main issues tend to be theoretical and practical questions of right and wrong may be swept aside.

Let's now examine in detail the 14 arguments already alluded to.

ARGUMENTS AND REPLIES

1. *Adam Smith's Argument.* Whether or not the 18th century economist endorsed exactly the following argument, it is often attributed to him and is generally consistent with his views. Simply stated, the argument is that if each person would pursue his or her own interests in a fairly enlightened way, then in the long run social well-being or welfare would be maximized. Moreover, people do seem to be naturally inclined to pursue their own interests rather than anyone else's. Therefore, it is pointless for businesspeople or anyone else to concern themselves with morally responsible action. In short, if people would do what comes naturally instead of trying to perform the relatively unnatural actions recommended by moralists, the very results that the latter desire would be achieved. Clearly then, the recommendations of the moralists are at best redundant.

Reply. The trouble with this argument is that its premises are empirically incorrect. If it is true that people are naturally inclined to pursue their own interests and it is also true that such activity will naturally maximize social well-being, then why has the latter not occurred? Presumably, a world that has recessions and depressions, unemployment, poverty, and inefficiencies resulting from near monopolies is not a world in which social well-being is being maximized. Moreover, it cannot plausibly be argued that we have not waited long enough to obtain the benefits of unbridled, universal, self-interested action, because virtually all of the restraints and remedial activities introduced into allegedly free markets have only been introduced when the destructiveness of unbridled self-interested action was obvious to everyone. For example, because self-interested monopolists would try to exploit everyone else (as long as that was perceived to be in their own interests), practically everyone has been willing to introduce antimonopoly laws a priori into allegedly free-enterprise systems. What's more, empirical research has repeatedly shown that the closer one comes to monopolistic domination of a market (in food, cars, fuel, etc.), the more consumers are robbed through gross inefficiencies in production and inflated prices. Again, unemployment insurance was introduced only after it became clear that the unbridled avarice of some people would keep many other people without any adequate means of support. Similarly, social insurance systems were initiated only after it became clear that many old people, single-parent mothers, and children would live and die in poverty unless the state intervened for them.

Instead of arguing that we have not waited long enough to obtain the benefits of unbridled self-interested action, one might argue, following Plato nearly four hundred years before Christ, that people don't always know what is really in their own interests. Whatever their natural inclinations might be, people tend to misperceive, misrepresent, and generally make mistakes when they try to look out for themselves. In fact, one might add a heavy dose of stupidity to human avarice to account for the fact that things haven't turned out as Smith predicted. That, I suppose, is a bit extravagant. It's bad enough to have a theory that leads to false predictions. To suggest that one's theory leads to false predictions because most people are too stupid to make the most of their avarice really adds insult to injury. It would be simpler and wiser to just abandon the theory altogether.

2. *Agnosticism Regarding Ends.* A second argument that might be used to argue that businesspeople should not be concerned with morally responsible action involves agnosticism regarding the appropriate ends of such action. According to this view, no one knows exactly what goals, objectives, aims, or ideal ends are really desirable for all the people in any society. Therefore, it is pointless at best and possibly dangerous, at worst, to try to get businesspeople (or anyone else, for that matter) to pursue such allegedly desirable ends.

Reply. Given the great variety of human interests, abilities, and resources, as well as what the economist Frank Knight called the "perversity of folks," it is indeed unlikely that there are many ideal ends that are desirable for every person in every society. Fortunately, however, it is also irrelevant. Just as it would be silly to abandon rules of the road because some people can't tell their right hand from their left, it would be silly to abandon the pursuit of all ideals because some people can't benefit from their pursuit or realization. There are plenty of identifiable goals whose realization *would* be desirable for the vast majority of people in any society, that is, there are plenty of socially and morally desirable goals. For example, most people would benefit from full employment, an equitable distribution of wealth and incomes, safety from environmental pollutants, the elimination of dangerous food additives and unsafe consumer durables (cars, toys, household appliances, etc.), universal and adequate health care and education, good housing and transportation, and equitable access to political power.

3. *Agnosticism Regarding Means.* Supposing it is granted that there are clearly identifiable socially and morally desirable ends to pursue, it might be argued that it is pointless and perhaps even dangerous to urge businesspeople to pursue them because no one knows exactly what any particular person, in particular circumstances, must do to achieve such ends. The road to hell is certainly paved with good intentions. Among those who believe that full employment is a desirable goal, for example, some seem to think the most efficient means of achieving this would involve government regulation only to prevent monopolies or obviously harmful activities; others think some government planning can be useful in the allocation of private resources and public resources; and some think total government control of all means of production is the best strategy. Again, according to some people, children are most likely to get an adequate education if schools are controlled by local communities, whereas others believe that because of the great disparities in local community resources, the best strategy involves some national intervention and contribution. Thus, in view of such controversies over the appropriate means to obtain recognized desirable ends, agnosticism is justifiable, for businesspeople as well as everyone else.

Reply. This argument proceeds from relatively reasonable premises to an unreasonable conclusion. From the facts of controversies and difficulties regarding the identification of optimal strategies to be used to pursue shared ends, it is concluded that total agnosticism is warranted. But if such agnosticism means the denial of any knowledge regarding appropriate means to obtain shared desirable ends, then the argument involves a non sequitur. It is plainly false that we know of no appropriate strategies to follow to try to realize our goals. In the case of the pursuit of full employment, for example, we know that it is useful in the first place for governments to obtain reliable and valid labor force statistics, including numbers of available workers by geographic region, age, sex, education, skill training, and employment status. It is useful to have a thorough understanding of a nation's resource production and consumption, past, present, and estimated future supplies and demands. In the third place it is useful to set relatively realistic employment targets, and finally to experiment with a variety of tactics for hitting those targets. Of course, there will be controversies and difficulties in the pursuit of shared goals because all knowledge is fallible, all activities have some unintended consequences, and very often the intended consequences of social engineering will not equally satisfy every affected person. Still, to grant all this is to grant nothing sufficient to warrant total agnosticism and abandonment of attempts to find optimally desirable means to obtain similar ends.

4. *Absence of Right.* Roughly speaking, we may say that one has a right to something insofar as one has a special entitlement or claim to it that everyone else has a duty or obligation to recognize. Rights may be described as positive or negative, depending on whether people have a duty to provide things in someone else's interests, or merely to avoid doing some things or to prevent some things that would harm someone else, from being done. For example, in Canada, children are supposed to have a positive right to at least a primary school education, which means that adults have an obligation to provide it. All people are supposed to have a negative right to life, which means, at a minimum, that all of us have a duty to avoid wantonly destroying other people's lives, or at a maximum, that all of us have a duty to prevent the wanton destruction of people's lives. Hence, in the interests of ensuring that Canadians have these rights protected, we are taxed to pay for the operation of educational institutions, our systems of criminal justice punish people legally for intentionally taking people's lives, and in some instances we morally condemn people for failing to prevent such destruction.

A fourth argument leading to the conclusion that businesspeople should not be concerned with morally responsible action *as* businesspeople is based on the simple premise that businesspeople do not have a right to engage in such action. According to this view, there is nothing in the special role, expertise, or character of such people that would give them such a right, and in any case few people outside the class would recognize any obligation to provide or prevent anything in the interest of protecting the alleged right.

The idea behind this argument is that businesspeople have certain roles to play and a certain kind of expertise that are relatively limited. To suppose or demand that an obligation to perform morally responsible action can or should be included in the definition of those roles, or in every sort of expertise, is a mistake. Thus, for example, the business of selling shoes, insurance, or cars can and should be defined without any appeal to moral responsibilities, and one may be a good shoe salesperson, insurance agent, or car dealer without having anything to do with such responsibilities. On the contrary, one's responsibilities would include, say, knowledge of the different qualities of shoes, the requirements of different people for different shoe styles, the appropriate prices to pay to suppliers and to charge to consumers, and so on. These sorts of things, it would be said, cannot reasonably be expected to create rights to making moral decisions.

Reply. In response to this argument, it may be insisted that businesspeople *as* businesspeople certainly have a right to act rationally. This may be regarded as a positive right insofar as some education, training, and socialization is a necessary condition of rational action, and initially someone (without specifying the particular agent) has to provide it. Indeed, it may be said that education, training, and socialization must be provided precisely in the interest of protecting people's right to act rationally. Without some of the former, most human babies would not even survive to adulthood, because rational action is typically necessary for survival.

If it is granted that businesspeople have a right to act rationally, then it must be granted that they have a right to estimate all the consequences of their actions, as far as that is possible in different circumstances. Without such estimates, people could not assess the ratio of benefits achieved to costs expended. In other words, without such estimates, people couldn't determine if their actions were self-constructive or self-destructive, that is, they couldn't assess the survival value of their actions. That ignorance, of course, should be resisted. Thus, it must be insisted that people have a right to estimate all the consequences of their actions, and that must include all the moral and immoral consequences of their actions too. Insofar as businesspeople are interested in performing rational actions, they must also have a right to perform them. Moreover, this implies a right to consider and perform morally responsible actions, because these also produce benefits and costs.

5. *Level of Competence.* Supposing it is granted that businesspeople have a right to perform morally responsible actions as businesspeople, it might still be argued that because they will have such low levels of competence regarding moral actions, they should not be encouraged to perform them. Given a society in which most people are relatively free to choose their occupations, it is likely that people who choose the world of business or competitive enterprise probably are more interested in engaging in the activities characteristic of this world than in those of its alternatives. Similarly, those who choose careers in government service, social work, or, broadly speaking, in any of the "helping professions"

(such as the ministry or priesthood, teaching, lawyers working in legal aid, and public health personnel) probably are more interested in engaging in the activities characteristic of these occupations than in those of business. Clearly, the career interests of those in the helping professions are more compatible with those of moralists than the career interests of businesspeople. Moreover, it is likely that interest is usually a necessary condition of competence, because people are not likely to be or become good at doing things that they are not interested in doing. Thus, in fact, the most competent people regarding morally responsible actions will probably be outside the world of business and, therefore, these are the people who should be urged to perform such actions rather than businesspeople. The latter will almost certainly botch the job.

Reply. Those who use the preceding argument incorrectly assume that competence in performing morally responsible actions is an exclusive trait that people develop at the expense of other traits. In this view, becoming a morally responsible person is analogous to developing a special skill or becoming a specialist in a particular area of knowledge. Becoming a morally responsible person, in this view, is like becoming a good dentist or historian. It is simply another kind of specialization. In this view, if, for example, *Macleans* or *Time* wanted to include reports of morally responsible actions, they would merely add another section. Besides their traditional sections on business, sports, books, international affairs, and so on, there would be a section on morality. Presumably, it would be a section reporting on who did what morally good or bad thing to whom, for what, and with what interesting consequences.

If one adopts what I earlier called the narrow way to identify morally responsible actions, there is a strong tendency to think of morality in precisely this way, that is, as a specialized field with special interests, principles and practitioners. Then one is hard-pressed to find good reasons for most people, who typically would not think of themselves as specialists in moral matters, to be interested in such matters. Short of striving to become some sort of new renaissance person or the local champion at *Trivial Pursuit,* there would appear to be little motivation for most people to try to keep up with the news in yet another area of specialization. Might as well leave it to those who go in for that sort of thing.

As you might have expected, the unhappy scenario just described provided one of the motivating factors for my adoption of what I called the broad way of identifying morally responsible actions. With this view of such actions, there would be no special section of *Macleans* devoted to morality because there is no such specialization. In this view, *any* action has moral significance insofar as it is appraised from a moral point of view. In other words, *any* action has moral significance insofar as it is assessed from the point of view of its being reasonably intended to impartially maximize human well-being. Thus, if, to continue my illustration, the editors of *Macleans* wanted to include reports of morally responsible actions, they would not add any new reports or any new sections. Instead, they would merely appraise the actions routinely reported in their specialized sections from a moral point of view. Competence in making such appraisals is not, therefore, an exclusive trait of moral specialists. On the contrary, because such appraisals involve the most comprehensive review of any and every human action, urging people to adopt a moral point of view is tantamount to urging them to develop a uniquely inclusive trait. It is a habit of mind, a mental set or disposition to think of all actions from the point of view of their moral impact, which is thoroughly inclusive rather than exclusive.

6. *Reduced Economic Efficiency.* In the interest of trying to impartially maximize human well-being, one might fail to maximize profits. In that case, one would also fail to be economically maximally efficient. Insofar as one fails to be economically maximally efficient, one is being wasteful, because inefficiency simply means there is less output per unit of input than there could be. Thus, because wastefulness is inexcusable, it should not be allowed to occur for the sake of achieving other goals.

Reply. This objection represents the tip of an iceberg involving a variety of more or less controversial arguments concerning an alleged trade-off between the aims of economic efficiency and morality. In the fifth volume of my *North American Social Report*, I presented nearly two dozen arguments that have been used by proponents of one side or the other. For present purposes, it is enough to report two main conclusions of that analysis. First, it is of course possible to imagine situations arising in which one would be faced with a choice between economic efficiency and morality. Second, given the distribution of wealth and income in Canada (and even more in the United States), it is highly probable that such choices do not arise. Because the richest 20% of Canadians own around 70% of the wealth, the other 80% of the population has to get along on the remaining 30%. Under these circumstances, it is virtually impossible for the wealthy fifth actually to use much of their wealth. In the simplest terms, one can only consume so much lobster and champagne, take so many trips, wear so many suits or dresses, live in so many houses, and even enjoy the natural beauty of one's own land, to a certain point of saturation.

Moreover, except for the very needy, few people make the maximum use of things they own. So one would expect that those who can accumulate goods at the relatively lowest personal cost would also be the most wasteful. They would have more things lying around idle and they would be least concerned with apparent waste. In short, given the current distribution of wealth and the likely uses to which that wealth can be and is put, it is highly probable that *any* activity that would tend to redistribute wealth in the direction of greater equality (in the interest of morality) would reduce waste and would, therefore, be economically efficient. Put more bluntly, I think that the current distribution of wealth in Canada creates such gross economic inefficiency that it is practically impossible to make adjustments toward greater equality in the interest of morality that would not create greater economic efficiency.

7. *Increased Government Control.* Ignoring my first reply to the argument concerning reduced economic efficiency, further developments in that scenario may be elucidated. In particular, the "nonmoralists" may argue that the immediate result of excessive wastefulness will be shortages, and that excessive shortages will lead directly to increased demands for government intervention. When the government finally intervenes, it will probably be in the form of regulating production and prices, and rationing consumption. The latter combination of activities, then, will probably lead directly to so-called black markets, that is, to illegal transactions in which the unscrupulous few rip off those who may or may not be able to afford to be ripped off. Increased illegal activities, of course, tend to generate increased demands for greater law enforcement, meaning additional government bureaucracy to manage additional taxation, to pay for more salaries of more law enforcement personnel (police officers, clerks, court officials, correctional officers and institutions), and to pay for more buildings and the sophisticated technological hardware characteristic of our modern enforcement agencies. Thus, because no one in his or her right mind wants to live through this scenario, everyone should be reluctant to suffer economic inefficiency even if it requires ignoring alleged moral responsibilities. Indeed, faced with the specter of such an outrageous scenario, many people would be inclined to describe their perceived obligations in fairly moralistic terms. That is, they would be inclined to insist that in the interests of humanity, civilization, or a free society such a scenario should be resisted.

Reply. Naturally, I would welcome the move from talk about economic efficiency to talk about humanity or, more particularly, morality. It is always helpful to have agreement about relatively ultimate aims, or about that for the sake of which relatively immediate actions are being performed or recommended. For present purposes, however, it will be wise to ignore those who might accept my aims and to concentrate on those who might not.

Because, for the sake of argument (i.e., Argument No. 6), I have allowed the other side to assume that actions performed in the interest of morality would lead to reduced economic efficiency, it is worthwhile to remember that standard practices allegedly leading to increased efficiency are notoriously inefficient. To avoid any misunderstanding or confusion about apparent paradoxes, one must never forget that all measures of efficiency are ratios of benefits to costs, and that there is no standard rule book to tell people exactly *how* to measure *which* benefits and costs to *whom* in *what* time period. Thus, it is easy for an employer to replace relatively expensive human labor (people, that is) with relatively cheap machines and to increase efficiency defined as a greater benefit-to-cost ratio *for the employer.* On the other hand, because the very same replacement (by hypothesis) puts some people out of work, it is easy for these employees to show a decrease in efficiency defined as a smaller benefit-to-cost ratio *for the employee.* Hence, the fact that efficiency measures are essentially ratios with controversial numerators and denominators largely explains the apparent paradoxes involved when certain actions are claimed to be both efficient and inefficient. Without first getting some agreement about how to measure which benefits, and so on, it is logically impossible to obtain generally recognized definitive answers.

In the absence of the required agreement about how to measure whose benefits, I would merely remind those who use this seventh argument that widespread poverty and unemployment are two extremely wasteful by-products of the sort of economic efficiency they are recommending. As the economists of the "small is beautiful" or "appropriate technology" view have argued, it cannot be rational to try continually to replace labor with capital when there is relatively plenty of the former and little of the latter. In more human terms, it cannot be reasonable to insist on capital accumulation for a few in the interest of a kind of "efficiency" that makes relative paupers of many others.

Consideration of waste aside, the main reply I would offer to the argument before us is that the alleged choice between a free society and a society highly controlled by government is a false dichotomy. All highly industrialized societies are characterized by high levels of functional interdependence. In such societies almost everyone is more or less dependent on many other people to maintain his or her lifestyle.

Although it is possible for people to raise their own sheep, spin the wool, weave cloth, manufacture needles, design clothes, carve buttons, make clothes, and so on, few people have the inclination to engage in such activities. The vast majority of people prefer a style that makes them more dependent on the productive activities of others. In highly industrialized societies, this preference has the unfortunate by-product that most people are probably even more dependent on others than they would like to be or should be for their own best interests. Indeed, the whole field of business ethics is largely a response to the realization that a system of production, distribution, and consumption of goods and services is almost synonymous with a way of life.

Such a system necessarily socializes, conditions and, finally, even controls people in fundamental ways. Thus, if one were going to insist on any dichotomy, I would suggest at the risk of oversimplification, that between control by elected officials in the public interest, and control by private industrial officials in their own interests. Given the fact that people will certainly become socialized with certain kinds of expectations, aspirations, and ideas about a good life, the real issue is how such a life should be defined and what strategies should be used to achieve it. It is a raw red herring to suggest that it is possible to just let everyone do whatever turns them on. That never happens. Moreover, as argued earlier, it is highly unlikely that the result of such unconditioned activity would benefit most people. Finally, granted that in fact elected officials do not always act in the interests of society as a whole and that private industrial officials do not always act in their own interests narrowly defined, this sort of dichotomized thinking is probably not particularly helpful in the long run.

8. *Loyal Agent's Argument.* In Chapter 4, I examine this argument in considerable detail. I will summarize that discussion here. The argument runs as follows: (a) As a loyal agent of some principal (i.e., employer), I ought to serve his or her interest as he or she would serve them if the latter had my expertise. (b) Such a principal would serve his or her own interests in a thoroughly egoistic way. Therefore, (c) as a loyal agent of such a principal, I ought to operate in a thoroughly egoistic way in the interests of that principal. In other words, loyal agency seems not only to permit but to require that people should be selfish in the interests of their employers.

Reply. One may be regarded as operating in a thoroughly egoistic way if all one's actions are designed to optimize one's own interests and one has no inclination at all to identify the interests of anyone else with one's own. One may very well be a self-confident, self-starting, self-sustaining, and self-controlled individual. These are all commendable personal characteristics. But one must be selfish, self-centered, and/or self-serving. In conflict situations when there are not enough benefits to satisfy everyone, an egoist will try to see that his or her own needs are satisfied whatever happens to the needs of others. One is more interested in being first than in being nice, and one assumes that everyone else is too. One may even believe that if everyone behaved this way, the world's resources would be used in a maximally efficient way and everyone would be materially better off. But that is a secondary consideration. One's first consideration—the only prudent one—is to look out for Numero Uno, oneself.

The trouble with the loyal agent's argument is that both premises are problematic. The second premise assumes that all people are egoists; but people who try to defend their actions with this argument assume that their own actions are *not* egoistic. Their basic assumption is that they are loyal agents motivated by a desire to serve the best interests of their employers. However, if it is possible for them to have such nonegoistic motives, then it must be possible for other people to have such motives too. Hence, the very assumption required to make the argument look plausible in the first place makes the second premise look implausible. So the argument is self-defeating.

The first premise—that an employee's responsibility is to the employer alone—looks as innocuous as motherhood and apple pie, and in a way it is. Its only weakness is that its limitations are not built into it. In this respect it is like most moral principles and rules of law. Short of turning every principle and rule into a self-contained treatise, it is impossible to indicate every possible exception. For example, no one should kill anyone, except *maybe* in self-defense, war, capital punishment, euthanasia, or suicide. Similarly, a loyal agent ought to pursue the interests of his or her employer with certain exceptions. In the famous Nuremberg trials, the Charter of the International Military Tribunal recognized, for instance,

> that one who has committed criminal acts may not take refuge in superior orders nor in the doctrine that his crimes were acts of states. These twin principles working together have heretofore resulted in immunity for practically everyone concerned in the really great crimes against peace and mankind. Those in lower ranks are protected against liability by the orders of their superiors. The superiors were protected because their orders were called acts of the state. Under the Charter, no defense based on either of these doctrines can be entertained.

Canadian and American laws relating to loyal agency do not sanction any illegal or unethical actions. Thus, there is no doubt at all that the first premise of the loyal agent's argument cannot be regarded as a license to break laws. No respectable court would permit it. In fact, although the courts have no special jurisdiction over moral law, they have shown no reluctance to condemn immoral acts allegedly performed in the interests of fulfilling fiduciary obligations.

9. *Materialist Orientation.* In the fifth argument above it was indicated that people whose primary interests are in business would probably have low levels of competence in performing morally responsible actions. I replied that the flaw in this argument was the assumption that competence in performing morally responsible actions was an exclusive trait or skill, and that the broad way of understanding morality that I have adopted is more inclusive than exclusive. One might still argue that, given the materialistic orientation of businesspeople, when they try to make a broad benefit-cost analysis in the interest of morality, they are bound to spoil it. As Aristotle said a long time ago, as a person's character is, so is the world seen. People who spend most of their time evaluating things from a materialistic point of view will tend to make moral evaluations from the same point of view. So, when they try to do things in the interests of everyone impartially, they will probably not be doing the sorts of things moralists would like them to be doing. For example, from the point of view of Canadian businesspeople, the support of economic research designed to show that Adam Smith's argument (Argument No. 1) was basically sound might be regarded as impartially benefiting everyone. Quite generally, then, such people might regard anything that reinforces their view of the world as impartially benefiting everyone. Thus, urging these people to be universally beneficent might lead to universal materialism, which most moralists would find unacceptable.

Reply. As suggested earlier, it is almost certainly an oversimplification to say that businesspeople usually have a materialistic orientation. Given the variety of businesses that people can enter, the variety and ambiguity of human motivations, and the variety of personal philosophies of life and lifestyles, it is unlikely that people in business, broadly construed, are uniformly materialistic. If there is any reliable and valid research indicating such bias, I haven't seen it. Second, it would be a mistake to think that all materialism is dangerous and objectionable. Some material goods do make positive contributions to the quality of life, for example, reliable consumer durables such as cars, household appliances, dwelling units, and communications hardware (telephones, radio, television). Finally, Aristotle's remark is obviously not the whole truth. As much as people's interests influence what they perceive and believe, what they perceive and believe also influences their interests. Indeed, my reading of the evidence accumulated so far indicates that perception and belief contribute more to interest than the reverse. But the literature on this subject is diverse, complicated, and controversial.

10. *Need for Pluralism.* In a pluralistic society like Canada, there are many perspectives from which controversial issues may be viewed. There are many important issues about which various people have unsettled opinions, and there are others about which there are solid and contradictory opinions. To expect businesspeople to have uniform and settled opinions, and to urge them to see that these are predominant is unwarranted and unwise. It is unwarranted because there is no good reason to expect businesspeople as such to be intellectually more tidy or clearheaded than the rest of the population and, therefore, it is unwise to urge these people to strive to make their views predominant over all others. Given the enormous overt and covert power of businesspeople, they might go even farther than they already have to create a one-dimensional society. The only reasonable course to follow is a pluralistic one.

Reply. This argument, too, is a red herring. To urge businesspeople to engage in morally responsible action is not to urge *only* businesspeople to engage in such action. Of course pluralism will and ought to continue, if that means that there should be a variety of perspectives from which important issues may be viewed. No one in his or her right mind would insist on silencing all voices but one, or on excluding all points of view but one. It would be as bad to have only businesspeople steering the ship of state as it would be to have only philosophers, moralists, or gymnasts doing so.

The other problem with this argument is that it is self-defeating. If it is true that businesspeople are so powerful that they represent a threat to the rest of society, then morally irresponsible businesspeople would represent an even greater threat. Hence, if this argument has any value at all, it is only to reinforce the view that urges businesspeople to be morally responsible.

11. *Overload.* The world of competitive enterprise is notoriously complicated already. Compared to those in other occupations, business executives have a relatively high incidence of heart attacks and strokes.

To insist that such overloaded people should take on yet another responsibility and, indeed, such a controversial and inherently complex one as moral decision making, is to risk complete systemic failure. Quite apart from the arguable facts that the engagement of businesspeople as such in morally responsible action would be redundant and incompetent, there is no good reason to risk destroying currently reasonable business practices by overloading decision makers.

Reply. If this argument proves anything, it proves too much. Life, after all, is complicated. So, if complexity were sufficient to eliminate the burden of attending to moral responsibilities, then all of us could take a permanent moral holiday. Clearly, however, a society in which no one attended to any moral responsibilities would have virtually nothing to recommend it as a human and humane community. In such a society, if it could even be called that, life would be "nasty, brutish and short," as the 17th-century British philosopher Thomas Hobbes said. Second, the argument still seems to presuppose that morality is some kind of specialization that people can get into or not, as they choose. As I have indicated above, this is a mistake. The moral point of view is not another specialized perspective, but is inherent in all major decisions.

12. *Inconsistency.* Perhaps one of the most frequently heard arguments against businesspeople engaging in morally responsible action is that such action is logically inconsistent with competitive enterprise. To engage in competition in an open market is essentially to try to do better than others. The rough rule is to buy cheap and sell dear. To engage in morally responsible action is essentially to try *not* to have some come out better than others. The rule then is to buy and sell at no monetary gain. Thus, those who recommend that businesspeople as such should be morally responsible are talking literal nonsense and recommending that businesspeople should perform actions that are aimed both to make someone and no one come out better, which is absurd.

Reply. I believe the unsoundness of this argument may be demonstrated by consideration of competitive games of fair play. For example, there is apparently nothing immoral about such competitive games as chess, tennis, golf, and track-and-field events, to name only a few. Rules are designed to ensure that, in principle, all competitors have an equal probability of winning. Each chess player gets the same number of pieces, uses the same board, has the same time constraints, and so on. Moreover, each player is free to play, or not, depending on the relative benefits and costs of playing. Hence, because chess games are thoroughly competitive and morally unobjectionable, it is logically possible for something to be so. Thus, those who think there is some logical absurdity involved in recommending that businesspeople should be moral and competitive are plainly wrong. If there is any inconsistency involved, it is certainly not a matter of logic or conceptualization.

13. *The Godfather's Argument.* The Godfather's argument in that excellent book and series of movies was simply that as long as a business provides goods and services demanded by some consumers and a substantial family income for producers, few people should ask anything more of it. After all, business is business, and businesspeople are not saints any more than the rest of us. Life, as the great British-American philosopher Alfred North Whitehead said, is robbery. All living things draw their sustenance from other living things. So, a Godfather-type disciple might have concluded, we are doomed to be predators. The most we can hope for is to make a reasonable living for ourselves and our families, granting always that there is an unattractive aspect to our business activities.

Reply. Dazzling—and pragmatic—as the rhetoric may sound, it's still nonsense. Granting that all living things live by consuming the corpses of other living things, it does not follow that we are all robbers, thieves, or murderers. Poetic license is not a license to commit logical fallacies. There are important differences between, for example, chopping up vegetables for a Caesar salad and chopping up Caesar. The facts that some people may be willing to pay to have someone murdered and that some other people are willing to perform the murder are not sufficient to justify the transaction. The person whose life is being negotiated also has an interest that ought to be protected, as do the rest of us whose lives would be at risk if such business transactions were legal.

14. *Particular Morality.* Finally, one might argue that the basic presupposition of this essay is a red herring, because few if any businesspeople have to be persuaded to be morally responsible. How many people in business have you ever heard saying that they should be morally irresponsible, immoral, morally bad, or evil? Not many, probably. No one is born a businessperson. Most people in business were taught roughly the same moral maxims at home and in school, and most of these maxims had roughly the same origins in the Judeo-Christian religions. So most people have been socialized to be morally responsible. Businesspeople generally intend to act and are expected to act the

same as everyone else. Thus, to assume that businesspeople are in need of special remedial training, encouragement, or admonitions to be nice is simply to make a false assumption.

On the other hand, it is true that the moral maxims to which virtually everyone is exposed are not necessarily predominant in the world of competitive enterprise. Just as chess players and golfers agree to accept particular rules of behavior for the sake of their games, businesspeople also adopt special rules for the sake of their work. Like chess players, then, businesspeople may be said to have particular codes of ethics in addition to and occasionally in opposition to ordinary or universal ethics. Many actions that would appear to have questionable moral status, judged by the maxims of universal morality, may be morally good judged by the maxims of the particular morality of the world of business. Therefore, instead of condemning businesspeople for acting immorally, one ought at least to appreciate their particular ethical positions and perhaps praise them for steadfastly adhering to the rules of their own game.

Reply. This apparently tolerant approach to the identification and appraisal of morally responsible action is yet another self-defeating argument. Insofar as the argument has any strength at all, it tends to undermine *all* morality. One of the basic aims and functions of morality or codes of ethics is the resolution of disputes involving conflicting interests. Moral maxims and, more important, the ideal of universal beneficence are designed to provide rules for settling disputes without resorting to legislated civil or criminal laws. The recognition of a supreme moral principle of action, namely, the intention to impartially maximize human well-being, is a necessary condition of morality achieving its basic aims. Without such a tiebreaking principle, a principle to adjudicate between conflicting interests or lower level maxims, appeals to morality are useless.

Thus, the concept of particular moralities is logically incoherent, for it entails maxims of action that both include and exclude a supreme principle. In other words, it posits a set of maxims that are relatively equal in status but also not relatively equal to one supreme principle. Unless the maxims of any so-called particular morality are roughly equal to those of other particular moralities, one cannot use them to claim special privileges for one's behavior. However, granting them such equal status implies eliminating the possibility of appealing to them to resolve conflicts. If, for example, businesspeople, bandits, and baseball players all have equally important ethical codes to live by, then, when there are conflicts between people in different groups, each can retreat to his or her own special code, with the result that no resolution of the conflict is possible. If one would take the additional step that some people seem to recommend, namely, that everyone should have his or her own moral code, then morality would be radically relativized and absolutely useless. Clearly, the way out of this logical and moral morass is simply to abandon the idea of particular morality. There can be only one kind of morality, and it is universal. Businesspeople, like everyone else, must be judged morally responsible or irresponsible in terms of this morality. There is no third option.

The Loyal Agent's Argument

According to the Report of the Special Review Committee of the Board of Directors of Gulf Oil Corporation:

> It is not too much to say that the activity of those Gulf officials involved in making domestic political contributions with corporate funds during the period of approximately fourteen years under review [1960-1974] was shot through with illegality. The activity was generally clandestine and in disregard of federal, as well as a number of state, statutes. (McCloy, Pearson, & Matthews, 1976, p. 31)

Nevertheless, and more important for our purposes, the Committee apparently endorsed the following judgment, which was submitted by their lawyers to the U.S. Securities and Exchange Commission.

> No evidence has been uncovered or disclosed which establishes that any officer, director or employee of Gulf personally profited or benefited by or through any use of corporate funds for contributions, gifts, entertainment or other expenses related to political activity. Further, Gulf has no reason to believe or suspect that *the motive of the employee or officer* involved in such use of corporate funds was anything other than *a desire to act solely in what he considered to be the best interests of Gulf and its shareholders*. [italics added] (McCloy et al., 1976, p. 13)

AUTHOR'S NOTE: Adapted from "The Loyal Agent's Argument" by A. C. Michalos (1991). In *Business Ethics in Canada* (2nd ed., pp. 236-241), edited by D. C. Poff & W. J. Waluchow. Scarborough, ON: Prentice Hall Canada. Used with permission of the publisher.

If we accept the views of the Committee and their lawyers, then we have before us an interesting case of individuals performing illegal actions with altruistic motives. What they did was admittedly illegal, but they meant well. They had good intentions, namely, to further "the best interests of Gulf and its shareholders." Furthermore, there is no suggestion in these passages or in the rest of the report that the officials were ordered to commit such acts. They were not ordered. On the contrary, the acts seem to have emerged as practically natural by-products of some employees' zeal in looking after their employer's interests. They are, we might say, the result of overzealous attempts of agents to fulfill their fiducial obligations.

In the following paragraphs I am going to pursue this apparently plausible account of overzealous behavior to its bitter end. That is, I'm going to assume for the sake of argument that there really are reasonable people who would and do perform immoral and illegal actions with altruistic motives, that is, there are people who would and do perform such actions with reasons that they regard as good in some fairly general sense. It's not to be assumed that they are shrewd enough to see that their own interests lie in the advancement of their employer's or clients' interests. They are not, I'm assuming, cleverly egoistic. If anything, they are stupidly altruistic by hypothesis. But that's beside the point now. What I want to do is construct a generalized form of an argument that I imagine would be attractive to such agents, whether or not any of them has or will ever formulate it exactly so. Then I want to try to demolish it once and for all.

THE ARGUMENT

What I will call the Loyal Agent's Argument (LAA) runs as follows:

1. *As a loyal agent of some principal, I ought to serve his interests as he would serve them himself if he had my expertise.*
2. *He would serve his own interests in a thoroughly egoistic way.*

   Therefore, as a loyal agent of this principal, I ought to operate in a thoroughly egoistic way in his behalf.

Some clarification is in order. First, to make full use of the fairly substantial body of legal literature related to the *law of agency*, I have adopted some of the standard legal jargon. In particular, following Powell (1965), I'm assuming that *"an agent is a person who is authorized to act for a principal and has agreed so to act, and who has power to affect the legal relations of his principal with a third party"* (p. 7). The standard model is an insurance agent who acts on behalf of an insurance company, his principal, to negotiate insurance contracts with third parties. More generally, lawyers, real estate agents, engineers, doctors, dentists, stockbrokers, and the Gulf Oil zealots may all be regarded as agents of some principal. Although for some purposes one might want to distinguish agents from employees, such a distinction will not be necessary here. The definition given above is broad enough to allow us to think of coal miners, Avon Ladies, zoo attendants, and Ministers of Parliament as agents.

Second, as our definition suggests, there are typically three important relationships involved in agency transactions, namely, those between agent and principal, agent and third party, and principal and third party. The law of agency has plenty to say about each of these relationships, whereas LAA is primarily concerned with only the first, the fiducial relation between agent and principal. It would be a mistake to regard this as mere oversight. Few of us are immune to the buck-passing syndrome. Most of us are inclined to try to narrow the range of activities for which we are prepared to accept responsibility and, at the same time, widen the range of activities over which we are prepared to exercise authority. Notwithstanding the psychological theory of cognitive dissonance, most human beings seem to have sufficient mental magnanimity to accommodate this particular pair of incompatible inclinations. Like the insects, we are very adaptable creatures.

Third, I imagine that someone using an argument like LAA would, in the first place, be interested in trying to establish the fact that agents have a moral obligation to operate in a thoroughly egoistic way in their principals' behalf. If most LAA users in fact are primarily concerned with establishing their legal obligations, then perhaps what I have to say will be less interesting than I imagine to most people. Nevertheless, I'm assuming that the force of *ought* in the first premise and conclusion is moral rather than legal. For our purposes it doesn't matter what sort of an ontological analysis one gives to such obligations or what sort of a moral theory one might want to use to justify one's moral principles. It only has to be appreciated that LAA is designed to provide a moral justification for the behavior prescribed in its conclusion.

Fourth, an agent may be regarded as operating in a thoroughly egoistic way if all his actions are designed to optimize his own interests and he has no inclination at all to identify the interests of anyone else with his own. (Throughout the chapter I usually let the masculine "he" abbreviate "he or she.") He may very well be a self-confident, self-starting, self-sustaining, and self-controlled individual. These are all commendable personal characteristics. But he must be selfish, self-centered, and/or self-serving. In conflict situations when there are not enough benefits to satisfy everyone, he will try to see that his own needs are satisfied, whatever happens to the needs of others. He is more interested in being first than in being nice, and he assumes that everyone else is too. He may harbor the suspicion that if everyone behaved as he does, the world's resources would be used in a maximally efficient way and everyone would be materially better off. But these are secondary considerations at best. His first consideration, which he regards as only prudent or smart, is to look out for *Numero Uno*, himself.

Fifth, to say that an agent is supposed to operate in a thoroughly egoistic way in behalf of his principal is just to say that the agent is supposed to act as he believes his principal would act if his principal were an egoist. The agent is supposed to conduct the affairs of his principal with the single-minded purpose of optimizing the latter's interests and not yielding them to anyone else's interests.

THE SECOND PREMISE

Now we should be talking the same language. The question is: Is the Loyal Agent's Argument sound? Can its conclusion be established or even well supported by its premises? I think there are good reasons for giving a negative answer to these questions. Moreover, because the argument has been deliberately formulated in a logically valid form, we may proceed immediately to a closer investigation of the content of its premises.

Let's consider the second premise first. This premise can only be regarded as true of people a priori if one of the assumptions we have made for the sake of argument about human motivation is false. Following the quotations from the Special Review Committee, it was pointed out that the case involved agents who apparently performed illegal actions with altruistic motives. What they did wrong, they did in behalf of Gulf Oil Corporation. Fair enough. However, if it's possible to perform illegal but altruistically motivated acts, it must be possible to perform legal but altruistically motivated acts as well. The very assumption required to give the argument initial plausibility also ensures that its second premise cannot be assumed to be generally true a priori. Because some people can perform nonegoistically motivated actions, the second premise of LAA requires some defense. Moreover, broadly speaking there are two directions such a defense might take, and I will consider each in turn.

Granted that users of LAA cannot consistently regard every individual as a thoroughly egoistic operator and hence guarantee the truth of the second premise a priori, it is still possible to try to defend this premise as a well-confirmed empirical hypothesis. That is, admitting that there are exceptions, one might still claim that if one acted as if the second premise were true, much more often than not one would be right. This is the sort of line economists have traditionally taken toward their idealized rational economic man. They realize that people are capable of altruistic action, but they figure that the capability is seldom exercised and they design their hypotheses, laws, and theories accordingly.

So far as business is concerned, the egoistic line seems to be translated into profit maximization. According to Goodman, for example,

> The Wall Street rule for persons legally charged with the management of other people's money runs as follows: Invest funds in a company with the aim of gaining the best financial return with the least financial risk for the trust beneficiaries. If you later come to disagree with the company's management, sell the stock. (Baum, 1975, p. 206)

Similarly, in a cautious version of LAA, Friedman (1970) has claimed that,

> In a free-enterprise, private-property system, a corporate executive is an employee of the owners of the business. He has a direct responsibility to his employers. That responsibility is to conduct the business in accordance with their desires, which generally will be to make as much money as possible while conforming to the basic rules of the society, both those embodied in law and those embodied in ethical custom. (p. 8)

Instead of challenging the accuracy of these assessments of the motives of people generally or of businessmen in the marketplace in particular now, I want to grant it straightaway for the sake of the argument. The question is: How does that affect LAA?

As you may have guessed, users of LAA are not much better off than they were. If it's a good bet that the second premise is true, then it's an equally good bet that anyone inclined to defend his actions with LAA is not an altruistic operator. No one can have it both ways. Evidence for the empirical hypothesis that people generally act as egoists is evidence for the truth of the second premise and the falsehood of the alleged altruistic motives of anyone using LAA. In short, the premise is still self-defeating.

Corporate Principals

Instead of regarding the second premise as an empirical claim about real people and attempting to support it inductively, one might treat it as a logical claim justifiable by an appeal to the definitions of some of its key terms. This looks like a very promising strategy when one considers the fact that many contemporary principals, like Gulf Oil Corporation, for example, are abstract entities. Corporate persons are, after all, nothing but fictional persons invented by people with fairly specific aims. In particular, corporations have been invented to assist in the accumulation of material assets. Although they typically accomplish many different tasks, the accumulation of assets is generally regarded as their basic aim. Thus, if one's principal happens to be a corporation, one might reasonably argue that it is by definition thoroughly egoistic. The business of such entities is certainly business, because that is their very reason for being, the very point of inventing them in the first place. So, the second premise of LAA could be substantiated by definitional fiat.

Apparently, then, morally conscientious corporate agents may find themselves facing lawsuits if they assume their principals are not self-serving profit maximizers and act accordingly. Legal niceties aside, there is a thought-provoking moral argument in favor of agents acting as if their principals were just as the designers of corporate law imagine them. That is, if any particular stockholder wants to give his money away or to pursue any aims other than profit maximization, he is free to do so. Investors should be and almost certainly are aware that corporations are designed to make money. If they have other aims, they shouldn't be investing in corporations. If they don't have other aims and they go into corporations with their eyes wide open, then they should appreciate and respect the interests of others who have gone in with them.

In principle, the defense of the second premise of LAA on the grounds of the defining characteristic of corporations may be challenged as before. Insofar as corporations are defined as egoistic corporate persons (a rough abbreviated definition, to be sure), a serious question arises concerning the morality of becoming an agent for them—not to mention inventing them in the first place. The evils of unbridled egoism are well known and they aren't mitigated by the fact that the egoist in question is a corporate person. If anything, they are magnified because of the difficulties involved in assigning responsibility and holding corporations liable for their activities. It is demonstrably certain that if everyone only attends to what he perceives as his own interests, a socially self-destructive result may occur. That is the clear message of prisoner's dilemma studies. It's also the message of two kids in a playpen who finally tear the toys apart rather than share them.

As before, it will not help to argue that in developed countries most people work for corporations or they don't work at all. Again, self-preservation is not altruism. To serve an evil master in the interests of survival is not to serve in the interests of altruism, and users of LAA are supposed to be motivated by altruism. On the other hand, insofar as corporations are not defined as egoistic corporate persons and are granted more or less benevolent if not downright altruistic aims, the truth of the second premise of LAA is again open to question. In either case, then, an agent trying to salvage LAA with this sort of definitional defense is bound to find the task self-defeating.

THE FIRST PREMISE

Let's turn now to the first premise of LAA. In a way it's as innocuous as motherhood and apple pie. Every discussion I've read of the duties of agents according to agency law in North America and the United Kingdom has included some form of this premise. For example, Powell (1965) says, "An agent has a general duty to act solely for the benefit of his principal in all matters connected with the execution of his authority" (p. 312). The *American Restatement of the Law of Agency* (Section 387) says that "an agent is subject to a duty to his principal to act solely for the benefit of the principal in all matters connected with his agency" (Blumberg, 1973, p. 87). According to a standard Canadian textbook on business law, "Good faith requires that the agent place the interest of his principal above all else except the law" (Smyth & Soberman, 1968, p. 360).

The only trouble with the premise is that its limitations are not clearly built into it. In this respect it is like most moral principles and rules of law. Short of turning every principle and rule into a self-contained treatise, it's impossible to indicate every possible exception. . . . However, the *American Restatement of the Law of Agency* (Section 385) makes it quite clear that "In no event would it be implied that an agent has a duty to perform acts which . . . are illegal or unethical" (Blumberg, 1973, p. 86). Moreover, "In determining whether or not the orders of the principal to the agent are reasonable . . . business or professional ethics . . . are considered" (Blumberg, 1973, p. 86). Powell (1965) also remarks that agents have no duty "to carry out an illegal act" (p. 302). Thus, there is no doubt at all that the first premise of LAA cannot be regarded as a license to break the law. No respectable court would permit it. In fact, although the courts have no special jurisdiction over moral law, they have shown no reluctance to condemn immoral acts allegedly performed in the interests of fulfilling fiduciary obligations.

Illegality and immorality aside, the first premise still gives up much more than any sane person should be willing to give up. It virtually gives a principal license to use an agent in any way the principal pleases, so long as the agent's activity serves the principal's interest. For example, suppose a life insurance agent agrees to sell State Farm Insurance on commission. It would be ludicrous to assume that the agent has also committed himself to painting houses, washing dogs, or doing anything else that happened to give his principal pleasure. It would also be misleading to describe such an open-ended commitment as an agreement to sell insurance. It would more accurately be described as selling oneself into bondage. Clearly, then, one must assume that the first premise of LAA presupposes some important restrictions that may have nothing to do with any sort of law.

Because they are apparently drawn from and applicable to ordinary affairs and usage, perhaps it would be instructive to mention some of the principles developed in the law of agency to address this problem. You may recall that the definition of an agent that we borrowed from Powell explicitly referred to a person being "authorized to act for a principal." An agent's duties are typically limited to a set of activities over which he is granted authority by his principal. This would be sufficient to prevent the exploitation of the hypothetical insurance agent in the preceding paragraph.

Besides a carefully developed set of principles related to the granting of authority, the law of agency recognizes some other general duties of agents, like the previously considered duty of good faith. For example, an agent is expected to "exercise due care and skill in executing his authority" (Powell, 1965, p. 303). This obviously serves the interests of all concerned, and there are plenty of principles and precedents available to explain "due care and skill." He is expected to "keep proper accounts," that is, accounts that clearly distinguish his principal's assets from his own (Powell, 1965, p. 321).

Keeping the preceding guidelines in mind, perhaps some form of LAA can be salvaged by tightening up the first premise. Let's suppose I'm in the advertising business and I want to use LAA by suitably restricting the scope of the first premise thus:

1a. *As a loyal advertising agent of some company, I ought to advertise its products as they would advertise them if they had my expertise.*

That would require a consistent modification of the second premise and conclusion, but we need not worry about that. The question is, Does this reformulated Premise 1a escape the kinds of criticism leveled against Premise 1?

Certainly not. If the company happens to be run by a bunch of thoroughly unscrupulous thugs, it could be immoral and illegal to advertise their products as they would if they had the agent's expertise. Even if the company is run by fools who really don't know what they make, it could be immoral and illegal to advertise their products as they would if they had the agent's expertise. For example, if the company's directors are smart enough to know that they can make more money selling drugs than they can make selling candy, but dumb enough to think that the candy they make is an effective drug, an agent could hardly be under any obligation to advertise their product as a marvelous new drug, that is, assuming that the agent was smart enough to know that his employers were only capable of producing candy.

If you think the agent could have such an obligation, what would be its source? Clearly it is not enough to say that the agent is employed by the company. That would be tantamount to appealing to LAA to establish a version of its own first premise; that is, it would be a circular salvaging effort. Something else is required to support Premise 1a.

CONCLUSION

The announced aim of this chapter was to destroy LAA once and for all. I think that has been done. It is perhaps worthwhile to emphasize that if people use LAA when, as we saw earlier, the real reason for their actions is fear (or job preservation) then they will be circulating a distorted view of the world and decreasing the chances of reform. Thus, in the interests of a clear perception and resolution of social problems related to responsible human agency, LAA deserves the sort of treatment it has received here.

REFERENCES

Baum, R. (Ed.). (1975). *Ethical arguments for analysis*. New York: Holt, Rinehart & Winston. (Reprinted from W. Goodman, "Stocks without sin." *Minneapolis Star and Tribune*)

Blumberg, P. I. (1973). Corporate responsibility and the employee's duty of loyalty and obedience: A preliminary inquiry. In D. Votaw & S. P. Sethi (Eds.), *The corporate dilemma*. Englewood Cliffs, NJ: Prentice Hall.

Friedman, M. (1970, September 13). The social responsibility of business is to increase its profits. *The New York Times Magazine*, p. 8.

McCloy, J. J., Pearson, N. W., & Matthews, B. (1976). *The great oil spill.* New York: Chelsea House.

Powell, R. (1965). *The law of agency.* London: Pitman.

Smyth, J. E., & Soberman, D. A. (1968). *The law and business administration in Canada.* Toronto: Prentice Hall of Canada.

5

The Best and Worst Arguments
for Business Ethics

In the preceding two chapters I presented every apparently plausible argument someone might use to establish the legitimacy of businesspeople either by ignoring or by explicitly opposing the application of ordinary moral principles to business practices. There were 14 initial arguments, and against each one I constructed criticisms that seemed sufficient to destroy them. At this point, then, according to the traditional structure of a philosophical treatise outlined in the introductory chapter, arguments should be presented in defense of my thesis that businesspeople ought to actively endorse moral principles and apply them in the market. Rather than provide a long list of arguments in defense of this thesis, I am going to provide what I think is the single best argument for my thesis and the single worst argument for it. Each one will be analyzed in turn.

The single best argument in defense of business ethics runs as follows:

1. In order for business or a market economy to exist, there must be some sort of community of potential buyers and sellers.
2. In order for a community of potential buyers and sellers to exist, there must be morality.
   Thus, in order for business or a market economy to exist, there must be morality.
3. Anyone with an interest in preserving business or a market economy should help maintain those conditions, like morality, that are necessary for its preservation.

4. Businesspeople have such an interest.
Therefore, businesspeople should help maintain those conditions that are necessary for the preservation of business, including morality.

In brief, the argument says, first, that because community is necessary for business and morality is necessary for community, morality is necessary for business. Then, with the latter conclusion established, it is reasonable to suppose that anyone with an interest in the existence or sustainability of business or a market economy should be an active supporter of morality. Presumably, that would include all businesspeople.

Considering the first premise, what is being asserted is that business, market economies, or exchange economies cannot exist without communities or societies. Imagine Robinson Crusoe on his island before the appearance of Friday. In his solitary state, Crusoe could not have had a marketing problem. In fact, when Friday appeared, Crusoe's first thought was that he had a security problem. Once the two men established some communal understanding and relationship, it became possible to think about a division of labor and appropriate exchanges. If they had immediately set out to mislead and/or destroy each other rather than to establish a community, their story would have been much shorter. Thus, because Crusoe's story is quite generalizable, some sort of community is necessary for a market economy or, quite simply, for business.

Considering the second premise, what is being asserted is that communities or societies cannot exist without a minimum sort of morality based on at least two moral principles, one proscribing killing people at will and the other proscribing lying to people. In other words, in order for a community to exist, people must, at a minimum, adhere to the principles of not indiscriminately killing people and lying to them.

To see that such a minimum morality is necessary for community, imagine the opposite. Imagine a community in which people are told that they ought to kill people at will and to lie to everyone and anyone. Such a community would be short-lived, if it could even get started. If members of the community did what they ought to do, they would literally destroy each other in the worst case and find it impossible to communicate with each other in the second worst case. If they literally destroy each other, there would obviously be no community. On the other hand, if they systematically lie to each other then there will be no useful communication and, what is worse, there may be danger in trying to communicate because everyone would be misleading everyone. So, in this case too there would be no community. Clearly, then, a minimum amount of morality is necessary for community.

Considering the third premise, what is being asserted is justifiable on the grounds of fairness and reasonable self-interest. Unless there are good reasons for doing otherwise, it is reasonable to perform actions that are likely to help one get what one wants. Presumably everyone would accept this much pragmatism, because the alternative is waiting for life's desires to fall into one's lap. The fairness of performing such actions arises from applying something like a User Pays Principle of Taxation. Insofar as one is able to pay for some benefit one is receiving, it seems fair that one should pay for it.

The fourth premise seems trivially true, that is, businesspeople have an interest in the preservation of business.

Plausible as this argument appears to be, a businessperson might still resist the idea that it is reasonable to actively support morality, at least in the sense of conducting one's business in accordance with moral principles. Taking a cue from Machiavelli's advice to his Prince, a businessperson might argue as follows.

To say that morality is necessary for community and therefore for business is to speak in very general terms that do not capture the real situation. More precisely, one should say that it is the institution of morality or the common practice of acting on moral principles that is necessary for community and business. It is certainly not necessary for each and every person to be moral. Indeed, if it were, there would be no communities because the world is full of immoral rascals. However, the institution of morality is a pure public good in the straightforward sense that even people who do not share its costs may share its benefits, perhaps provided that they do not get caught. Because it is a pure public good, it creates a free-rider problem. A Machiavellian businessperson would grant the necessity of publicly appearing to act in accordance with moral principles, but covertly she or he would try to take a free ride on everyone else's good behavior. As long as it remained common practice for most people to play by the rules, to act in accordance with moral principles, the institution of morality and business would be secure. Then, by pretending to play the game, a Machiavellian business-person would be able to enjoy the benefits of the institution of morality and business plus the additional payoffs resulting from her or his duplicity.

Machiavelli's advice makes as much sense today as it ever did and, broadly speaking, there are only two ways to address a free-rider problem. One can use coercion or rational persuasion, including moral arguments. The two approaches are not mutually exclusive, because a rational person might find herself or himself coerced by excellent arguments and might even come to see the wisdom in such arguments as a result of being appropriately coerced (i.e., punished). Nevertheless, it is useful to think of the two approaches as alternatives. Books like this one are obviously designed in the interests of persuasion.

As I explain in a later chapter in this volume (Chapter 6) on trust, I think most people are nicer than most people seem to give them credit for. I do not doubt, however, that some people would take a free ride on their neighbors at any opportunity and maybe there are some situations that would bring down the most virtuous among us. Apart from such extreme cases, it may be possible to persuade many potential free riders to pay a fair share of the costs of sustaining the institution of morality. For instance, one might suggest that others are more likely to believe one's preaching in support of business ethics if one is perceived to be practicing what one is preaching, and one might be more likely to be perceived to be engaged in such practice if one really is engaged in it. One might add that because one's own covert treachery undermines the institution of morality that is necessary for one's own good (business), one is engaging in potentially self-destructive activities. For this or that potential free rider in this or that particular situation, either or both of these arguments might carry some weight.

There is another argument that carries some weight with some businesspeople, but seems to me to be very dangerous to use. This argument runs as follows.

1. Rational businesspeople ought (prudentially, in their own self-interest) to do whatever is profitable for business.
2. It is profitable to conduct business in accordance with principles of morality.
   So, rational businesspeople ought to conduct business in accordance with principles of morality.

In brief, a businessperson ought to be morally good because there is money in it or, at least, there is more money in moral goodness than in moral evil.

The danger that I see in this argument comes from the fact that it clearly makes profits or increased money-making capacity the reason or motive for doing what is morally required and being morally good. This raises two problems. In the first place, insofar as one is acting primarily in the interest of increasing profits, it is trivially true that one's primary interest is not in doing what is morally right. So, there would be nothing morally praiseworthy about one's motive for action. Consequently, one of the most important features of virtuous action, namely, a morally virtuous or good intention, would be absent. Second, because profits are accepted as legitimate motives even for moral action, in all those cases where estimated greater profits were connected with morally evil deeds, it would be acceptable for businesspeople to engage in the latter. In other words, the trouble with making the bottom line in a business sense (increasing profits) the bottom line for moral purposes is that the two lines are not the same. So, in conflict situations when both cannot be realized, morality would be abandoned in favor of profits, which is precisely the opposite conclusion that a defender of business ethics would want to see.

The question now is: What, if anything, is the difference between the earlier argument that I claim is the best argument in defense of business ethics and this other argument that I claim is the worst argument? Evidently both arguments appeal to a businessperson's self-interest. The first appeals to one's interest in sustaining a market economy or business itself, and the second appeals to one's interest in increasing one's own profits.

I think there is a fundamental difference in these interests, which is disguised by referring to them both as self-interests. The difference is that a market economy or business is a public good, whereas personal profits are private goods. Business or a market economy is a public good in the sense that it is a functioning institution of a community and people who live in communities with such institutions enjoy their benefits even if they do not pay for them. For example, even Canadians who do not own cars or television sets benefit from the fact that they live in a country in which taxes are collected from people who buy, sell, and service such items and the taxes pay for many public goods and services, like environmental clean-ups, education, and health care facilities. Without getting into arguments about whether or not there might be even more public goods and services if we had a command economy or some sort of an economy without any form of business, it seems fair to say that the particular type of mixed market economy we enjoy, including business as a fundamental feature, does generate benefits from which nonpurchasers cannot be excluded. Accordingly, business or a market economy may be regarded as a pure public good.

In contrast to such functioning institutions, the private profits that a business or businessperson makes are not public goods, although one could correctly say that the institution or common practice of profit-making is a public good. In the usual case, other people and nonpurchasers in particular cannot enjoy the benefits of someone else's private enterprise. If this were not so, there would be little meaning left in the idea of private enterprise and in the distinction between private and public goods.

Thus, the important difference between the alleged self-interest of the best argument and that of the worst argument is that the motive in the former case is the pursuit of a public good whereas the motive in the latter case is the pursuit of private profit. Presumably, then, people acting on the former motive know that others cannot be excluded from any benefits that they obtain whereas people acting on the latter motive know that others can be excluded from any benefits that they obtain. Therefore, unlike the former, the latter people really are acting in their own self-interest in the exclusionary sense usually contemplated by those describing any action as self-interested. Furthermore, because the most important aim of the institution of morality is to resolve conflicts of interest among people pursuing their own selfish interests, any argument in support of the institution that appealed to selfish interests would be self-defeating, if not literally self-contradictory. In effect, it would be an argument asserting that selfishness is both morally praise-worthy and blameworthy, which is logically absurd.

Finally, then, if I am right about the difference in the motives involved in the best and worst arguments for business ethics, then that would provide a good reason to distinguish the two arguments as I have distinguished them here. The first argument really is supportive of my thesis that businesspeople ought to endorse moral principles and apply them in the market, and the second argument really is dangerously subversive for my thesis. Although there is no guarantee that the best argument will be decisive in every situation that every businessperson finds herself or himself in, the argument does seem to provide a good reason for accepting my general thesis.

6

The Impact of Trust on Business,
International Security, and the Quality of Life

In this chapter I am bringing together three lines of research that I have been engaged in for some years in relative isolation, namely, research on social indicators and quality-of-life measurement, on international peace and security, and on business ethics. The three areas overlap in many ways, but the common thread passing through all three areas that is the focus of attention here is trust. I am not going to undertake a logical analysis of the concept of trust. Bluhm (1987) claimed that trust is a "heroic concept" worthy of detailed analysis, while Baier (1985, 1986) and Govier (1989) have already begun the task in earnest. For present purposes it is enough to think of trust as a relatively informed attitude or propensity to allow oneself and perhaps others to be vulnerable to harm in the interest of some perceived greater good. As will be explained below, trust is a necessary but certainly not a sufficient condition of a

AUTHOR'S NOTE: Adapted from "The Impact of Trust on Business, International Security and the Quality of Life" by A. C. Michalos (1990). In *Journal of Business Ethics, 9*, pp. 619-638. Used with permission of Kluwer Academic Publishers. Earlier versions of this chapter were presented at the International Conference on Social Reporting at the Science Center of Berlin, Federal Republic of Germany, September 18-20, 1989, and at a luncheon meeting of the Centre for Ethics and Corporate Policy, Toronto, ON, Canada, February 1989.

I would like to thank the following people for helpful comments: Deborah C. Poff, Frank M. Andrews, Bruce Headey, Wolfgang Zapf, M. Harvey Brenner, Leo Groarke, Trudy Govier, Jean Smith, and Shirley Farlinger.

high quality of life, international peace and security, and a market or exchange-based economy.

Virtually all contemporary research on subjective well-being, quality of life, happiness, and satisfaction with life as a whole shows that good interpersonal relations contribute more than anything else to these desirable states. If one were to list plausible necessary conditions for good interpersonal relations, trust would certainly be included in the list. For nearly 2 decades there have been more than 1,100 titles published every year on the general topic of subjective well-being (Michalos, 1987). Much of this literature deals with the psychological dynamics of subjective well-being, including the relations between relatively objective features of the world and people's perceptions and evaluations of those features.

According to Macintosh (1985), there are nine "serious generic problems" in the literature of Western nations' international Confidence Building and Security Measures, including the following two:

1. A failure to explicitly discuss the actual psychological processes that are assumed to (a) mediate or facilitate the creation of "confidence" and (b) overcome the "misperception" of intentions and ambiguous actions;
2. A general failure to appreciate the ramifications of the fact that Confidence-Building *is an intrinsically psychological process* (i.e., there is stunning disregard for the intellectual and emotional distortions that cognitive processes can wreak on perceptions of "trust," "predictability," "confidence," and "certainty"—all vital features of meaningful Confidence-Building). (p. 87)

When I did a computer search of the Social Science Citation Index in January 1989 on the general topics of trust and confidence, I found more than 3,000 titles. Macintosh (1985) was only able to scratch the surface of this research, mentioning some salient work in decision theory and cognitive psychology. But he emphasized the need for and the potentially great benefits of a more thorough review of the literature. He did not mention the literature from the field of social indicators research and quality-of-life studies, but this area represents an enormous untapped resource, a resource that I am just barely going to be able to tap here. Earlier attempts to connect some aspects of social indicators/ quality-of-life research to peace and security studies may be found in Michalos (1980a, 1989).

According to Sellerberg (1982), confidence and trust have always been necessary conditions of people living together in communities. Following insights of such sociological authorities as Georg Simmel and

Max Weber, "Trade," she wrote, "needs for its existence confidence and trust" (p. 39). Then she shows how the trust and confidence based on familiarity and personal relations that was characteristic of earlier social arrangements increasingly tends to be based on nonpersonal information, consumer laws, technological devices, and other forms of regulation.

Lewis and Weigert (1985) claim that "society is possible only through *trust* in its members, institutions and forms" (p. 455), and Short (1984) takes a similar line, arguing that contemporary assessments of risk are largely assessments of the trustworthiness of institutions and institutional arrangements designed to cope with risks.

Clearly, research on trust and confidence is directly relevant to research on quality of life, peace and security, and business ethics. Although one of the aims of this chapter is to review enough relevant research to provoke others to undertake their own investigations, that is not my fundamental aim. My basic theses are that the world is to some extent constructed by each of us, that it can and ought to be constructed in a more benign way, that such construction will require more trust than most people are currently willing to grant, and that most of us will be better off if most of us can manage to be more trusting in spite of our doubts.

PERCEPTION, TRUST, AND MEASURABLE RISK

In Michalos (1980a), I showed that in 1973 to 1974, although Americans were more than five times as vulnerable to violent crime as Canadians,

> there was no significant difference in the proportion of people in both countries who expressed some fear of walking alone at night in their own areas. In both countries close to 40% of the respondents [in national Gallup polls] felt this way. (p. 16)

Clearly, there was something intervening between people's perceived security and the objectively measured risk of victimization and, with some justification, Canadians might have felt and expressed greater security than Americans.

Studies of rural residents of Ohio (Mullen & Donnermeyer, 1985; Phillips & Wurschmidt, 1982) and Indiana (Donnermeyer, 1982) showed that concern with crime was considerably disproportionate to the probability of victimization indicated by crime rates. More important, for our purposes, Conklin (1976) and Mullen and Donnermeyer (1985) found that higher trust was related to less perceived crime and more perceived safety in one's neighborhood. According to the latter two authors, trust of neighbors functioned as a mediating variable between isolation and perceived safety for the rural elderly of Ohio.

Some observers think the media create the "reality" to which people react. MacKuen (1984) matched American concerns with crime against actual crime rates and media reports of crime in the period 1966 to 1976 and concluded that "the public's attention is directed by editorial judgments and not, at least in the aggregate, by awareness of the objective conditions" (p. 456). When he looked at concerns with Vietnam, inflation, unemployment, and energy shortages, the same tidy correlation did not appear. The media do not seem to be responsible for all kinds of perceived risks.

Citrin and Green (1988) reviewed American national opinion polls regarding trust and confidence in presidential leadership and government from the early 1960s to 1984. They found that

> the so-called Misery Index (the sum of the inflation and unemployment rates) and confidence in government . . . moved in tandem. Throughout the 1970s, the American economy stagnated and political cynicism increased. In the 1980s, first inflation and then unemployment abated; during this period trust in government began to rise . . . economic outcomes influence approval of the president's job performance, which in turn affects more generalized feelings of confidence in government. (pp. 438-441)

MacKuen also found that people's judgments about the seriousness of unemployment were closely related to relatively objectively measured unemployment rates, but their judgments about inflation were more closely related to media reports.

Several studies have shown that people living relatively near to nuclear plants tend to have more confidence in the safety of nuclear power than people living relatively far from them (Manning, 1982), although following the 1979 accident at the Three Mile Island Nuclear Station in Pennsylvania local residents reported levels of perceived threat considerably greater than what might have been justified on the basis of reported actual radiation levels.

Newcomb (1986) reported results of a 1980 survey of 722 young adults in Los Angeles County showing that, compared to males, females were more troubled by nuclear power and weapons, and had less nuclear denial. He ominously concluded that

> Results of this study show clearly the emotional (depression, lowered quality of life) and social (drug use and its attendant problems) concomitants of living in a world in which a nuclear atrocity is a very real danger. The consequences

for emotional and psychological development are staggering because a feeling of security and trust is fundamental to healthy growth and maturation. In one way, denial and psychic numbing may be adaptive mechanisms to cope with living with the unthinkable. . . . Although it relieves depression and anxiety on a temporary basis, the long-term outcome of such defenses may be nuclear war because of apathy and lack of involvement. (Newcomb, 1986, p. 918)

Driedger and Munton (1988) reported that Francophones found the USSR to be more of a threat than English-speaking Canadians perceived it to be, and younger Canadians expressed greater trust in the Soviets than in the Americans.

SOCIAL CONSTRUCTION OF PERCEPTION, KNOWLEDGE, AND VALUE

I am enough of an epistemological realist or objectivist to grant that there is a world relatively independent of this or that person, containing things with more or less objectively measurable properties, which are more or less objectively comparable. But these points must be made with some care because there is a big difference between what one may grant and what one can prove.

To some extent all knowledge is relative in several respects. All human artifacts, including methods, practices, principles, and bodies of knowledge are constructed by people with a variety of interests and purposes precisely to serve those interests and purposes. The foundation of our most impressive and apparently certain empirical knowledge consists of nothing more than fallible, negotiated agreements among diverse research communities regarding what is the case and what are to count as good reasons for accepting some claims as well warranted and rejecting others as not well warranted. In short, assuming that one's knowledge extends precisely as far as one's good reasons and that what counts as a good reason is determined by negotiations within some research community, it follows that one's knowledge is finally determined by and relative to those negotiations (Michalos, 1980b).

Besides all the aspects of human artifacts that are built in by design, there are many that result from the fact that people cannot choose their biological parents or the latter's socioeconomic class; the time, place, and circumstances of their birth; the events that surround them; all the people whose lives interact with theirs, such as their parents' friends and their friends' parents, relatives, school teachers, classmates, next-door neighbors, neighborhood bullies; and so on. We are creative and adaptive creatures of history and culture, and there is no way to decide once and for all time exactly which features of our world we have merely constructed and which are found. It seems highly unlikely that the whole universe has somehow been constructed out of our imagination, but there is no way, I think, to say just how much has been constructed.

An overview of the sort of symbolic interactionist point of view assumed here may be found in House (1977). Evidence for the social construction of perception, knowledge, and evaluation may be found in Angel and Thoits (1987) involving the construction of illness; LaRocco (1985) regarding working conditions; O'Reilly and Caldwell (1970, 1985) for job task perceptions, job enrichment perceptions, and job satisfaction; White and Mitchell (1979) for perceptions of job enrichment; Durbin (1980) for scientific knowledge; Zalesny, Farace, and Kurchner-Hawkins (1985) for trust in an organization's administration; Bella, Mosher, and Calvo (1988) for trust in the organizational process involved with nuclear waste disposal; Bella (1987) for trust in the professional judgment of engineers; Linsky, Colby, and Straus (1986) for alcohol-related problems; Schlenker (1987) for self-identity; Shepelak (1987) for self-evaluations and the legitimation of socioeconomic status; Lavee, McCubbin, and Olson (1987) for family crises; Short (1984) for judgments of the risk of criminal victimization; and Adams (1988) for assessments of risk on highways and in playgrounds. Generally speaking, the more ambiguous the environment and the more cohesive one's group, the more influence the latter will have on one's constructions (Hackman, 1976).

O'Reilly and Caldwell (1985) summarize some of the important dynamics in the social construction of reality in the workplace as follows:

> Within work groups, there may emerge a consensus about what are the important features of the work environment. In this manner, groups may act to make salient certain aspects of the job and downplay others. Newcomers to a group are quickly made aware of what is important, how one should feel about certain aspects of the job, and what are acceptable standards of behaviour. This may lead to identical tasks being perceived of and responded to differently across groups. Thus, in addition to the effects of informational social influence, groups may also develop a normative framework for interpreting and responding to facets of the work environment resulting in a stable social construction of reality that may vary across work groups faced with objectively similar circumstances. (p. 195)

If one's "workplace" happens to be an institution responsible for negotiating international peace and security, the latter may hang in a precarious socially constructed balance.

Snyder (1984) summarized his excellent review by saying that:

investigations of the reality-constructing consequences of social beliefs make clear just what it is that is inherently and fundamentally *social* about social beliefs. That is, these investigations sensitize us to the links between social beliefs and social reality. Social beliefs can and do create their own social reality. The very events of the social world . . . may be products of preconceptions about the social world. . . . Social beliefs are *social* beliefs precisely because of their intimate involvement in the construction and the reconstruction of social reality in ongoing and continuing social relationships. Social beliefs are *social* beliefs precisely because of the links they create between the domain of thought and the domain of action. (pp. 293-294)

PERSONAL EXPECTATIONS, BIAS, AND CONSTRUCTIONS OF REALITY

Evidence for the impact of personal expectations on constructions (including perceptions, evaluations, and beliefs about the world and one's own self) may be found in Miller and Turnbull (1986) and Snyder (1984). A substantial amount of evidence of personal bias in the organization of systems of cognitions, conations, and affects (belief systems broadly construed) has been gathered by Schlenker and Miller (1977), Greenwald (1980, 1981), Greenwald and Pratkanis (1984), and Greenwald and Breckler (1985).

According to Greenwald and Pratkanis (1984), most people's belief systems have a bias toward

egocentricity, the tendency of judgment and memory to be focused on self, . . . *beneffectance*, the tendency for self to be perceived as effective in achieving desired ends, while avoiding undesired ones, and . . . *cognitive conservatism*, the tendency to resist cognitive change.

The second characteristic includes a

tendency to recall successes more readily than failures . . . the acceptance of responsibility for successes but not for failures on individual or group tasks . . . denial of responsibility for harming others . . . [and] . . . the tendency to identify with victors and to disaffiliate with losers.

The third characteristic includes the tendency to adopt

information-seeking strategies that selectively confirm initial hypotheses . . . selective recall of information that confirms previously established beliefs . . . selective generation of arguments that support opinions under attack . . . researchers' selective evaluation of their own data as a function of the data's agreement with their hypotheses . . . rewriting of memory . . . so as to obscure the occurrence of opinion change . . . believing that newly acquired facts have had lengthy residence in memory . . . [and] . . . overestimating the validity of inaccurate memories. (pp. 139-140)

The tendency for people to be overconfident about their beliefs and alleged knowledge has been demonstrated in a number of studies. For example, Fischhoff and MacGregor (1982) reviewed research on groups of psychology graduate students, executives, civil engineers, bankers, clinical psychologists, and untrained and professional weather forecasters and concluded that

Knowledge generally increases as confidence increases. However, it increases too swiftly, with a doubling of confidence being associated with perhaps a 50 percent increase in knowledge. With all but the easiest of tasks, people tend to be overconfident regarding how much they know. (p. 155)

Faust and Ziskin (1988) reviewed several studies on the comparative accuracy of judgments of expert clinical psychologists and psychiatrists versus those of laypersons, and concluded that "Confidence and accuracy can be inversely related, and yet [a] jury may well accept the opinion of an expert who exudes confidence over that of an opposing expert who expresses appropriate caution" (p. 35).

Koriat, Lichtenstein, and Fischhoff (1980) claimed that

People who are interested in properly assessing how much they know should work harder in recruiting and weighing evidence. However, that extra effort is likely to be of little avail unless it is directed toward recruiting contradicting reasons. (p. 117)

These researchers found that the most effective way of resisting one's inclinations to consider only arguments supporting one's own position is to routinely insist on a review of arguments opposed to it. The Scholastic philosophers who typically reviewed objections to their theses before presenting arguments for them would have been pleased to see the experimental evidence uncovered by Fischhoff and his colleagues.

What actually can be recalled from one's past depends to some extent on how far away it is, how it was encoded in one's memory, and how long and hard one tries. But people's memories play tricks on them by obliterating some things and embellishing others. Sometimes they will put several events together to create an experience that never happened (Bradburn, Rips, & Shevell, 1987). If asked what particular stimulus provoked what response, they frequently will pick the wrong stimulus.

> Even when they are thoroughly cognizant of the existence of both stimulus and response, they often deny that a genuinely influential stimulus affected their response and assert that a noninfluential stimulus did affect their response. (Nisbett & Bellows, 1977, pp. 613-614)

They seem to be more influenced by their own or generally accepted theories and rationalizations of why they behave, think, and feel as they do than they are by having some privileged and private access to their own mental and behavioral processes (Nisbett & Wilson, 1977).

At least since Festinger's (1957) research on cognitive dissonance, some people have wondered whether the troublesome thing about discrepancies between what one expects to happen and what actually happens is the mere fact of a perceived inconsistency in beliefs (the so-called consistency model) or the more personal fact that holding inconsistent beliefs might affect one's own self-esteem (the incentive model). Schlenker (1975) provided part of an answer. Although his research was limited to people's presentations of their own selves to themselves and to others, his results were fairly decisive in this area. "Under public performance conditions," he wrote,

> (where future public events could invalidate an unrealistically positive self-presentation), self-presentations were consistent with subjects' expectations of actual performance. However, under anonymous conditions, self-presentations were quite favourable and unaffected by expectations of actual performance. The results support an incentive model and fail to support a consistency model. Subjects seemed to desire as self-enhancing and approval gaining a public image as possible but conceded to the demands of public reality when necessary. (Schlenker, 1975, p. 1030)

In a later study, Schlenker and Leary (1985) reported that

> people with larger discrepancies between the real self and the ideal self on particular traits were prone to anxiety and self-doubt and also lacked interpersonal skills. Those with smaller discrepancies were characterised as being more socially poised, confident, and adept in their dealings with the problems of everyday life. (p. 177)

They also found that the combination of low expectations of goal achievement and a very important goal produced not only negative affect, but also

> physical or psychological withdrawal from the situation, and self-preoccupation with one's limitations . . . a protective self-presentational style . . . a lowered level of participation in interactions (e.g., initiating fewer conversations, talking less frequently), the avoidance of topics that might reveal one's igno- rance . . . minimal disclosure of information about the self . . . and a passive yet pleasant interaction style that avoids disagreement (e.g., reflective listen- ing, agreeing with others, smiling).

On the other hand,

> high as compared to low outcome expectations prompt people to begin difficult tasks sooner rather than procrastinate or avoid the tasks, work harder on them, and persist longer in the face of obstacles. (Schlenker & Leary, 1985, pp. 171-176)

People's expectations are so influential that Levenson and Gottman (1985) were able to explain over 60% of the variance in a person's marital satisfaction by that person's physiological reactions (heart rates, bodily movement, and skin conductance levels) to the presence of the person's partner. Experiments were designed so that participants' physiological reactions were monitored 5 minutes prior to and throughout some social interaction. To their surprise, physiological data from the first 5 minutes were highly predictive of the reported marital satisfaction of both partners. Levenson and Gottman (1985) concluded that

> In happy marriages, there may be an expectation of pleasure and a sense of optimism that becomes associated with the anticipation of interaction. . . . In unhappy marriages, an expectation of displeasure, dread, and pessimism may evolve because past interactions . . . have been experienced as highly punish- ing. We believe that it is these pleasurable or unpleasurable expectations that account for the arousal differences we have observed during baseline periods when couples sit facing each other for 5 minutes in silence, knowing that they will soon be engaged in interaction. (p. 92)

According to Liebrand, Messick, and Wolters (1986), others have referred to egocentric biases as "self-handicapping" biases. Messick and Sentis (1983) reviewed evidence of an egocentric fairness bias, which is a tendency for people to see arrangements that favor themselves over others as fairer than arrangements that favor others.

> People will judge the efforts that they make to achieve a favourable outcome to be appropriate and proper, whereas the behaviors that the other party or parties employ to achieve their ends may be viewed as inappropriate or unfair. (Liebrand et al., 1986, p. 591)

Using samples mainly of Dutch undergraduates, these authors replicated studies undertaken by Messick and others in the United States, and concluded that

> Since the replication was conducted in a different country and different language, the results suggested that these fairness biases have transcultural generality. (Liebrand et al., 1986, p. 602)

Shepelak's (1987) survey in Indiana led to the conclusion that "those in relatively advantaged positions believe their advantage to be fair whereas those in relatively disadvantaged positions question the fairness of their rewards" (p. 499). Similarly, Feather and O'Brien (1986) claimed that "cross-sectional studies show that the unemployed tend to blame their condition on external factors while the employed are relatively more inclined to appeal to internal factors when accounting for unemployment" (p. 123).

Liebrand, Jansen, Rijken, and Suhre (1986) replicated other research showing that although some people think of cooperation and competition in relatively moralistic terms as good or bad, others think of these behavioral options in terms of strength or weakness; that is, in terms of social potency. Thus, for example, behavior that one person characterizes as cooperative and morally praiseworthy, another might characterize as weak willed and ineffective. Add this dimension to those described above and it is easy to imagine a scenario in which I might offer you a package that I believe is fair to you but is really favorable to me; you might accept it out of generosity, and I might interpret your generosity as weakness. Indeed, because it is likely that you would recognize my interpretation and grant that there may be something in it, in time I might even get you to interpret your behavior as I do. Of course, what one would like to see happen is that I would come to see the world as you do, in which case I might be inclined to make offers in the future that were genuinely fair.

Jones (1986) reviewed evidence indicating that people's constructions of reality have some creative impact on the latter. Thus,

> An approach orientation (for example, one involving smiles and eye contact) is the most likely behavioral reaction to the expectation of warmth, friendli-

ness, and liking. Expectations of hostility or competitiveness tend to breed hostility or competitiveness in response. If we think someone is emotionally fragile, we will typically respond with cautious and accommodating behavior. (Jones, 1986, p. 43)

To make matters worse, at least from the point of view of descriptive accuracy, when people construct explanations for the constructed behavior of others, they have a distinct bias for character-disposition accounts versus situational accounts. For example, I expect you to be untrustworthy and treat you as if you are; then, after you show some sign of untrustworthiness, I attribute it to a latent character flaw in you rather than a set-up by me. Jones refers to this sort of bias as "correspondence bias" and claims that

> people almost inevitably prefer to make personal attributions for behaviors that can be fully explained by the circumstances of situational constraint . . . even when the constraint is extreme and even when it is induced by the perceiver himself or herself. (Jones, 1986, p. 44)

According to Bell, Daly, and Gonzales (1987), both Ross and Sicoly (1979) and Thompson and Kelley (1981) reported that "individuals within close relationships tend to perceive themselves as more responsible than their partners for its positive aspects" (p. 451). Bell et al.'s own sample of 109 women "believed they were more responsible than their husbands for the maintenance of their marriages" (p. 451).

Rempel, Holmes, and Zanna (1985) studied trusting relationships among 47 couples and claimed that "there was a tendency for people to view their own motives as less self-centered and more exclusively intrinsic in flavor than their partner's motives" (p. 95). For these authors, a task motivation is intrinsic for someone insofar as the latter engages in it for its own sake rather than for the sake of something else. Thus, what they observed was a tendency for people to think of themselves as doing things for their partners for their mutual satisfaction and to think of their partners as doing things for them to get something else, something besides mutual satisfaction.

To some extent, one's own sense of personal security and self-esteem influence one's capacity for developing intimate and trusting relationships (Barry, 1970; Rempel et al., 1985). Several studies show that good communication is one of the most important influences on marital satisfaction (Michalos, 1986), and among the most important things one can communicate to a loved one or friend is information about one's own self and internal states. Such communication is facilitated by trust (Franzoi, Davis, & Young, 1985; Gibbs, 1978).

TABLE 6.1 Red Cross Study

Percentage Who Would Give Blood		*Percentage Who Would Not Give Blood*	
60		40	
% estimating others would give blood	% estimating others would not give blood	% estimating others would give blood	% estimating others would not give blood
39	61	30	70

60% said they would give blood, but 32% thought others would.

SOURCE: From "Fabricating and Ignoring Social Reality: Self-Serving Estimates of Consensus," by G. R. Goethals (1986). In *Relative Deprivation and Social Comparison*, edited by J. M. Olson, C. P. Herman, & M. P. Zanna. Hillsdale, NJ: Lawrence Erlbaum, p. 152. Copyright 1986 by Lawrence Erlbaum. Reprinted with permission.
NOTE: N = 50 undergraduates.

EXPERIMENTAL RESEARCH ON TRUST

Goethals (1986) reported results of several small group undergraduate studies of the following sort. Students are informed that a Red Cross blood donor clinic will be set up on campus for the next few days. They are asked if they will give blood and if they think others will do the same. Table 6.1 shows the responses from 50 undergraduates. Sixty percent of the students said they would give blood, but only 32% thought others would. Of those who said they would give, 61% thought others would not; and of those who said they would not give, 70% thought others would not. Thus, neither the givers nor the nongivers were very optimistic about the generosity of their peers, but the nongivers were more pessimistic than the givers. If we assume that the students were making honest reports about their own behavior and judgments about that of their peers, then most students were more pessimistic about their peers than the circumstances warranted. Most students were apparently more generous with their blood than most students believed they would be.

In May 1989, I tried out a couple similar scenarios on my own students in introductory business ethics and philosophy of science courses. Results from both classes are combined and displayed in Tables 6.2 and 6.3.

In the stranded seniors case, the story is that

you and a friend are driving down a country road one night just before dusk and you see an old man and woman beside their car with its hood up. There are no homes or stores in sight, and the people are flagging passing cars in order to get someone to stop to help them out. Do you think you would

TABLE 6.2 Stranded Senior Strangers Case

Percentage Who Would Stop to Help				Percentage Who Would Not Stop to Help			
88				12			
% estimating others would stop		% estimating others would not stop		% estimating others would stop		% estimating others would not stop	
62		38		18		82	
M	F	M	F	M	F	M	F
61	39	61	39	0	100	67	33

88% said they would stop, but 57% thought most people would stop.

NOTE: N = 93 University of Guelph undergraduates, May 1989.

TABLE 6.3 Lost Wallet Case

Percentage Who Would Return Everything				Percentage Who Would Not Return All			
91				9			
% estimating others would return everything		% estimating others would not return all		% estimating others would return everything		% estimating others would not return all	
51		49		29		71	
M	F	M	F	M	F	M	F
59	41	55	45	50	50	40	60

91% said they would return everything, but 49% thought most would return everything.

NOTE: N = 74 University of Guelph undergraduates, May 1989.

probably stop to help them? (Yes or no.) Do you think most people would probably stop to help them? (Yes or no.) Are you male or female?

Table 6.2 shows that although 88% said they would stop, only 57% thought most people would stop. Unlike the Goethals study, of those who said they would stop, a minority of 38% thought most others would not stop; but 82% of the nonstoppers thought most people would not stop. So, we have a fairly clear case of what some people call a false consensus bias according to which people are inclined to estimate that the behavior and attitudes of other are similar to their own; see, for example, Fields and Schuman (1976), Ross, Green, and House (1977), Judd and Johnson (1981), and van der Pligt (1984). Nisbett and Kunda (1985) claimed that

> the false consensus bias is a very useful heuristic to employ in the absence of other knowledge: For most of the distributions we examined, the majority of people would be right to assume that most other people's stances are not very different from their own. (p. 309)

On the basis of the responses shown in Table 6.2, the false consensus bias would have been a useful heuristic for most people for the stranded seniors scenario too. More important, if most people would have granted that most people were like themselves, they would have found most people nicer than they imagined them to be.

Table 6.2 also provides some data regarding male and female differences. Of those who said they would stop, more males than females thought others would stop and more males than females thought others would not stop. Of those who said they would not stop, only females thought others would stop, and twice as many males as females thought others would not stop. So, the nonstopping females seemed a bit more optimistic than the nonstopping males, but the stopping females were not generally more optimistic or pessimistic than the males. Johnson-George and Swap (1982) reported that their own research and that of at least three other authors indicated that females typically scored higher on measures of "generalized trust in others."

I made up the lost wallet case after it occurred to me that some people, especially young women, as a matter of self-defense might never stop to pick up strangers on the road. The story goes as follows:

> Suppose you are walking down the street and you find a wallet containing $50, some credit cards, and a driver's license. Do you think you would probably try to return the wallet and all its contents to its owner? Do you think most people would probably try to return the wallet and its contents to its owner? Are you male or female?

Table 6.3 shows that although 91% said they would return everything, only 49% thought most people would. The false consensus bias does not appear to operate for the returners, but it does for the nonreturners. Seventy-one percent of the nonreturners thought others would not return everything. There do not seem to be any clear distinctions between male and female returners and nonreturners. Again, however, the most important message of this experiment is that most people could justifiably have more confidence in most people if they simply grant that others are probably as decent as they are themselves.

Table 6.4 reviews some of the results of a survey of 280 American marketing managers by Ferrell and Weaver (1978). There are 17 questionable kinds of business activities listed (e.g., padding expense accounts, bribing people, falsifying documents, stealing, etc.), and respondents were asked to rate each one with respect to how unethical they thought it was and how frequently they engaged in it. Then they were asked to estimate their peers' beliefs and behavior. Every one of the 34 answers indicated that respondents thought their peers' beliefs and behavior were not as ethical as their own.

Table 6.5 reviews results of a survey of 500 American marketing researchers, corporate planners, and business librarians by Beltramini (1986). Seven questions concerning relatively unethical competitive information acquisition strategies were put to respondents, and they were asked if they themselves, their companies, and other companies would use the various techniques. In every case, more respondents thought other companies were less scrupulous than their own company and themselves. Cohen and Czepier (1988) replicated these results with a sample of 451 American business personnel attending seminars on gathering competitive intelligence.

Table 6.6 lists some results of three American surveys from three different years, involving a national sample of managers and 118 executives of manufacturing firms reported by Vitell and Festervand (1987). Respondents were asked about their own behavior and that of average executives with respect to padding expense accounts and paying fees to win contracts. For every one of the 18 comparisons, respondents judged others more harshly than themselves.

Table 6.7 gives the results of a survey of 301 members of the American Institute of Certified Public Accountants by Finn, Chonko, and Hunt (1988). Respondents were asked about the opportunities for and frequency of unethical behavior of CPAs in their own and others' firms. As one would expect now, respondents thought that people in other firms had more opportunities for unethical behavior and that they took advantage of those opportunities with more frequent unethical activities.

All of these studies are limited, perhaps outrageously so when they are compared to international peace and security negotiations with their enormous potential costs and benefits, their number and variety of stakeholders, and so on. The first three of the studies suffer the limitations of being confined to university undergraduates, and the other four studies are constrained by the fact that all of them involve surveys of

(text continued on page 78)

TABLE 6.4 Comparison of Beliefs for Respondents, Peers, and Top Management (Mean Scores)

	What I Believe X (Note 1) A	What I Think My Peers Believe X (Note 1) B	What I Do X (Note 2) C	What I Think My Peers Do X (Note 2) D
1. Using company services for personal use	3.23	2.67	1.91	3.01
2. Padding an expense account up to 10%	4.35	3.25	1.47	2.84
3. Giving gifts/favors in exchange for preferential treatment . . .	3.90	3.31	1.20	2.29
4. Taking longer than necessary to do a job	3.77	2.96	1.65	2.70
5. Divulging confidential information	4.71	4.32	1.17	1.91
6. Doing personal business on company time . . .	3.06	2.47	2.11	3.07
7. Concealing one's errors . . .	3.72	3.17	1.53	2.63
8. Passing blame for errors to an innocent coworker . . .	4.84	3.89	1.02	2.17
9. Claiming credit for someone else's work	4.72	3.42	1.11	2.62
10. Falsifying time/quality/ quantity reports	4.73	4.06	1.08	2.17
11. Padding an expense account more than 10%	4.72	3.50	1.08	2.29
12. Calling in sick to take a day off	3.86	3.00	1.29	2.28
13. Authorizing a subordinate to violate company rules . . .	4.24	3.74	1.34	2.00
14. Pilfering company materials and supplies	4.50	3.56	1.59	2.50
15. Accepting gifts/favors in exchange for preferential treatment . . .	4.33	3.44	1.14	2.35
16. Taking extra personal time (lunch hour, breaks, early departure). . .	2.60	2.29	2.22	3.15
17. Not reporting others' violations of company policies . . .	2.89	2.87	2.35	2.65

SOURCE: From "Ethical Beliefs of Marketing Managers," by O. C. Ferrell & K. M. Weaver (1978), *Journal of Marketing, 42*, p. 71. Reprinted with permission of the American Marketing Association.
NOTE 1: A high mean score indicates that the behavior is believed to be highly unethical.
NOTE 2: A low mean score means that the behavior is practiced infrequently.
N = 280 marketing managers.

TABLE 6.5 Use of Competitive Acquisition Strategies

Research Strategies	Percentage of Affirmative Responses		
1. Researcher poses as graduate student working on a thesis. Researcher tells source that dorm phones are very busy, so researcher will call back rather than have phone calls returned. This way, researcher's real identity is protected.	39.6[a]	42.6[b]	75.6[c]
2. Researcher calls the V.P. while she or he is at lunch, hoping to find the secretary who may have information but is less likely to be suspicious about researcher's motives.	60.6	68.7	81.7
3. Researcher calls competitor's suppliers and distributors, pretending to do a study of the entire industry. Researcher poses as a representative of a private research firm and works at home during the project so that the company's identity is protected.	46.1	54.6	81.0
4. The competitor's representative is coming to a local college to recruit employees. Researcher poses as a student job-seeker to learn recruiting practices and some other general information about competitor.	30.1	35.4	62.0
5. The researcher is asked to verify rumors that the competitor is planning to open a new plant in a small southern town. The researcher poses as an agent from a manufacturer looking for a site similar to the one that the competitor supposedly would need. Researcher uses this cover to become friendly with local representatives of the Chamber of Commerce, newspapers, realtors, etc.	42.4	49.1	75.5
6. Researcher corners a competitor employee at a national conference, such as American Marketing Association, and offers to buy drinks at the hotel bar. Several drinks later, the researcher asks the hard questions.	70.6	67.1	86.8
7. Researcher finds an individual who works for the competitor to serve as an informant to researcher's company.	39.1	39.1	73.8

SOURCE: From "Ethics and the Use of Competitive Information Acquisition Strategies," by R. F. Beltramini (1986), *Journal of Business Ethics*, 5, p. 309. Reprinted by permission of Kluwer Academic Publishers.
NOTES: a. Researcher's own company would use this technique.
b. Researcher would use this technique.
c. Researcher believes other companies use this technique.
$N = 500$ marketing researchers, corporate planners, and business librarians.

TABLE 6.6 Oneself Versus the Average Executive

Situation 1: Padding an Expense Account

	1961*		1976*		1985	
	Oneself	Average Executive	Oneself	Average Executive	Oneself	Average Executive
Unacceptable, regardless of circumstances	86%	60%	89%	53%	98%	54%
Acceptable, if other executives in company do the same thing	6%	27%	4%	28%	0%	26%
Acceptable, if the executive's superior knows about it and says nothing	11%	28%	9%	33%	2%	20%

Situation 2: Paying Fee to Get a Contract

	1976		1985	
	Oneself	Average Executive	Oneself	Average Executive
Refuse to pay, even if sale is lost	42%	9%	51%	21%
Pay the fee, feeling it was ethical in the moral climate of the foreign nation	36%	45%	16%	27%
Pay the fee, feeling it was unethical but necessary to help ensure the sale	22%	46%	33%	52%

SOURCE: From "Business Ethics: Conflicts, Practices and Beliefs of Industrial Executives," by S. J. Vitell & T. A. Festervand (1987), *Journal of Business Ethics, 6*, pp. 118-119. Reprinted by permission of Kluwer Academic Publishers.
NOTES: * Sum of percentages exceeds 100% due to multiple responses. $N = 118$ executives of manufacturing firms.

American businesspeople of one sort or another. Still, the most remarkable fact about all the studies is their complete consistency. Every single one makes the same point: Most people think most people are not as nice as they are themselves and, therefore, cannot be trusted to behave as well. Taking respondents at their words, the same studies provided clear evidence that most people were wrong about most people. A more realistic assessment of others' moral virtue would have been more optimistic.

EXPLAINING LACK OF TRUST

Can the respondents be taken at their words? Of course, I don't know. They may be giving honest reports badly distorted by egocentric biases.

TABLE 6.7 Questionnaire Items for Ethics

Questionnaire Items	Average Response[a]	Standard Deviation	Percentage Agree[b]
A. Opportunities for unethical behavior			
1. There are many opportunities for CPAs in my firm to engage in unethical activities	4.6	2.1	35
2. There are many opportunities for CPAs outside my firm to engage in unethical activities	2.7	1.6	76
B. Frequency of unethical behavior			
1. CPAs in my firm often engage in behaviors that I consider to be unethical	6.2	1.2	3
2. CPAs outside my firm often engage in behaviors that I consider to be unethical	3.9	1.7	4.2

SOURCE: From "Ethical Problems in Public Accounting: The View From the Top," by D. W. Finn, L. B. Chonko, & S. D. Hunt (1988), *Journal of Business Ethics, 7*, p. 612. Reprinted by permission of Kluwer Academic Publishers.
NOTES: a. Each respondent was asked to indicate a response on a 7-point Likert scale from strongly agree (1) to strongly disagree (7).
b. Percentage responding "slightly agree," "agree," or "strongly agree."
$N = 301$ members of the American Institute of Certified Public Accountants.

Indeed, one might hypothesize that the egocentric biases are so strong that they virtually wipe out false consensus biases. Even though people are inclined to suppose that most others are like themselves, people may find their self-esteem threatened too much by the supposition that most others are as morally virtuous, trustworthy, or nice as they are themselves. In the interest of protecting their own self-esteem, they might find it necessary to think that they are at least as good as others; that is, others are at best equal to or less virtuous than they are themselves.

Some of the respondents may have seen some of the studies cited earlier regarding fairness biases, social and individual constructions of knowledge, and so on. If so, they would have had considerable evidence of human frailties and might have judged others harshly on the basis of extrapolating some sort of halo effect. But the same extrapolation should have extended to themselves too.

Maybe respondents just judged others on the basis of their own experiences. Insofar as egocentric biases are operative, people will be inclined to experience others as less impressive than themselves, whether or not they are. But just as the fact that one is paranoid does not imply that others are *not* out to get one, the fact that one judges others as less impressive does not imply that they are *not* less impressive than oneself. Maybe most respondents had relatively bad experiences with most people. I doubt that, because I think most people are like most people in most ways. Of course, if that is true, then most people think most people are like most people in most ways, which implies that most people expect most people to be as morally virtuous as they are. If most people ever did have such expectations, then they were either dashed by experience prior to the studies I have just reviewed, or they were not dashed. If they were dashed then respondents were simply making harsh judgments based on their harsh experiences. If they were not dashed, then we are back to square one; maybe their harsh judgments were the result of egocentric biases or intentional distortion, or something else. Again, I just don't know.

According to Headey and Wearing (1988),

> a sense of relative superiority is the usual state for most people. To feel "above average" is normal. If events happen which cause one to feel "average" or "below average," then one has plunged below the normal baseline. To repeat: SRS [the sense of relative superiority] is a crucial mechanism accounting for high levels of SWB [subjective well-being]. (p. 499)

As I report in detail in Michalos (1991a), my own survey of more than 18,000 university undergraduates in 38 countries yielded results that were not quite consistent with Headey and Wearing's claim. Although most of my respondents perceived their status to be "at least average" or "average or above average," it would not be true to say that most respondents perceived their status to be "above average." So, it would not be true to say that the perception of such a status "is a crucial mechanism accounting for high levels of SWB." Still, it does seem fair to say that the feeling that one is at least as good as the next person (similar other) is crucial in accounting for subjective well-being.

Both Glatzer (1987) and Davis (1984) reported social comparison results similar to mine. Glatzer noted that in 1980, 70% of West Germans "classified their own household income as equal to or higher than the household income of the average citizen" (p. 44). Davis looked at the period from 1972 to 1980 covering 9,297 responses to the NORC General Social Survey item asking people to compare their family incomes to "American families in general" and found that 80% of respondents thought they were average or above average (p. 324).

It is likely that most respondents were taught to be nice and to not trust strangers. So, maybe most people were just reporting what they learned at their parents' knees. I guess the prescriptions are not inconsistent, but they are an odd couple because if most people obey the former, then most people can safely ignore the latter. Still, the prescriptions are not unique in this way. The same ethical codes that urge people to be self-reliant also urge them to be generous in helping their neighbors. Odd as these couples appear when given some thought, maybe most people do not give them much thought, especially in rather contrived experimental circumstances.

It is possible, though perhaps unlikely, that respondents are familiar with the economic theory of public goods and the free-rider problem, and their responses are guided by theoretical considerations. A public good may be defined by either of two characteristics, namely, jointness and nonexclusiveness. Roughly speaking, something has the quality of jointness if using it does not imply using it up. For example, any number of people may use the same information or knowledge at the same time and virtually forever. Something has the quality of nonexclusiveness if nonpurchasers cannot be excluded from it. For example, if Canada is internationally secure, then all its inhabitants can enjoy that security whether every person pays for it or not. Furthermore, because everyone benefits whether they pay for it or not, self-interested people have a reason to try to avoid paying for it altogether. That is, they have a reason to try to take a free ride on other peoples' payments. This is the so-called free-rider problem.

The free-rider problem arises in the case before us because things like moral virtue, generosity, and trustfulness are public goods. Not only does using, exercising, or expressing such qualities not imply using them up, but on the contrary, they tend to grow stronger with use. The more people appeal to and display moral virtue, the more others are inclined to behave in the same way. The more people display their trustfulness, the more others are inclined to be trustworthy. Moral virtue in general and trust in particular feeds on itself (Gibbs, 1978; Jones, 1986). Unfortunately, what works for most people most of the time does not work for everyone always. Because most people can enjoy the benefits of most people's good behavior even if some people do not behave well, at least some of the latter will be inclined to and will take a free ride. They will therefore enjoy the benefits of most people's good behavior and any additional benefits they can scrounge out of their own treachery. Thus, maybe most respondents are cautious and even harsh about other people because virtually everyone knows that such free riders exist and no one wants to be taken in by them. In these cases, then, respondents' mistrust is based more on theoretical considerations than on actual experiences.

Finally, we cannot rule out the possibility that respondents do some rough and relatively unconscious calculations patterned after classic textbook decision strategies (Michalos, 1969). Maybe they do a rapid minimax loss assessment, and respond in a manner that would yield the smallest of the greatest possible losses with each option. For example, if they imagine that they will give blood but that most people will not, then they can avoid any great feeling of disappointment when most people do not give blood. On the other hand, the adoption of a pessimistic attitude toward the moral virtue of most people typically would not create any great disappointment. There is some international evidence suggesting that most people are not optimistic about their future (Michalos, 1988). Maybe most people are not optimistic about anything, including other people.

ADDRESSING THE PROBLEM OF LACK OF TRUST

So much seems to hang on trust and trustworthiness, that one ought to have some principled and well-warranted strategy for addressing the problem of what appears to be a significant lack of trust in most people by most people. Because moral reasons are generally regarded as supreme among any reasons that might be offered for intentional human action, it will be worthwhile to begin our search for a strategy in the area of moral philosophy.

Generally speaking, moral philosophers may be divided into two groups, depending on which of the following two principles they regard as the fundamental basis of morality.

1. *Principle of Beneficence*: One ought to try to act so that one's actions tend to impartially improve the human condition.
2. *No-Harm Principle*: One ought to try to act so that one's actions tend not to harm anyone.

So far as I know, there is no absolutely irrefutable argument for either position. People operating on the Principle of Beneficence will try to do as much good as possible. People operating on the No-Harm Principle will try to do as little harm as possible. Personally, I favor universal beneficence because I think moral goodness ought to require more of people than a life of anxious inactivity mixed with pious hopes for our common future. I have no illusions about anyone's ability to behave ideally all or even most of the time, with respect to morality or anything else. But that is not a serious objection to any ideal. Insofar as one has a choice about what sort of moral ideal one ought to be guided by, what sort one ought to recommend to family, friends, and the rest of the human race, I think it is wise to aim high rather than low. So, I prefer universal beneficence.

At least one author has come out in favor of the No-Harm Principle in a way that connects it directly to trust. Gewirth (1987) claimed that

> the moral principle which is at the basis of a civilized society . . . is a principle of mutual trust, of mutual respect for certain basic rights: that persons will not, in the normal course of life, knowingly inflict physical harm on one another, that they will abstain from such harms insofar as it is in their power to do so, insofar as they can informedly control their relevant conduct. (p. 108)

Garfinkel (1963) and Bok (1978) seem to have taken a similar line. From this point of view, then, one might say that one has a right to expect that one will not be harmed intentionally by another person, that one therefore has a right to trust people, and that the latter (meaning everyone) have a duty or moral obligation to be trustworthy. Alternatively, one might say that insofar as adherence to the No-Harm Principle is necessary for a civilized society or a moral community, so is trusting people and being trustworthy. Thus, although I prefer the Principle of Beneficence, even those who prefer the No-Harm Principle as the fundamental basis of morality would have a good reason to take trust and trustworthiness seriously.

Baier (1985) made a provocative and persuasive case for regarding the concept of trust as central for a theory of morality that would be broad enough to include the moral insights of most male theorists concerning the importance of obligations and the moral insights of most female theorists concerning the importance of love. "To trust," she wrote,

> is to make oneself or let oneself be more vulnerable than one might have been to harm from others—to give them an opportunity to harm one, in the confidence that they will not take it, because they have no good reason to. Why should one take such a risk? . . . If the best reason to take such a risk is the expected gain in security which comes from a climate of trust, then in trusting we are always giving up security to get greater security, exposing our throats so that others become accustomed to not biting. A moral theory which made proper trust its central concern could have its own categorical imperative, could replace obedience to self-made laws and freely chosen restraint on freedom with security-increasing sacrifice of security, distrust in the promoters of a climate of distrust, and so on. (pp. 60-61)

In the famous exchange of views on the ethics of belief by William James and W. K. Clifford at the turn of the century (Michalos, 1978), James (1956) wrote:

There are . . . cases where a fact cannot come at all unless a preliminary faith exists in its coming. *And where faith in a fact can help create the fact,* that would be an insane logic which should say that faith running ahead of scientific evidence is the "lowest kind of immorality" into which a thinking being can fall. . . . *A rule of thinking which would absolutely prevent me from acknowledging certain kinds of truth if those kinds of truth were really there, would be an irrational rule.* (pp. 25-28)

As I explained in Michalos (1978), James thought his line of argument was strong enough to justify his belief in God. Because the argument turns on an estimate of one's own costs and benefits of belief versus disbelief, James was probably right. That does not make it right for the rest of us, who might perceive very different costs and benefits. But it does provide a general approach to our problem. I think the following argument is consistent with James's view and reasonable in itself.

From a logical point of view, there are four relevant possible worlds to consider. The world might be such that most people are actually

1. trustworthy and trusted,
2. trustworthy but not trusted,
3. not trustworthy but trusted,
4. not trustworthy and not trusted.

With some exaggeration, the first case may be regarded as Real Paradise. One's trust is completely justified by the "real" world. Assuming that there is little or nothing especially pleasing or satisfying about distrust, the second case may be regarded as a Fool's Hell. One's distrust is not justified by the world and one continues to distrust even though one gets no particular pleasure out of it. The third case may be regarded as a Fool's Paradise. One's trust is not justified by the world, although one continues to trust people anyhow. The fourth case may be regarded as Real Hell. One distrusts most people and one's distrust is completely justified.

Given these possible circumstances, if one usually does not trust most people, then the most one can usually expect to achieve is either a Real Hell or a Fool's Hell. If one usually does trust most people, then the most one can usually expect to achieve is Real Paradise or a Fool's Paradise. One can probably imagine cases in which it would be preferable to have a Real Hell rather than a Fool's Paradise, and vice versa. Still, as a long-range strategy, because trust is a necessary condition of Real Paradise, which is the best of the four possibilities, one ought to try to be trustful. One ought to try to take the extra step, to risk something to achieve the finest human community and the highest quality of life.

It would be foolish for anyone to imagine that trust could be elevated to some sort of a supreme moral principle, the way Royce (1908) recommended loyalty to loyalty as a supreme moral principle. Neither trust nor loyalty can bear such weight (Baier, 1986; Michalos, 1991b). But it does seem to me that the argument in the previous paragraph has some merit, if not as the last word, at least as a first. It is both an argument from prudence and morality. It is prudential to adopt a strategy of trust because, considering the four possible worlds, that will finally lead to Real Paradise if anything will. It is morally right to adopt a strategy of trust from the point of view of the No-Harm Principle, as Gewirth argued, and from the point of view of trust as a necessary condition of impartially improving the human condition, that is, the alternative Principle of Beneficence.

The moral arguments of James, Baier, and myself do not have to be taken on trust. For those who think of prudence as at least as important as, and not implied by, moral virtue, we may improve the case for adopting a strategy of trust with the following considerations.

A necessary and sufficient condition of having a world in which most people trust most people is, obviously, that most people have to trust most people. On a more personal level, it is virtually impossible to have good friends if one does not trust people and is not in turn trustworthy. Furthermore, as indicated earlier, virtually all contemporary research on subjective well-being shows that without good interpersonal relations, it is virtually impossible to have high levels of subjective well-being. Hence, one would expect to find some positive association between measures of trust and subjective well-being.

Fortunately, the presumed relations between trust and subjective well-being were explored in detail by Rotter (1980) and his colleagues, using mainly university undergraduates as subjects. Among other things, Rotter (1980) reported that (a) "The high truster is less likely to be unhappy, conflicted, or maladjusted; . . . " (b) "Regardless of the sex of either the subject or the target person, the high truster was seen as happier, more ethical, and more attractive to the opposite sex, as having had a happier childhood, and as more desirable as a close friend than the low-trust target." (c) "People who trust more are less likely to lie and are possibly less likely to cheat or steal. They are more likely to give others a second chance and to respect the rights of others." (d) "The low trusters of both sexes showed significantly greater feelings of being distrusted, . . . " (e) "The high truster is no less capable of determining who should be trusted and who should not be trusted, . . . It may be true that the high truster is fooled more often by crooks, but the low truster is probably fooled equally often by distrusting honest people, thereby forfeiting the benefits that trusting others might bring." (f) "Some people, obviously low trusters, believe that high trusters are just plain dumb. . . . [but] . . . we have correlated scholastic aptitude scores with trust scores and have in each case found a nonsignificant relationship" (pp. 3-6).

On top of all these characteristics, Williams and Barefoot (1988) claimed that "the available evidence suggests that a cynical, mistrusting attitude toward others and a willingness to express openly the anger and contempt engendered by such an attitude lie at the heart of coronary-prone behavior" (p. 206). The literature on Type A behavior and a variety of diseases is substantial (e.g., see Houston & Snyder, 1988), but Williams (1989) claims, "Hostility and cynical mistrust are now regarded as the lethal elements of Type A behavior by several researchers, and driving ambition is no longer viewed as dangerous" (p. 36).

Inglehart and Rabier (1986) reported

a remarkable congruence between the levels of interpersonal trust and subjective well-being observed in given societies. . . . In the World Values Surveys [1981], overall life satisfaction shows a mean correlation of 0.125 with interpersonal trust, while happiness correlates with trust at the 0.109 level: A given individual is significantly more likely to be happy if he trusts those around him. (p. 53)

Personally, I do not find the indicated correlation coefficients as impressive as Inglehart and Rabier find them.

Finally, it is probably worthwhile to mention the fact that at least two studies showed that a promisor's credibility increased directly with the frequency with which he or she actually fulfilled promises and that subjects relied more often on the former's promises as their perceived credibility increased (Gahagan & Tedeschi, 1968; Schlenker, Helm, & Tedeschi, 1973). This is encouraging evidence for those who are inclined to try to be trustworthy in the interest of generating others' trust.

CONCLUSION

I have tried to make a case for the theses that the world is to some extent constructed by each of us, that it can and ought to be constructed in a more benign way, that such construction will require more trust than most people are currently willing to grant, and that most of us will be better off if most of us can manage to be more trusting in spite of our doubts. It has not been my intention to close the subject, but to open it up for further discussion and exploration. I think Macintosh (1985) was right in his judgment that international peace and security research could profit from contributions by psychologists and sociologists of one sort or another, and I hope that this chapter has established that point. The same may be said of the field of business ethics. The field of social indicators and quality-of-life research is already dominated by psychologists and sociologists. So my message to people in this field is simply the central theses advocated above.

REFERENCES

Adams, J. G. U. (1988). Risk homeostasis and the purpose of safety regulation. *Ergonomics, 31*, 407-428.

Angel, R., & Thoits, P. (1987). The impact of culture on the cognitive structure of illness. *Culture, Medicine and Psychiatry, 11*, 465-494.

Baier, A. (1985). What do women want in a moral theory? *Nous, 19*, 53-63.

Baier, A. (1986). Trust and antitrust. *Ethics, 96*, 231-260.

Barry, W. A. (1970). Marriage research and conflict: An integrative review. *Psychological Bulletin, 73*, 41-54.

Beltramini, R. F. (1986). Ethics and the use of competitive information acquisition strategies. *Journal of Business Ethics, 5*, 307-312.

Bell, R. A., Daly, J. A., & Gonzales, M. C. (1987). Affinity-maintenance in marriage and its relationship to women's marital satisfaction. *Journal of Marriage and the Family, 49*, 445-454.

Bella, D. A. (1987). Engineering and erosion of trust. *Journal of Professional Issues in Engineering, 113*, 117-129.

Bella, D. A., Mosher, C. D., & Calvo, S. N. (1988). Establishing trust: Nuclear waste disposal. *Journal of Professional Issues in Engineering, 114*, 40-50.

Bluhm, L. H. (1987). Trust, terrorism, and technology. *Journal of Business Ethics, 6*, 333-342.

Bok, S. (1978). *Lying*. New York: Pantheon.

Bradburn, N. M., Rips, L. J., & Shevell, S. K. (1987). Answering autobiographical questions: The impact of memory and inference on surveys. *Science, 236*, 157-161.

Citrin, J., & Green, D. P. (1988). Presidential leadership and the resurgence of trust in government. *British Journal of Political Science, 16*, 431-453.

Cohen, W., & Czepier, H. (1988). The role of ethics in gathering corporate intelligence. *Journal of Business Ethics, 7*, 199-204.

Conklin, J. E. (1976). Robbery, the elderly, and fear: An urban problem in search of a solution. In J. Goldsmith & S. Goldsmith (Eds.), *Crime and the elderly* (pp. 142-163). Lexington, MA: Lexington.

Davis, J. A. (1984). New money, an old man/lady and "two's company": Subjective welfare in the NORC General Social Surveys, 1972-1982. *Social Indicators Research, 15*, 319-350.

Donnermeyer, J. F. (1982). Patterns of criminal victimization in a rural setting: The case of Pike County, Indiana. In T. J. Carter, G. H. Phillips, J. F. Donnermeyer, & T. N. Wurschmidt (Eds.), *Rural crime: Integrating research and prevention* (pp. 201-226). Totowa, NJ: Allanheld, Osmun.

Driedger, M., & Munton, D. (1988). *Security, arms control and defence: Public attitudes in Canada.* Ottawa: Canadian Institute for International Peace and Security.

Durbin, P. T. (Ed.). (1980). *A guide to the culture of science, technology and medicine.* New York: Free Press.

Faust, D., & Ziskin, J. (1988). The expert witness in psychology and psychiatry. *Science, 241,* 31-35.

Feather, N. T., & O'Brien, G. E. (1986). A longitudinal study of the effects of employment and unemployment on school-leavers. *Journal of Occupational Psychology, 59,* 121-144.

Ferrell, O. C., & Weaver, K. M. (1978). Ethical beliefs of marketing managers. *Journal of Marketing, 42,* 69-73.

Festinger, L. (1957). *A theory of cognitive dissonance.* Stanford, CA: Stanford University Press.

Fischhoff, B., & MacGregor, D. (1982). Subjective confidence in forecasts. *Journal of Forecasting, 1,* 155-172.

Fields, J. M., & Schuman, H. (1976). Public beliefs about the beliefs of the public. *Public Opinion Quarterly, 40,* 427-448.

Finn, D. W., Chonko, L. B., & Hunt, S. D. (1988). Ethical problems in public accounting: The view from the top. *Journal of Business Ethics, 7,* 605-615.

Franzoi, S. L., Davis, M. H., & Young, R. D. (1985). The effects of private self-consciousness and perspective taking on satisfaction in close relationships. *Journal of Personality and Social Psychology, 48,* 1584-1594.

Gahagan, J. P., & Tedeschi, J. T. (1968). Strategy and the credibility of promises in the Prisoner's Dilemma Game. *Journal of Conflict Resolution, 12,* 224-234.

Garfinkel, H. (1963). A conception of, and experiments with, trust as a condition of stable concerted actions. In O. J. Harvey (Ed.), *Motivation and social interaction: Cognitive determinants* (pp. 187-238). New York: Ronald Press.

Gewirth, A. (1987). Human rights and the prevention of cancer. In D. Poff & W. Waluchow (Eds.), *Business ethics in Canada* (pp. 105-115). Toronto: Prentice Hall of Canada. (Originally published in the *American Philosophical Quarterly,* 1980)

Gibbs, J. R. (1978). *Trust: A new view of personal and organizational development.* Los Angeles: Guild of Tutors Press.

Glatzer, W. (1987). Income. *Social Indicators Research, 19,* 39-46.

Goethals, G. R. (1986). Fabricating and ignoring social reality: Self-serving estimates of consensus. In J. M. Olson, C. P. Herman, & M. P. Zanna (Eds.), *Relative deprivation and social comparison* (pp. 139-159). Hillsdale, NJ: Lawrence Erlbaum.

Govier, T. (1989). *Trust: Some competing accounts in social science and philosophy.* Unpublished manuscript, Philosophy Department, University of Calgary, Alberta.

Greenwald, A. G. (1980). The totalitarian ego: Fabrication and revision of personal history. *American Psychologist, 35,* 603-618.

Greenwald, A. G. (1981). Self and Memory. In G. H. Bower (Ed.), *The psychology of learning and motivation* (pp. 201-236). New York: Academic Press.

Greenwald, A. G., & Breckler, S. J. (1985). To whom is the self presented? In B. R. Schlenker (Ed.), *The self and social life* (pp. 126-145). New York: McGraw-Hill.

Greenwald, A. G., & Pratkanis, A. R. (1984). The self. In R. S. Wyer & T. K. Srull (Eds.), *Handbook of social cognition* (pp. 129-178). Hillsdale, NJ: Lawrence Erlbaum.

Hackman, J. R. (1976). Group influences on individuals. In M. Dunnette (Ed.), *Handbook of industrial and organizational psychology* (pp. 1455-1525). Chicago: Rand McNally.

House, J. S. (1977). The three faces of social psychology. *Sociometry, 40,* 161-177.

Headey, B., & Wearing, A. (1988). The sense of relative superiority—Central to well-being. *Social Indicators Research, 20,* 497-516.

Houston, B. K., & Snyder, C. R. (Eds.). (1988). *Type A behavior pattern: Research, theory and intervention*. New York: John Wiley.

Inglehart, R., & Rabier, J.-R. (1986). Aspirations adapt to situations—But why are the Belgians so much happier than the French? A cross-cultural analysis of the subjective quality of life. In F. M. Andrews (Ed.), *Research on the quality of life* (pp. 1-56). Ann Arbor: University of Michigan, Institute for Social Research.

James, W. (1956). *The will to believe and other essays in popular philosophy*. New York: Dover.

Johnson-George, C., & Swap, W. C. (1982). Measurement of specific interpersonal trust: Construction and validation of a scale to assess trust in a specific other. *Journal of Personality and Social Psychology, 43*, 1306-1317.

Jones, E. E. (1986). Interpreting interpersonal behavior: The effects of expectancies. *Science, 234*, 41-46.

Judd, C. M., & Johnson, J. P. (1981). Attitudes, polarization, and diagnosticity: Exploring the effect of affect. *Journal of Personality and Social Psychology, 41*, 26-36.

Koriat, A., Lichtenstein, S., & Fischhoff, B. (1980). Reasons for confidence. *Journal of Experimental Psychology: Human Learning and Memory, 6*, 107-118.

LaRocco, J. M. (1985). Effects of job conditions on worker perceptions: Ambient stimuli vs. group influence. *Journal of Applied Social Psychology, 15*, 735-757.

Lavee, Y., McCubbin, H. I., & Olson, D. H. (1987). The effect of stressful life events and transitions on family functioning and well-being. *Journal of Marriage and the Family, 49*, 857-873.

Levenson, R. W., & Gottman, J. M. (1985). Physiological and affective predictors of change in relationship satisfaction. *Journal of Personality and Social Psychology, 49*, 85-94.

Lewis, J. D., & Weigert, A. J. (1985). Social atomism, holism, and trust. *The Sociological Quarterly, 26*, 455-471.

Liebrand, W. B. G., Jansen, R. W. T. L., Rijken, V. M., & Suhre, C. J. M. (1986). Might over morality: Social values and the perception of other players in experimental games. *Journal of Experimental Social Psychology, 22*, 203-215.

Liebrand, W. B. G., Messick, D. M., & Wolters, F. J. M. (1986). Why we are fairer than others: A cross-cultural replication and extension. *Journal of Experimental Social Psychology, 22*, 590-604.

Linsky, A. S., Colby, J. P., & Straus, M. A. (1986). Drinking norms and alcohol-related problems in the United States. *Journal of Studies on Alcohol, 47*, 384-393.

Macintosh, J. (1985). *Confidence (and security) building measures in the arms control process: A Canadian perspective*. Ottawa: Department of External Affairs, The Arms Control and Disarmament Division.

MacKuen, M. B. (1984). Reality, the press and citizens' political agendas. In C. F. Turner & E. Martin (Eds.), *Surveying subjective phenomena* (Vol. 2, pp. 443-474). New York: Russell Sage.

Manning, D. T. (1982). Post-TMI perceived risk from nuclear power in three communities. *Nuclear Safety, 23*, 379-384.

Messick, D. M., & Sentis, K. P. (1983). Fairness, preference and fairness biases. In D. M. Messick & K. S. Cook (Eds.), *Equity theory: Psychological and sociological perspectives* (pp. 61-94). New York: Praeger.

Michalos, A. C. (1969). *Principles of logic*. Englewood Cliffs, NJ: Prentice Hall.

Michalos, A. C. (1978). *Foundations of decision-making*. Ottawa: Canadian Library of Philosophy.

Michalos, A. C. (1980a). *North American social report: Vol. 2. Crime, justice and politics*. Dordrecht, the Netherlands: D. Reidel.

Michalos, A. C. (1980b). Philosophy of science: Historical, social and value aspects. In P. T. Durbin (Ed.), *A guide to the culture of science, technology and medicine* (pp. 197-281). New York: Free Press.

Michalos, A. C. (1986). Job satisfaction, marital satisfaction and the quality of life: A review and a preview. In F. M. Andrews (Ed.), *Research on the quality of life* (pp. 57-83). Ann Arbor: University of Michigan Press.

Michalos, A. C. (1987). What makes people happy? *Levekårsforskning Konferanserapport* (Proceedings of the Seminar on Welfare Research) (pp. 12-93). Oslo: Norwegian Research Council for Science and the Humanities.

Michalos, A. C. (1988). Optimism in thirty countries over a decade. *Social Indicators Research, 20,* 177-180.

Michalos, A. C. (1989). *Militarism and the quality of life.* Toronto: Science for Peace/Samuel Stevens.

Michalos, A. C. (1991a). *Global report on student well-being: Vol. 1. Life satisfaction and happiness.* New York: Springer-Verlag.

Michalos, A. C. (1991b). The loyal agent's argument. In D. C. Poff & W. J. Waluchow (Eds.), *Business ethics in Canada* (2nd ed., pp. 236-241). Scarborough, ON: Prentice Hall Canada.

Miller, D. T., & Turnbull, W. (1986). Expectancies and interpersonal processes. *Annual Review of Psychology, 37,* 233-256.

Mullen, R. E., & Donnermeyer, J. F. (1985). Age, trust, and perceived safety from crime in rural areas. *The Gerontologist, 25,* 237-242.

Newcomb, M. D. (1986). Living with the bomb: Nuclear anxiety and emotional health. *Journal of Personality and Social Psychology, 50,* 906-920.

Nisbett, R. E., & Bellows, N. (1977). Verbal reports about causal influences on social judgments: Private access versus public theories. *Journal of Personality and Social Psychology, 35,* 613-624.

Nisbett, R. E., & Kunda, Z. (1985). Perception of social distributions. *Journal of Personality and Social Psychology, 48,* 297-311.

Nisbett, R. E., & Wilson, T. D. (1977). Telling more than we can know: Verbal reports on mental processes. *Psychological Review, 84,* 231-259.

O'Reilly, C., & Caldwell, D. (1970). Informational influence as a determinant of perceived task characteristics. *Journal of Applied Psychology, 64,* 157-165.

O'Reilly, C., & Caldwell, D. (1985). The impact of normative social influence and cohesiveness on task perceptions and attitudes: A social information processing approach. *Journal of Occupational Psychology, 58,* 193-206.

Phillips, G. H., & Wurschmidt, T. N. (1982). The Ohio Rural Victimization Study. In T. J. Carter, G. H. Phillips, J. F. Donnermeyer, & T. N. Wurschmidt (Eds.), *Rural crime: Integrating research and prevention* (pp. 186-200). Totowa, NJ: Allanheld, Osmun.

Rempel, J. K., Holmes, J. G., & Zanna, M. P. (1985). Trust in close relationships. *Journal of Personality and Social Psychology, 49,* 95-112.

Ross, L., Green, D., & House, P. (1977). The false consensus phenomenon: An attributional bias in self-perception and social perception processes. *Journal of Experimental Social Psychology, 13,* 279-301.

Ross, M., & Sicoly, F. (1979). Egocentric biases in availability and attrition. *Journal of Personality and Social Psychology, 37,* 322-336.

Rotter, J. B. (1980). Interpersonal trust, trustworthiness, and gullibility. *American Psychologist, 35,* 1-7.

Royce, J. (1908). *Philosophy of loyalty.* New York: Macmillan.

Schlenker, B. R. (1975). Self-presentation: Managing the impression of consistency when reality interferes with self-enhancement. *Journal of Personality and Social Psychology, 32,* 1030-1037.

Schlenker, B. R. (1987). Threats to identity: Self-identification and social stress. In C. R. Snyder & C. E. Ford (Ed.), *Coping with negative life events: Clinical and social psychological perspectives* (pp. 273-321). New York: Plenum.

Schlenker, B. R., Helm, B., & Tedeschi, J. T. (1973). The effects of personality and situational variables on behavioral trust. *Journal of Personality and Social Psychology, 25,* 419-427.

Schlenker, B. R., & Leary, M. R. (1985). Social anxiety and communication about the self. *Journal of Language and Social Psychology, 4,* 171-192.

Schlenker, B. R., & Miller, R. S. (1977). Egocentrism in groups: Self-serving biases or logical information processing. *Journal of Personality and Social Psychology, 35,* 755-764.

Sellerberg, A. M. (1982). On modern confidence. *Acta Sociologica, 25,* 39-48.

Shepelak, N. J. (1987). The role of self-explanation and self-evaluations in legitimating inequality. *American Sociological Review, 52,* 495-503.

Short, J. F. (1984). The social fabric at risk: Toward the social transformation of risk analysis. *American Sociological Review, 49,* 711-725.

Snyder, M. (1984). When belief creates reality. *Advances in Experimental Social Psychology, 18,* 247-305.

Thompson, S. C., & Kelley, H. H. (1981). Judgments of responsibility for activities in close relationships. *Journal of Personality and Social Psychology, 41,* 469-477.

van der Pligt, J. (1984). Attributions, false consensus, and valence: Two field studies. *Journal of Personality and Social Psychology, 46,* 57-68.

Vitell, S. J., & Festervand, T. A. (1987). Business ethics: Conflicts, practices and beliefs of industrial executives. *Journal of Business Ethics, 6,* 111-122.

White, S., & Mitchell, T. (1979). Job enrichment versus social cues: A comparison and competitive test. *Journal of Applied Psychology, 64,* 1-9.

Williams, R. B. (1989, January/February). The trusting heart. *Psychology Today,* pp. 36-42.

Williams, R. B., & Barefoot, J. C. (1988). Coronary-prone behavior: The emerging role of the hostility complex. In B. K. Houston & C. R. Snyder (Eds.), *Type A behavior pattern: Research, theory and intervention* (pp. 189-210). New York: John Wiley.

Zalesny, M. D., Farace, R. V., & Kurchner-Hawkins, R. (1985). Determinants of employee work perceptions and attitudes: Perceived work environment and organizational level. *Environment and Behavior, 17,* 567-592.

7

Ethical Considerations Regarding Public Opinion Polling During Election Campaigns

Commercial public opinion polling is an increasingly important element in practically all elections in democratic countries around the world. Poll results and pollsters are relatively new and autonomous voices in our human communities. Here I try to connect such polling directly to morality and democratic processes. Several arguments have been and might be used for and against banning such polling during elections, that is, for and against effectively silencing these voices. I present the arguments on both sides of this issue, and try to show that there are reasonable responses to all the arguments in favor of banning polls. Then I review some proposed Canadian legislation concerning banning polls and, alternatively, requiring disclosure of methodological features of polls. Finally, I offer a model set of disclosure standards for the publication of poll results during election campaigns.

INTRODUCTION

This chapter is divided into eight sections. It begins with an account of my understanding of ethics and morality and proceeds to a brief

AUTHOR'S NOTE: Adapted from "Ethical Considerations Regarding Public Opinion Polling During Election Campaigns" by A. C. Michalos (1991). In *Journal of Business Ethics, 10,* pp. 403-422. Used with permission from Kluwer Academic Publishers. An earlier and longer version of this chapter was written for and presented to the Canadian Royal Commission on Electoral Reform and Party Financing in June 1990.

section on social indicators and quality-of-life measurement. The two sections are connected by the fact that I regard ethics as essentially concerned with improving the human condition or the quality of human existence.

Because one way to discover whether or not people's lives are getting better or worse is to ask them, survey research or public opinion polling has emerged as an important resource for people with my particular moral point of view. Such research is always liable to sampling and nonsampling measurement errors of various sorts, with the latter type being much less familiar to most people than the former. So, the third section is devoted to reviewing many kinds of nonsampling errors. Although there is no simple mathematical formula that would allow one to estimate the total amount of error resulting from the variety of sampling and nonsampling problems, the 3 or 4 percentage point sampling error margins usually mentioned in commercial polls probably represents at best only half of the total error.

Sixteen arguments in favor of banning the publication of the results of public opinion polls during election campaigns are presented in the fourth section, and I try to show that each of them is defective. Although some of them do have some merit, I think reasonable replies may be offered to all of them.

I then present 16 arguments, in the fifth section, against banning the publication of poll results during elections. Insofar as my arguments (many of which are borrowed from other sources) in these two sections are sound, a case is made for not banning the publication of poll results. However, I do suggest in these sections that there is a need for some legislation regarding the disclosure of information relevant to evaluating opinion polls.

In the sixth section I review some private members's bills that have been introduced in the Canadian House of Commons with the intention of banning the publication of some or all poll results during election campaigns. Although I am opposed to such legislation, I think it is useful to document what has actually been proposed on this score in recent history.

The seventh section reviews bills that have been proposed that would require disclosure of information necessary for those interested in assessing the results of opinion polls conducted during elections. I consider each recommended requirement with a view to accepting or rejecting it. Finally, in the eighth section, I propose a model set of disclosure requirements. Although my focus of attention throughout this chapter is on public opinion polling during election campaigns and possible legislation regarding such polling, I think my model set of disclosure requirements should be voluntarily adopted by all pollsters for the publication of all poll results.

A MORAL POINT OF VIEW

I use the terms *ethics* and *morality* as synonyms. What is morally good or evil is ethically good or evil, and vice versa. If I say that something is morally or ethically good or evil, I mean that it is good or evil from a moral point of view. Thus, in my view, nothing is inherently morally good or evil. The institution of morality, and the ideas of moral goodness and evil are human artifacts designed by human beings to serve a variety of purposes. One important purpose is the resolution of conflicts of interest without resorting to civil or criminal law. Insofar as people are willing and able to perceive, judge, and act in accordance with a moral point of view, morality exists. If we stop caring, morality will cease to exist.

Because morality rests on the adoption of a moral point of view, the latter must be defined. Such a definition would be tantamount to the articulation of a principle or principles that may be used as a foundation for morality. Generally speaking, moral philosophers may be divided into two groups, depending on which of the following two principles they regard as the fundamental basis of morality.

1. *Principle of Beneficence*: One ought to try to act so that one's actions tend to impartially improve the quality of life.
2. *No-Harm Principle*: One ought to try to act so that one's actions tend not to harm anyone.

The principles are not exclusive and there are other ways to express them. For example, what I call the Principle of Beneficence might be expressed in terms of the impartial maximization of utility, happiness, satisfaction, or well-being. Theological ethicists might capture much of what is in this principle with their insistence on loving one's neighbor, and contemporary feminist ethicists' emphasis on care and nurturing might capture it from a slightly different point of view. Instead of a single No-Harm Principle, one might capture the same idea with a list of duties, freedoms, or rights. This is the moral significance of the United Nations Declaration of Human Rights and Freedoms and Canada's own Charter of Rights and Freedoms. For example, when nations or individuals grant that everyone has a right to life, they are implying that everyone else has a duty or a moral obligation to refrain from taking people's lives for the fun of it. They are creating moral codes as an immediate implication of their declarations. Although everything important about duties, rights, respect for persons, and so on, may not be captured in my two general principles, enough can be captured for our purposes.

So far as I know, there is no absolutely irrefutable argument leading to the conclusion that one or the other of these principles must be taken as fundamental. People operating primarily on the Principle of Beneficence will try to do as much good as possible. People operating primarily on the No-Harm Principle will try to do as little harm as possible. Personally, I favor universal beneficence because I think moral goodness ought to require more of people than a life of anxious inactivity mixed with pious hopes for our common future. I have no illusions about anyone's ability to behave ideally all or even most of the time, with respect to morality or anything else. But that is not a serious objection to any ideal. If one has a choice about what sort of moral ideal one ought to be guided by primarily, what sort one ought to recommend to family, friends, and the rest of the human race, I think it is wise to aim high rather than low. So, I am inclined to regard universal beneficence as more fundamental than the mere avoidance of intentional harm.

Goldfarb and Axworthy (1988) seem to be inclined to the opposite point of view when they write that

> Ethics demand that pollsters portray the reality their research has made apparent. . . . There are . . . ethical questions that all pollsters face. Should we know? Should information gleaned from polling be made available? Should we find out what we don't want to know? These questions are crucial to the ethics of polling. Should politicians, for example, have access to the results of polls taken during election campaigns? Should polls form part of the context of decision-making? Indeed, the formative and abiding commitment of the pollster is to discern reality, not to withhold or change the findings. . . . Pollsters, however, must be true to the portrait of reality that has emerged from their work. . . . Can anyone become a client? (pp. xiii-xiv)

These remarks suggest, to me at least, that the authors believe that there are some questions that are inherently ethical. On the contrary, I think that nothing is inherently ethical, whether ethically good or evil. In my view, everything is inherently neutral but subject to appraisal from a moral point of view. Ethical or moral principles in my view are constructs or artifacts designed by humans in the interest of building a good life, and everything is subject to appraisal in the light of such principles. So, every question can be regarded as an ethical question when it is considered from a moral point of view.

SOCIAL INDICATORS

Assuming that one is going to try to conduct one's human relations from a moral point of view as expressed in the Principle of Beneficence, there are, again broadly speaking, two ways to go. One can:

1. Try to improve relatively objective circumstances that are measured by things like full employment, cleaner and safer workplaces, equitable distributions of wealth and income, longer lives free of disability and disease, elimination of poverty and homelessness, and the reduction of crime.
2. Try to improve relatively subjective circumstances that are measured by people's reported peace of mind, contentment, happiness, and satisfaction.

Clearly, if one's relatively objective and subjective circumstances are improved, then the quality of one's life is improved. Since the fifth century B.C., people have haggled about what is objective, what is subjective, and which is more important. But it is evidently trivially true that if one's total circumstances are improved, one is better off and the quality of one's life has improved.

Social indicators are statistics that are supposed to have some significance for the quality of life. Statistical measures of relatively objective things, such as death rates, are referred to as *objective indicators* or indicators of objective well-being. Measures of relatively subjective states of affairs, such as personal satisfaction and happiness, are referred to as *subjective indicators* or indicators of subjective well-being. (More detailed accounts of these terms may be found in Michalos, 1980a.)

A review of *Psychological Abstracts* and *Sociological Abstracts* for the past 2 decades reveals that researchers around the world have been publishing articles and books on subjective well-being at a rate of more than a thousand titles a year.

SURVEY RESEARCH

Most of the research being done on subjective well-being employs some sort of surveying or interviewing technique, and these techniques have some fairly notorious limitations. The research may be broad-based involving a sample of all the members of some community or country, or it may merely involve a convenience sample of students, workers, patients, consumers, and so on.

In an excellent review article, Groves (1987) summarizes the roots of survey research's problems as follows:

> Survey research is not itself an academic discipline, with a common language, a common set of principles for evaluating new ideas, and a well-organized professional reference group. Lacking such an organization, the field of survey research has evolved through the somewhat independent and uncoordinated contributions of researchers trained as statisticians, psychologists, political scientists, and sociologists. . . . Such a *melange* of workers certainly breeds innovation, but it also spawns applications of the method for radically different purposes, suffers severe problems of communication, and produces disagreements about the importance of various components of quality. (p. S156)

One may assume that any measure taken of an individual's attitude will represent the attitude itself plus some measurement error. The latter will include both sampling and nonsampling errors. Excellent reviews of a wide variety of survey sampling and nonsampling errors may be found in Turner and Martin (1984), Frankel and Frankel (1987), Alwin and Campbell (1987), Groves (1987), and Hippler, Schwarz, and Sudman (1987).

Although most researchers have some familiarity with and are properly cautious about sampling errors (e.g., what size and sort of sample to draw to obtain a certain probability of error a certain percentage of the time), nonsampling errors are another matter. For the latter, there is less familiarity, less caution, and much more theoretical and empirical work to be done. Turner and Martin (1984) claimed that in their study of more than 1,000 newspaper reports of public opinion polls in the United States and Great Britain, "less than 3 percent . . . even vaguely refer to the possibility of nonsampling errors" (p. 69).

Under the rubric of nonsampling errors, there are all the problems related to interviewers, fieldwork, interviewees, questionnaire design, coding, editing, and the interview questions themselves. Regarding interviewers, for example, we know that females generally make better interviewers than males, and some interviewers will typically get more responses on more questions than others (Converse & Traugott, 1986). There will therefore be predictable percentages of nonresponses and judgments will have to be made about how to count these. Nonresponses imply additional possibilities of error, error arising from the interviewers' personality, techniques, expertise, and training, alone and in combination with some features of the interviewees. No one knows exactly how many percentage points of accuracy should be given up for such nonsampling errors. Sometimes all one can do is try to reduce or eliminate the errors rather than try to measure their impact (Groves, 1987).

There is an enormous amount of literature on the impact of experimenter and interviewer expectancies on the performance of respondents or target populations. Reviews may be found in Miller and Turnbull
(1986), Snyder (1984), and Michalos (1990). Besides affecting respondents' behavior, an experimenter's expectations affect both his or her as
well as the respondent's own perception and evaluation of that behavior. Expectations also have a direct and indirect impact on people's
self-concepts.

Even the time of day, weather, rural or urban setting, and the presence
of other people have affected responses to the relatively matter-of-fact
types of questions that appear in national labor force surveys (Bailar &
Rothwell, 1984).

As explained in Michalos (1990), what actually can be recalled from
one's past depends to some extent on how far away it is; whether the
source of one's information was perceived to be likeable, attractive, or
expert; whether there were arguments presented that seemed to be
cogent, whether the material or event was especially relevant to one's
interests or had particularly salient features; how it was encoded in
one's memory, and how long and hard one tries (DeBono & Harnish,
1988; Holtgraves, Srull, & Socall, 1989; Jacoby, Kelley, Brown, & Jasechko,
1989; Ottati, Fishbein, & Middlestadt, 1988).

There is a general tendency for people to overreport good things and
underreport bad things, the so-called social and trait desirability and
undesirability effects in polls (Beggan, Messick, & Allison, 1988; Moum,
1988). For example, there is more reported voting than actual voting,
less reported drunk driving than actual drunk driving, and less reported
tax evasion than officially documented evasion (Hessing, Elffers, &
Weigel, 1988).

Roos (1988) claimed that subjective well-being researchers face a
special kind of social desirability effect, which he called "the happiness
barrier." In his words, "it is an image of one's life, projected for the
benefit of others: neighbours, social authorities, research workers, the
society in general . . . a well-built happiness barrier becomes also an
image of one's life, projected for the benefit of the subject himself: it
becomes a double wall" (p. 141). Kozma and Stones (1988) demonstrated that one popular measure of social desirability, the Edwards
Scale of Social Desirability, has too much content reflecting subjective
well-being to be regarded as an independent, reliable, and valid measure
of social desirability.

There is a tendency for people to give responses that seem to be
popular at the time, the so-called bandwagon effect (DeMaio, 1984).
From several focused samples of Norwegians, Moum (1981, 1983, 1988)

found a tendency for females, people with low socioeconomic status, and elderly individuals to have their reported life satisfaction inflated by yea-saying and relatively high levels of resignation. Again, no one knows exactly how much of any response to most questions should be attributed to these kinds of effects.

Whether a question allows answers in two or more categories makes a difference. Asking for approval or disapproval is not equivalent to asking for strong approval, approval, disapproval, or strong disapproval. Crespi (1980) reported a study providing striking evidence of the crucial difference that numbers of response categories can make. Presidential approval scores were sought by a Gallup poll allowing one of two responses, a Harris poll allowing one of four, and a Post poll allowing one of five. "The gallup method produced a favorable rating of 62 percent for Carter, appreciably higher than either Harris's 48 percent or the Post's 41 percent. On the other hand, the Harris method produced a 4 percent 'don't know' compared with 10 percent for Gallup and 8 percent for the Post" (pp. 34-35).

Different pollsters prefer different question styles. Some like the take-it-or-leave-it style. Others like to creep up on a topic with a dozen or so questions and a variety of response categories (Converse & Schuman, 1984; Smith, 1978, 1982). According to Turner and Martin (1984), "Any question can be considered limited from some point of view, and single questions are inherently inadequate to convey a picture of any subjective phenomenon of importance. For this reason, a range of questions should be asked and the sensitivity of measurements to wording effects should be assessed" (p. 82).

Small changes in the wording of questions can radically alter responses. The simple substitution of the word *job* for the word *work* has produced differences of more than 20 percentage points in responses. Framing questions negatively rather than positively can alter responses by over 100% (Tversky & Kahneman, 1986). Although some people have thought that answers to attitude questions would be less affected by wording changes among people whose attitudes are "intense, important and held with great certainty," Krosnick and Schuman (1988) conducted 27 experiments in American national surveys designed to test this hypothesis and found no support for it.

The context of questions can make a difference (Strack & Martin, 1987). If, for example, you ask someone how happy they are with life right after asking them how happy they are with their marriage, the way they feel about the latter will have an impact on the way they feel and respond about the former (Turner, 1984). If you ask people how happy they are on a sunny day versus on a rainy day, the rain will depress their happiness scores (Schwarz, 1984). There are seasonal effects, with reported subjective well-being in the spring being typically higher than in the fall (Andrews & Withey, 1976). People's feelings about a certain event may also change if the event is preceded or followed by a series of distinctly pleasant or unpleasant events (Wedell & Parducci, 1988).

The vaguer or more ambiguous a question, the greater the variation in responses. People will just impute some particular meaning to the words uttered in order to provide some answer, some data. Many will even report reading books that do not exist and seeing movies that have not been made. Unfortunately, we have no neat way to quantify vagueness or ambiguity, and no way to know how many percentage points in confidence should be given up for people answering questions that were never asked (Turner, 1984).

It is sometimes asserted that questions about life satisfaction and happiness are especially vague and that because people seldom think about such things, they are likely to avoid responding to such questions. On the contrary, in the lead article of the first issue of the journal *Social Indicators Research*, Andrews and Withey (1974) reported that four nationwide American surveys regarding satisfaction with a wide variety of life domains revealed that usually fewer than 1% of any sample chose the response "never thought about it," and refusal rates for interviews ran about 15%. Davis and Fine-Davis (1978/1979) reported a refusal rate of 3.8% for their national quality-of-life survey in Ireland. Inglehart and Rabier (1986) reported that for their west European surveys covering nine countries from 1973 to 1983 and over 93,000 interviews, only 1% of respondents failed to answer a life satisfaction question and only 2% failed to answer a happiness question. The average nonresponse rate for other items in these surveys is about 10%.

Because survey research interviews tend to move along briskly and cover a wide variety of items in a relatively short space of time, results of such interviews are sometimes regarded as shallow. Some people suppose that much longer, in-depth interviews might yield very different results. When Wood and Johnson (1989) compared results of relatively shallow survey research with results obtained from intensive qualitative interviews of about 12 hours or more in length, they concluded that consistent assessments emerged from the two sources. As one would expect, the longer interviews uncovered nuances and suggested lines of exploration that the quantitative survey research missed. But there was substantial agreement between the findings of the qualitative and quantitative approaches.

Nobody knows exactly how much error is introduced by all of the above and other kinds of nonsampling errors. Useful work has been done and will certainly continue on the "concept of total error" (Frankel & Frankel, 1987), but so far there are no generally accepted statistical formulas to take account of the great variety of nonsampling errors. Most academic, government, and commercial pollsters will grant that nonsampling errors introduce at least as much error into public opinion poll results as sampling errors. But we are far from knowing what to do about it.

Lest anyone leave this section with a very pessimistic view of the "scientific status" of survey research, I offer the following quotation from Turner and Martin (1984):

> Not only can physical measurements vary wildly, but even well-publicized "discoveries" in the physical sciences have sometimes been shown to be experimental artifacts. For example, between 1963 and 1971 more than 500 articles in journals (including *Science* and *Nature*) discussed a supposed new substance: anomalous water or polywater. Although it resembled ordinary water, polywater was alleged to have a greater density, a reduced freezing point, and an elevated boiling point, among other anomalous properties. In the end, however, it was discovered that this "new substance" was nothing more than an impure solution of ordinary water. (p. 16)

Obviously, pollsters seldom, if ever, get even 5 kicks at the same can, let alone 500. If they did, they would surely develop better batting averages than they have developed so far. So, at this point I would not be pessimistic. On the contrary, I would be optimistic, and urge others to be cautious and to have patience.

ARGUMENTS FOR BANNING THE PUBLICATION OF SOME OR ALL POLL RESULTS DURING ELECTION CAMPAIGNS, AND REPLIES TO THEM

Following are 16 arguments that might be offered by someone in favor of banning the publication of some or all poll results during election campaigns. For each argument I have presented a reply or counterargument that I think is sufficient to seriously undermine the original argument.

1. "The polls, and the extensive commentary on them, have no beneficial effects" (Boyer, 1990, p. 33).

Reply. In the next section I review 16 allegedly beneficial effects.

2. "Polls trivialize a parliamentary election by turning it into a horse race" (Boyer, 1990, p. 33).

Reply. "Banning polls would not necessarily solve the problem. The public would be left with unreliable street surveys, self-serving leaks from political insiders, and selective canvassing of results" ("Banning Polls," 1990, p. A26; Reid in *Hearings* for Winnipeg, p. 5).

3. Polls "displace limited newspaper space and broadcast air time that otherwise could be used for coverage of issues, candidates and party programs" (Boyer, 1990, p. 33; Germond, 1980; Maureen McTeer in Hoy, 1989; Jones in *Hearings* for Vancouver, p. 5; Sperling in *Hearings* for Regina, p. 1).

Reply. The point is well taken, but no one knows if the trade-offs made have a net benefit or not. The critics apparently assume that most polls produce relatively trivial or useless information that ought to be replaced by something better. One can hardly argue with the view that we should have better information than we do have if it is available at a reasonable cost. I am just not persuaded that the elimination of all poll results would significantly improve our chances of getting something better. During one of the weeks while I was writing this chapter (June 1990), many of the media people in Canada were camped on the doorsteps of the Ottawa Convention Centre gathering tidbits from people involved in the constitutional discussions regarding the Meech Lake Accord. The debates were certainly important and worthy of coverage. However, very little useful information came out of the secret meetings and a considerable amount of resources was invested in broadcasting that information over and over and over. This example could be multiplied, but I think it illustrates the source of my doubts about Argument No. 3.

4. "They dishearten workers of parties seen to be losing, when in fact our system depends on supporters of all parties eagerly carrying their message to voters to enable an informed voting decision" (Boyer, 1990, p. 33).

Reply. This objection and the two that follow it suggest possibilities that are probably realized sometimes, but no one knows how often. This seems to be the view of Reid too (*Hearings* for Winnipeg, p. 4). One would suppose that in the long run such effects balance out, that we lose as much as we gain as a result of these sorts of influences. (Lemieux in *Hearings* for Quebec City takes this view, p. 4.)

5. "They encourage, on the part of those trailing, a 'negative' media advertising campaign to hit against whoever is leading" (Boyer, 1990, p. 33).

Reply. I think my reply to Argument No. 4 is appropriate here too.

6. They encourage workers for front-runners to be complacent ("Banning Polls," 1990; Gagne in *Hearings* for Montreal, p. 5).

Reply. Same as for Argument No. 5.

7. They "prompt people to switch their votes," perhaps for strategic reasons ("Banning Polls," 1990) or because they are caught up in a "bandwagon effect" (Campbell in *Hearings* for Charlottetown, p. 3; Robert Stanfield in Hoy, 1989, p. 222).

Reply. People must be allowed to change their minds as often as they like prior to and after voting. Although I already mentioned the fact that there is some evidence of some kinds of bandwagon effects for some kinds of people and some kinds of surveys (see Survey Research section), Reid claimed (*Hearings* for Winnipeg), "there is absolutely no evidence that there is a bandwagon effect associated with the publication of polls" (p. 4). Gagne made a narrower claim (*Hearings* for Montreal), namely, that "it had not been established that polls had an impact in moving votes in a specific direction" (p. 5).

Political observers have frequently complained about the bandwagon effects of polls and the compounding effects of media coverage. The more support a candidate or issue gets from the polls, it is supposed, the more media coverage there is and the more support there is likely to be, and so on. In fact, contradictory claims about such effects should be expected because interactions between media reports and poll responses are complex. As I mentioned in Michalos (1990), studies have shown that people's opinions about the seriousness of unemployment are closely correlated with objectively measured unemployment rates, regardless of the amount of media coverage. On the other hand, people's feelings about safety from violent crime are closely correlated with the amount of media coverage regardless of objectively measured crime rates (MacKuen, 1984).

Quite apart from polls, there is an enormous literature on the impact of the media on virtually every aspect of life. Good reviews may be found in Katz (1987), Beniger (1987), and Gollin (1987). Suffice it to say that the debate about the nature and extent of media influence on what, how, and why we think, feel, and act remains lively.

8. Polls can be manipulated to influence and mislead voters ("Banning Polls," 1990; Davis, Clark, Bourassa, & Hatfield in Hoy, 1989; Wilkinson & Kirwan in *Hearings* for Regina, p. 2).

Reply. The best protection against manipulators is widespread access to scientifically reliable and valid poll results ("Banning Polls," 1990; Lemieux in *Hearings* for Quebec City, p. 4). Regarding the issue of poll results simply influencing, but not misleading, voters, there does not seem to be any good reason for singling out such information as inappropriate, provided that it is reliable and valid. Hoy (1989) correctly remarked that "Political advertising influences voters too, and newspaper columns, and television commentary, and front-page news stories, and the physical appearance of candidates" (p. 227). Goldfarb and Axworthy (1988) seemed to want have their cake and eat it too when they claimed that

> Pollsters do not change society's [anyone's?] behavior: this is neither their role, nor their function. They are essentially private figures who are unlikely to have any *direct* influence on the public's behavior. This is not to say, however, that a pollster's findings do not potentially influence the decisions of other individuals who do wish to affect public behavior. (p. xiii)

According to Lee (1989), during the 1988 federal election, when polls indicated that the Tory government might be defeated by Liberals and New Democrats, the value of the Canadian dollar dropped. Noticing the relationship between these events, Canadians apparently altered their opinions on election day to keep the dollar up even at the expense of keeping Liberals and New Democrats down.

9. According to Stevens (1990a), "a majority of witnesses" before the Royal Commission on Electoral Reform and Party Financing "advocated banning the publication of opinion polls during at least the final stages of election campaigns" (p. B3).

Reply. At the time of the Stevens article, the hearings were still going on and briefs were still coming in. So, the majority may change by the end of the process. However, I have received and read summary transcripts from the commission's hearings in 14 of 30 (47%) projected cities, and these results confirm Stevens's comments. There were 247 speakers mentioned in these transcripts, which I suppose is fewer than actually appeared before the Commission. Twenty-five (10%) of the speakers addressed the issue of public opinion polling during elections, with 16 (64%) of these people recommending some banning of the publication of poll results and 9 (36%) recommending no banning. Six of the latter 9 people also explicitly rejected the idea of introducing some regulations or standards regarding poll data. Seven of the 9 (78%) people who opposed any sort of banning or regulations on the publication of poll results had some sort of commercial interest at stake.

Because this sample of contributors to the Royal Commission is so small and unrepresentative of the Canadian population as a whole, one cannot extrapolate results from the former group to the latter. To do so would be to engage in the kind of pseudo sample surveys that give legitimate polling a bad name (e.g., calling a 900 phone number, buying a hamburger to endorse a candidate, etc.). The best one can do is carefully weigh the arguments produced by all contributors and make a judgment. So, I have included all the arguments in my lists of those on both sides of the banning issue, and I will consider them in turn.

10. There are several democracies in which restrictions are imposed on polls and their publication through all or part of an election campaign, for example, France, the United Kingdom, Luxembourg, Portugal, Spain, Brazil, and Venezuela (Hoy, 1989).

Reply. This shows that some people have thought that such restrictions are consistent with democracy and that democracies do not crumble with their introduction. It does not show that there are good reasons to introduce such restrictions in all democracies or even in Canada, or that the introduction of such restrictions always produces benefits outweighing costs for most people. There are, after all, many democracies without any specific restrictions on the publication of polls. According to Hnatyshyn (1986), from 1939 to 1982 British Columbia had a law prohibiting the conduct of opinion polls during election campaigns. On the other hand, Gollin (1987) reported that in 1948 George Gallup claimed that, "The question of government regulation of polls has come up [unsuccessfully] in nearly every Congress during the last 20 years and is certain to be raised again in the eighty-first Congress" (p. S91).

11. Too much of the polling undertaken for the press and broadcast media during elections is methodologically sloppy, resulting in the publication of unreliable and invalid information advertised as scientifically warranted (Germond, 1980; Hoy, 1989; Repo in *Hearings* for Saskatoon, p. 2; Roper, 1980). Gollin (1987) reported results of a study of American

preelection polls that dealt with 446 state and local races (both primary and general elections) and found an appreciable difference in quality in polls carried out by independent pollsters vs. media ones, and (linked with this distinction) in polls done by interviewers in full-service polling firms vs. pickup interviewers hired by the media. In both cases, the former achieved greater accuracy. (p. S90)

Reply. In principle it seems that it should be possible to write a set of standards that pollsters and media publishers must follow in order to ensure that methodologically defective polls will not be published or that defects will be adequately noted for all potential consumers. I will return to this issue below in the section Proposed Bills Providing Disclosure Standards for the Publication of Poll Results During Election Campaigns. However, a good review of American pollsters' attempts to design such standards may be found in Turner and Martin (1984). According to Gollin (1987),

> Even the guidelines for minimal disclosure of polling methods, while less contentious as an issue than were (and are) performance or procedural standards, failed to win the assent of AAPOR [American Association for Public Opinion Research] members for almost 20 years after their initial proposal in 1947. And it wasn't until 1986 that these guidelines—formulated initially to assist polling firms and news media disseminators of poll results—were revised and made an integral part of AAPOR's Code of Professional Ethics and practices, binding upon AAPOR members as individuals. (p. S92)

12. "In Canada, we have a polling industry with no enforceable standards and a media industry that, even if it gave a damn, is plagued by such massive ignorance of the limitations of polling that it wouldn't much matter" (Hoy, 1989, p. 225).

Reply. Both problems are solvable in principle, at least. The former can be solved by introducing legislation with enforceable standards. Once such legislation is in place, the media industry will be obliged to hire competent editors in order to ensure compliance with the new legislation. Reid (*Hearings* for Winnipeg) claimed that "there were tremendous marketplace pressures on polling firms to be objective and to be accurate, so it was not necessary to address this issue by regulation" (p. 5). Gagne (*Hearings,* for Montreal, p. 5) took a similar line. For reasons that will become clear below (Proposed Bills Providing Disclosure Standards), I think these two pollsters are optimistic about the benevolent pressures of the marketplace.

13. There is a serious conflict of interest issue involved when the media conduct polls in order to generate news. According to Hoy (1989),

> No other group in society gets the relatively free ride from media scrutiny that pollsters enjoy. This surely is in part because the two crafts are sharing the same bed, a self-inflicted conflict-of-interest the media wouldn't tolerate under any other circumstances. If a newspaper or TV station hires a pollster, the results of the pollster's work, by definition, are big news for that newspaper or TV station, not subject to normal journalistic scrutiny. (p. 226)

Roper (1980) takes a similar line.

Reply. I do not think there is any conflict-of-interest issue in the situation Hoy describes. According to Crespi (1980),

> public opinion polling was started by the news media and has always depended upon them as the primary source of financial support. The first documented poll in the United States was conducted in 1824 by the *Harrisburg Pennsylvanian* to measure voting preferences in that year's presidential election. Today, most public opinion polls are conducted under contract to the news media or are conducted directly by them. (p. 28)

It seems to me that what the media are doing when they hire a pollster is merely an extension of what they have always done when they hire reporters, photographers, editorialists, and feature writers. Whatever their motives and however well or poorly they have accomplished their task, they have always created news. They have always and will always have to seek out events, issues, people, stories, and so on that seem relatively important and worth publishing. In the final analysis, the media make judgments about such things, and nowadays such judgments often favor the publication of poll results. Although there are problems with the latter, conflict-of-interest between media sponsors and pollsters is not one of them. The question of the extreme concentration of ownership of the media is, of course, a different matter of serious concern (Michalos, 1981a, 1981b, 1982, 1988a).

14. There is a tendency for people to regard poll results as an indication of "the collective will of Canadians," but survey research is not designed to and cannot serve that purpose. Vague as the idea is, one would suppose that a "collective will" would be the sort of thing that might be reflected by an election in which there is a fair and public debate over some issue. Because pollsters usually do not attempt to

present a balanced set of relevant considerations to a respondent prior to asking any questions, it is likely that a typical respondent is not giving answers in the light of such considerations. So, those who regard poll results as an indication of a "collective will" are misleading themselves and perhaps others (Hoy, 1989, p. 226).

Reply. I think this is a fair criticism of some people's views about the significance of public opinion polls, but I do not think the problem should be addressed by banning the publication of poll results. Granted that most people are not very sophisticated about polling, it must also be granted that there is considerable disagreement about the requirements of democratic decision making. I have personally shed an embarrassingly large amount of ink trying to specify necessary and sufficient conditions for good individual and group decision making in democracies (see, for example, Michalos 1970a, 1970b, 1971, 1972, 1978, 1980b, 1981c, 1985, 1987, 1988b).

According to Converse (1987),

> virtually all of the major figures before 1910—including George Gallup, Elmo Roper, and Archibald Crossley in the private sector, or Henry Wallace and Rensis Likert in the government at the [U.S.] Department of Agriculture—were strong on democratic principles and pleased to provide a means that the voice of the people might be more clearly heard to compete with the few voices in the ears of power. (p. S15)

Furthermore, I am sure that these pioneers recognized the danger in their becoming and reproducing a new elite group of technicians who might stifle and distort the very populist voices they were trying to amplify. That danger is still with us, and I hope my proposals in the final section, A Model Set of Disclosure Standards for the Publication of Poll Results During Election Campaigns, will significantly address it.

15. Polls "invade the privacy of respondents" (Hoy, 1989, p. 227).

Reply. This is a fairly old but pointless complaint about all survey research. People who feel that their privacy is invaded by pollsters usually just refuse to respond. There is some evidence indicating that in the United States refusal rates are increasing, for example, in Groves (1987), Gollin (1987), and Frankel and Frankel (1987). Indeed, the problem was perceived to be so serious there that in 1977 the Committee on National Statistics of the Commission on Behavioral and Social Sciences and Education of the U.S. National Academy of Sciences established a Panel on Incomplete Data. The Panel published a three-volume report in 1983. As I mentioned above (in Survey Research), nonresponse does create problems for pollsters and for anyone interested in correctly interpreting poll results. But none of these problems involves citizens' privacy. The latter is easily protected by the citizens themselves.

16. The publication of poll results can "make cowards of politicians, generating a reluctance for decision-making on issues that does not serve us well" (Hoy, 1989, p. 227).

Reply. If any politicians are disposed to abandon their principles or their own best judgment about what must be done in the interests of the good of the country as a result of hostile polls, it would be helpful to be able to identify and replace them.

ARGUMENTS AGAINST BANNING THE PUBLICATION OF ANY POLL RESULTS DURING ELECTION CAMPAIGNS

Following are 16 arguments that might be offered by someone opposed to banning the publication of any poll results during election campaigns.

1. Voters are entitled to as much information as they care to digest when making their decision ("Banning Polls," 1990; Reid in *Hearings* for Winnipeg, p. 5).
2. Favorable poll results can encourage workers to continue their efforts.
3. Candidates and other key players will always want to have polls for their internal use. So restricting publication of polls would make voters significantly disadvantaged compared to political elites regarding relevant information ("Banning Polls," 1990).
4. Any attempt to restrict publication of poll results might be challenged as a violation of the 1982 Charter of Rights and Freedoms (Hoy, 1989; Reid in *Hearings* for Winnipeg, p. 4). The prohibition of third-party advertising that was built into the 1974 Election Expenses Act was struck down as a violation of freedom of expression by the Alberta Supreme Court in 1984 and was not appealed.

Stevens (1990a) suggested that Section 33 of the Charter (the "notwithstanding" clause) might be invoked to override the freedom of expression clause, and in a later article, he indicated clearly that what would be at stake in such a move would be an assessment of the value of fair elections versus the right to free expression (Stevens, 1990b). I will have more to say about free expression and the pursuit of truth in the next section.

5. For all its limitations and disadvantages, polling may produce better information about what people think, feel, and want than any of the standard alternatives. That seems to be the view of academic and commercial pollsters, and their sponsors and clients. Converse (1987) was surely right when he wrote that "the political impact of public opinion data would be quite muffled indeed if politicians themselves gave such data no credence" (p. S16). But politicians are hardly alone. According to Sudman and Bradburn (1987), in the United States alone, "The number of firms conducting either public opinion polls or market research surveys now numbers in the thousands, with an annual dollar volume of over two billion dollars, . . . [and] . . . there are approximately 50 organizations conducting surveys in a university setting" (pp. S67-S68). As well, Turner and Martin (1984) noted that "survey research presently provides one of the prime sources of courtroom testimony as to community prejudice" (pp. 43-44) in the United States.

6. A national Gallup Poll taken in 1977 found that 57% of sampled Canadians opposed the banning of preelection polls, whereas 32% favored such banning (Hoy, 1989).

7. The issue of restricting publication of poll results might never have arisen and might be disposed of easily "if the media practised the social responsibility they claim to treasure" (Hoy, 1989, p. 224).

8. Polls can help citizens "understand where their opinions and values fit in the range of attitudes about issues that affect their lives and their country" (Goldfarb & Axworthy, 1988, p. xi).

9. According to Goldfarb and Axworthy (1988), "Polls are not plebiscites, . . . [but] . . . they provide instant feedback on the most important issues." Although it is certainly an exaggeration to claim that they provide "instant feedback" (p. xi) and, as I have already shown, many critics believe that during elections polls on "the most important issues" are neglected in favor of polls on who is winning for whatever reason (i.e., candidate popularity polls), it does seem fair to say that polls can provide timely information for average citizens and inside operators prior to election day.

10. Goldfarb and Axworthy (1988) also claim that "Polls create an involved citizenry. For the voter, polls may make the political process more gratifying, challenging and thought-provoking" (p. xi). (Whidden

in *Hearings* for Thompson, p. 2, takes a similar line.) I think there is a heavy dose of optimism in this assertion, but the optimism would have a good chance of being justified if pollsters would undertake more of the issue-oriented polling that critics charge they typically neglect.

11. We have seen that some people would restrict polls because poll results might frighten politicians. On the contrary, Goldfarb and Axworthy (1988) advocate polling during elections precisely because "Polls put pressure on politicians. In the shadow of public opinion and public accountability, politicians cannot lead blindly" (p. xi). Although one might argue that there is so much information overload and confusion created by having so many polls that politicians really are not faced with any constraints as a result of any particular poll results, I think that on particular issues the results of diverse polls frequently point fairly dramatically in one direction and do create some pressure. Francis Fox and Serge Joyal recommended banning the publication of poll results for the last 10 days prior to an election because of the "pollution" resulting from too many polls (*Hearings* for Montreal, p. 4). Steeves (*Hearings* for Moncton, p. 6) took a similar line.

Going a step farther, Goldfarb and Axworthy (1988) claim that

> Today's politicians have access to very little information that is not also available to the public. . . . No longer do we see ourselves electing, or hiring, politicians as wiser, more knowledgeable sages to protect us with their deeper insight into the means of attaining the public good. . . . What one knows, the other knows. What one wants, the other one can engineer. (p. xvii)

I am sure these optimistic remarks would be regarded as incredible to the Commissioner of Information for the federal Access to Information Act (Vienneau, 1989). Though I would agree that today's citizens are probably better informed than their predecessors, I would doubt that the publication of public opinion polls is especially responsible for our advantages. After all, besides having more polls, we also have an expanded educational system and more media outlets reaching more people than ever before.

12. Poll results can be useful in the generation of ideas regarding new policies and programs (Crespi, 1980; Goldfarb & Axworthy, 1988). Presumably this applies primarily to issue-oriented polls rather than to candidate preference polls, though results that are very positive or negative for candidates can generate plenty of ideas too.

13. Such results can be used for setting agendas for public discussion of important issues and "engineering" consent in the best sense of this

term (Goldfarb & Axworthy, 1988). Although these possibilities present opportunities for abuse along the lines suggested above, it cannot be denied that they also provide opportunities for significant benefits. Because there are many other ways to obtain such benefits, one must weigh the likely consequences of using polls versus other instruments in particular cases. But that seems to grant no more than any reasonable person would insist on regarding any course of action (Michalos, 1978).

14. Poll results may be used to obtain a balanced assessment of social conditions against mere economic assessments. Like the two previous points, this applies primarily to issue-oriented polls.

15. They might be used to facilitate comparisons among the attitudes and beliefs of different regions, cities, and other groups.

16. Given our proximity to American media, "no prohibition can be completely effective, . . . no statute to that effect would have any force outside Canada's boundaries" (Hnatyshyn, 1986, p. 27).

PROPOSED BILLS BANNING THE PUBLICATION
OF POLL RESULTS DURING ELECTION CAMPAIGNS

According to the *White Paper on Election Law Reform* published in June 1986,

> More than 20 Private Members' bills have been introduced in the Canadian House of Commons with the purpose of either prohibiting the publication of polls or to control the methodology of polls published in newspapers during campaigns. Several debates on this issue were held in the House in recent years. (Hnatyshyn, 1986, p. 26)

I was able to track down eight bills, including several duplicates, from the House and only one extensive debate. I also found one bill from the Ontario Legislature. Most of the bills that I found are little more than a paragraph long. So it will be easy to review them.

Bill C-213, "An Act to Amend the Canada Elections Act" was introduced by Robert C. Coates on October 15, 1974. It is virtually identical to Bill C-361 introduced by Harold T. Herbert on October 22, 1976.

According to Bill C-213, Section 105 of the Canada Elections Act would be amended by inserting after subsection (1), "(2a) No person, company or corporation shall, in any province after the issue of the writ for an election, or after the dissolution of Parliament or the occurrence of a vacancy in consequence of which a writ for an election is eventually issued, and before the hour of closing of the polls in such province, publish the result or purported result of a poll of the political opinions of the electors or any of them in any electoral district or districts in Canada, whether such publication is by radio or television, broadcast, or by newspaper, news-sheet, poster, bill-board, handbill, or in any other manner."

The explanatory note following the text says that "The purpose of this amendment is to prohibit, and to make punishable as an illegal practice, the publication in any manner before an election day of the results of a poll of the political opinions of the electors. The proposed amendment does not prohibit the taking of such a poll for private purposes."

Bill C-266, introduced by Harold T. Herbert on October 31, 1977, is very similar to C-213. Bill C-266 bans what C-213 bans, but the former explicitly mentions opinion polls related to referenda and candidates in federal elections.

Two points should be emphasized about C-213 and C-266. First, they would ban publishing poll results concerning all political opinions during an election, including opinions about issues as well as candidates. Second, because they are quite general prohibitions in terms of their temporal scope and types of polls, all of the arguments listed above against banning the publication of poll results would be applicable to them.

Bill C-364, introduced by Benno Friesen on October 31, 1977, would ban the publication of polls throughout election campaigns provided that the polls are about "any candidate or registered party." Although the explanatory notes for this bill are virtually identical to those for the previous bills, the text of this bill represents a significant departure from the others. This bill is apparently designed to eliminate the publication of the results of candidate and party popularity/preferences polls. If that is the correct reading of the bill, then it would directly address the second listed objection that critics raise against the publication of poll results during elections (i.e., section on Arguments for Banning, No. 2). The only bill on polling that I found in the Ontario Legislature had the same prohibition as C-364. It was numbered C-79 and was introduced by George Samis in 1979.

The only extensive debate I found in the House of Commons concerned Bill C-213 (House of Commons, 1974). Coates defended his bill by mentioning some version of arguments listed in Arguments for Banning above, namely Nos. 2 (turning elections into horse races), 7 (bandwagon effects), 8 (misleading polls), and 12 (absence of publication standards). Although the debate took place prior to the introduction of the 1982 Charter, he addressed a version of the freedom of expression argument (Arguments Against Banning, No. 4) as follows:

> I do not know about the radio and television stations, but many of the newspapers in this nation become very upset by any suggestion that they should be prevented from using polls. They say this would be curtailment of freedom of speech. I say in answer to that that any time the press does not provide accurate information to the public, based on sound facts, that information should not appear in the newspapers. I say there is no curtailment of freedom involved if the newspapers are prevented from using information which, in the first instance, is not authentic. All too often newspapers have neither the staff, the time nor the capability to produce accurate information in respect of what they endeavour to place before the public about an event that is taking place. (Recall Arguments for Banning, Nos. 11 and 12)

There is, of course, an enormous literature on freedom of speech or more generally of expression. Without pretending to address all of the important issues related to this freedom, I would like to present a brief overview based on one of my earlier writings. Interested readers can consult the longer and earlier discussion at their leisure.

> People have traditionally defended free speech or expression on two grounds. For some it has been a matter of moral principle that people ought to be allowed to express their views without fear of reprisals. While it may be a defeasible moral right, it is nevertheless a fundamental moral right, like the right to life, for example. For others, free expression has been defended as a matter of epistemological good sense. These people are more interested in the pursuit of truth and the avoidance of falsehood than they are in moral principles, and they see the free expression of ideas as a necessary condition of their epistemic aims.
>
> Of course, no one has to choose between these two different grounds for defending free expression, but historically I think people have tended to lean toward one or the other as especially weighty. If one is primarily interested in the free expression of fictional or visual material (stories, films, paintings, sculptures) then one's defence might run more smoothly from moral grounds, while if one is primarily interested in the free expression of nonfictional or descriptively accurate material, then one's defence might run more smoothly from epistemic grounds. The point I want to emphasize here, however, is that the two grounds often coalesce. Indeed, I suspect that this is typically the case. (Michalos, 1987, p. 353)

I suppose that people opposed to banning the publication of poll results during elections would be inclined to use the epistemic defense of free expression more than the moral defense, but in either case freedom of expression cannot be taken as a license intentionally to publish misleading or false reports. From an epistemic point of view, the publication of misleading or false reports would be objectionable because such reports directly undermine the epistemic grounds for free expression. So, insisting on allowing such reports would be inconsistent with the very goal that freedom of expression is supposed to be pursuing. From a moral point of view, the publication of misleading or false reports would be objectionable because such reports would undermine our pursuit of human well-being indirectly as a result of people believing and acting in accordance with an inaccurate view of reality.

Philosophical niceties aside, virtually everyone thinks that lying or intentionally spreading falsehoods is morally wrong and, in some circumstances, it is also illegal, for example, in cases of false advertising, libel, and slander. So, anyone inclined to argue for the moral supremacy of free expression over telling the truth would have an uphill battle at best. Indeed, insofar as free expression is regarded as taking precedence over telling the truth, the latter is significantly undermined. What good could it do to urge people to tell the truth, and then to allow that it is more important to say anything they like?

As a matter of fact, at the beginning of this century two great philosophers, the American William James and the Englishman W. K. Clifford, carried out a somewhat famous exchange of views over what is called the ethics of belief (Michalos, 1978). This is not the place to review that exchange, but I merely want to indicate that several of the arguments used by both James and Clifford were designed to establish that one has a moral obligation not only to tell the truth as one sees it, which everyone will grant, but also to make a reasonable attempt to pursue the truth and avoid falsehood. In general they argued as I did in the preceding paragraph. That is, it would be epistemologically and morally wrong to urge people to take truth-telling seriously but to allow them to be frivolous regarding the pursuit of truth and the avoidance of falsehood. In short, freedom of expression cannot be a license to express anything that takes one's fancy, under any and every possible circumstance.

Following Coates's remarks in favor of C-213, C. A. Gauthier offered his support using some versions of Arguments No. 8 (misleading polls) and No. 13 (media sponsored polls) in Arguments for Banning. Serge Joyal spoke against the bill. Although he granted that the publication of poll results could and probably did influence some voters, he thought the influence was exaggerated. In effect he rejected Arguments No. 1 through 8 in Arguments for Banning. Interestingly enough, he cited some survey research indicating that polls had no effect on voter turn-out or switches between one party or another. (Recall the comments of Reid and others above, Arguments for Banning, Reply to No. 7.) In defense of polling, he mentioned a version of Argument No. 5 (Arguments Against Banning, scientific status of polls) and the high credibility of survey research undertaken by reputable agencies like Statistics Canada, for example, regarding the measurement of unemployment rates. Rather than a ban on polls during elections, he recommended careful consideration of appropriate regulations and standards of good practice. In particular, he mentioned the importance of having surveys undertaken by agencies "famous" as specialists, with "a proven method," a "representative" sample and a clearly articulated time period for any surveys.

Joyal's bottom line seemed fairly close to that of Coates as the latter concluded his remarks. "At the same time," Coates said,

> so that members of Parliament cannot be charged with limiting freedom of the press in any way, I would accept as an alternative guidelines established by Parliament that would tell the media that if they are to produce the results of polls during an election campaign, and place these results before the public as accurate and authentic information on which the public should be able to rely, then the media will have to follow a set of rules and regulations to the effect that it must be shown how many people were encompassed by a poll, that the poll was national in its investigative function, or provincial if the poll being placed before the public purports to give a reading on the trends in a given province. . . . There are many other considerations, but I believe there should be a substantial contact with the people in the nation, that all parts of the nation must be involved, and that there should be a minimal doubt factor. (House of Commons, 1974, pp. 1817-1818)

The reference to surveying "all parts of the nation" is included because Coates believed that, "Far too often, especially in respect of Gallup polls produced in this country, there is no mention of the attitudes of the people who live in the four eastern provinces." Typical Gallup polls draw such small samples from the Atlantic provinces ($N <$ 150) that any comments made about the attitudes of people in those provinces have error margins too wide to make them useful. Unfortunately, instead of drawing larger samples in order to justify making reliable and valid comments about those provinces, usually pollsters have just gone ahead and made the comments anyhow.

Two other Members of Parliament made substantive comments on C-213. Jack Pearsall objected to the bill mainly on the grounds of Argument No. 3 (denying information to voters that is available to insiders) in Arguments Against Banning, whereas Stanley Knowles challenged it as a limitation of free expression or of a free press (i.e., Arguments Against

Banning, No. 4). The following remarks by Knowles are especially relevant to the moral point of view outlined above in the first section.

> A concern that is really hitting us in our society today is the extent to which freedom of thought and freedom of decision as to the kind of people we want to be is terribly thwarted by commercial interests. I am glad there is some legislation on the books regarding misleading advertising. I think we have to go a lot further. I hope that one day we will have media, print and electronic, educational forces, religious forces and all the rest, the aim of which will not be some particular axe to be ground and not some particular profit to be made, but the real enrichment of human life.

I suppose many of us share Knowles's hope, and I think some appropriate legislation can make a positive contribution toward realizing it.

PROPOSED BILLS PROVIDING DISCLOSURE STANDARDS FOR THE PUBLICATION OF POLL RESULTS DURING ELECTION CAMPAIGNS

Although banning the publication of poll results during an election would effectively eliminate many or all of the costs cited by critics, depending on how severe a blackout is legislated, many or all of the benefits cited by the other side would also be eliminated. Therefore, as I have already suggested, I think it would be preferable to provide standards for the publication of poll results. This strategy would allow Canadians to maintain and even increase the benefits of public opinion polling while significantly reducing the costs.

Although the bills that have been introduced have been intended to apply only to polls undertaken during elections, I think that any good reasons for insisting on quality standards at such periods would be applicable to the publication of poll results at any time. In the long run it would be self-defeating to insist on a certain quality for a 6-week period every 4 or 5 years and to allow substandard material to be published the rest of the time.

I suppose that once Canadians get a clear idea of the difference between a quality product and the quick and dirty imitations that are frequently published these days, there will be a decline in the marketability of the latter. So, it might be sufficient to legislate standards only for election periods and let nature take its course for nonelection periods. At any rate, I will proceed on the premise that legislation for election periods is sufficient.

Dean Whiteway introduced Bill C-265, "An Act respecting public opinion polls," on October 30, 1978. I believe it is substantially the same as Bill C-455 and Bill C-459, which he introduced on May 15, 1978, and June 7, 1978, respectively.

Bill C-265 would amend the Canada Elections Act so that immediately after Section 105, there would be inserted

105.1 (1) Where, during an election, a person publishes by radio or television broadcast or by newspaper or periodical publication a result or purported result of a survey of the political preferences of electors with respect to a candidate, registered party or election issue, he shall also publish the following additional data:

  a. who commissioned the survey, who paid for it, and who carried it out;
  b. when the survey was carried out;
  c. a description of the target population of the survey;
  d. a description of the procedure followed to select a sample of the target population;
  e. the size of the sample selected;
  f. a description of the procedure followed to collect the survey data;
  g. the amount of nonresponse to each survey question for which a result is published; and
  h. an estimate of the sampling error for each numerical result published.

Any violation of the provisions of the bill would be "punishable on summary conviction and liable to a fine of up to ten thousand dollars." Commenting on Bill C-455, Whiteway said,

Mr. Speaker, my bill would not disallow public opinion polls during the time of a writ period, but simply make certain requirements, namely, stating who took a poll, the sampling and the results of the poll, in order that Canadians are able to ascertain whether the poll was an adequate one and not simply one done by a political party with no real basis of sampling.   .

To get some idea of how demanding the eight items of C-265 are compared to current practice, one might consider the information provided in typical commercial polls published in a daily newspaper, for example, the *Toronto Star*. Usually we are given (a) who did it, (b) when, (c) the target population, (e) the sample size, and some of (h) the sampling error. That is, typically less than half of the information required by the items in C-265 is provided.

Item by item, what difference would the additional material make?

a. If we knew who commissioned and paid for all or part of a survey, would that allow us to judge the results any better? It often happens that a single survey is constructed of questions paid for by different people. We might discover exactly who paid for a survey or some of the questions, which would certainly be additional information. But it would not allow us to judge the results any better. Even if we found that whoever paid for the poll really wanted to mislead us somehow with the results of the poll, it is not clear that this information should have any effect on our judgment of the poll results. We would be able to make a harsh judgment about the purchaser and the pollster on the grounds of their intention to mislead us, but that is irrelevant to the reliability and validity of the poll results (Michalos, 1969, 1970c). The latter has to be assessed on the basis of the methodology employed, not on anyone's intentions.

On the other hand, the identification of the pollster is relevant to our judgment of the likely reliability and validity of poll results. After all, as we saw in Arguments for Banning, No. 12, neither commercial, government, nor academic pollsters work in a vacuum. They have peers, competitors, and concerned critics. Their peers and competitors frequently survey the same populations regarding the same issues. They develop relatively visible track records that allow us to assess their long-term reliability and validity compared to that of their peers and competitors. In polling as in other areas of life, a good reputation is not a guarantee of quality, but it is relevant. In the absence of specific data and the expertise to analyze it oneself, one may have little else to go on but the good name of the pollster. In short, regarding (a) I would keep the pollster's name and not require the other two names.

b. Because people's opinions may change with the passage of time and the occurrence of events, the dates of polls are certainly relevant to our judgments regarding their results. So, this requirement is uncontroversial.

c. Unless we know what population was supposed to be surveyed, either in part or as a whole, we cannot make any useful judgments about poll results. To be informed that certain percentages of anonymous respondents some place in the world answered some questions some way is simply worthless. So, the target population requirement must stay.

d. At some level of analysis, the procedure used to draw the sample (i.e., the sampling design) must be known. Different sampling procedures have different advantages and disadvantages, yielding different estimated reliabilities and validities for poll results. The problem I have with this requirement is knowing how much of this sort of information to insist on. For statisticians it is enough to say, for example, that a simple random probability sample was drawn from a list of all households in some area. They will know that means every household in the area had an equal chance or probability of being drawn. But for a variety of reasons related to the actual distributions of populations in different areas of our country and the costs of surveying them, simple random samples are virtually never drawn. Pollsters stratify, cluster, and weigh samples in various ways to accommodate geography, settlement patterns, costs, and so on. Descriptions of their sampling designs that are precise enough to be useful to experts interested in double-checking their calculations would be useless noise for most people. One might require that such information should be available to anyone who wants to contact the pollster directly, but it would be pointless to require the popular media to publish such information. I am not even sure that it would be fair to require pollsters to make such information available to everyone who asks for it. Although the fundamentals of sampling theory have been around for more than 40 years, there may be cost-effective competitive advantages to some procedures involving fieldwork and computers that ought to be enjoyed by their inventors. There may be proprietary rights involved similar to those for copyrights and patents. Still, the fact that academic and government pollsters are expected to provide complete information on sampling designs as requested by anyone inclines me to expect the same from commercial pollsters. So, even though I would not endorse item (d) as it stands, I would recommend that pollsters should be required to disclose their sampling designs on demand.

e. I suppose no one questions the requirement regarding disclosure of total sample sizes. Pollsters routinely provide such information. However, the fact that the same pollsters routinely fail to provide subsample sizes indicates a serious problem, and a serious moral problem at that. Pollsters know that the error margins applicable to their total samples usually do not apply to their subsamples, but they seldom say so. Though some people are aware of the need for greater caution in judging poll results for subsamples, most people probably are not. Most people probably just assume that the error margins mentioned at the end of the reports are roughly applicable to all the statistics mentioned in the report.

Insofar as all of these facts are as clear to commercial pollsters as they are to me, I concluded long ago that pollsters intentionally mislead the public on this score. Because I find it incredible to believe that the editors of our major media are any less informed than I am about this issue, I believe they also are guilty of intentionally misleading the public. It seems to me that the behavior of pollsters and media editors on this score is patently immoral and it ought to be illegal. So, in item (e), I would insist on full disclosure of every sample and subsample size about which any reports are made.

f. There are basically only three alternatives here, namely, face-to-face interviews, telephone interviews, and mail-out surveys, and most of the evidence indicates that very similar returns can be obtained from the three procedures. I would accept the requirement because it is very easy to satisfy, not because satisfying it provides especially useful information.

g. As suggested above in the Survey Research section, nonresponse figures are as important as response figures because originally specified sample and subsample sizes can be significantly distorted by nonresponse rates, resulting in very misleading percentages being reported. For all public opinion polls, it is highly unlikely that everyone is home when called, willing and able, and in fact answers all the questions. Typically, there must be some nonresponse and it must be accommodated somehow, with additional calls on other people, special weighting by quotas, substitution of mean values for missing values, or something. In the absence of information on nonresponse and its treatment, one cannot judge the percentages that pollsters report. Therefore, I would not only insist on the publication of nonresponse rates for each question reported, I would also want some indication of how nonresponses are treated. Because most pollsters will have preferred ways of dealing with nonresponse, most of them will only have to formulate a single sentence or phrase to be included with all their releases.

h. Perhaps enough has been said regarding the necessity of providing the sampling error margins for each question under (e) above. Because part of the point of publishing sample sizes is to allow one to estimate error margins, most people might be better served by simply publishing the latter. However, I think that the publication of sample sizes probably makes people a bit more cautious about poll results and that is probably beneficial. If there is one thing about which all pollsters agree, it is that though all information-gathering methods are subject to a variety of errors, public opinion polls based on probability sampling are subject to measurable errors. Thus there can be no excuse for not requiring the publication of measurable error margins with all poll results. Insofar as error margins are not strictly measurable, appropriate cautionary remarks should be required.

The federal government's *White Paper on Election Law Reform* (Hnatyshyn, 1986) included most of the eight items of C-265, arranged in a different order. The list in the former runs as follows:

(A) The name and address of the organization which conducted the inquiry;
(B) The population polled, the size of the sample and the percentage of completed interviews;
(C) The dates of the first and last completed interviews;
(D) The name and address of the person or organization who paid for the conduct of the inquiry;
(E) A summary description of any normalization procedure used in order to account for the under- or over-representation of some strata of the population in the sample. (p. 27)

The omitted items are those regarding (f) survey method and (h) error margins. I suppose (E) would cover the issues I discussed in relation to the treatment of nonresponse, and I suppose addresses are unnecessary.

The last bill introduced that I am aware of is Bill C-79, introduced for the government by Ray Hnatyshyn on June 30, 1987. It applies to polls concerning candidates and registered parties and would require disclosure of:

a. the name and address of the person or organization that conducted the inquiry;
b. the size of the sample;
c. the dates of the first and last completed interviews;
d. the name and address of the person or organization who paid for the conduct of the opinion poll;
e. the margin of error if calculable; and the exact wording of each question the answers to which led to the results so printed and broadcast.

Fines for individual violators of any of these provisions have a maximum value of $5,000 and for corporate violators $10,000.

The requirements of C-79 are similar to those of the *White Paper*, with the important addition of item (e) regarding the exact wording of questions. The latter is obviously absolutely necessary.

A MODEL SET OF DISCLOSURE STANDARDS FOR THE PUBLICATION OF POLL RESULTS DURING ELECTION CAMPAIGNS

The results of my consideration of alternative disclosure standards to be met in the publication of poll results during election campaigns may be summarized as follows. There should be routine disclosure of the

a. name of the person or organization that conducted the inquiry;

b. name or description of the target population;

c. size of the total sample and any subsamples used;

d. dates of the first and last completed interviews;

e. margins of sampling and (if calculable) nonsampling errors for any reported percentage results;

f. exact wording of each question about which results are reported;

g. nonresponse rates and method of treating nonresponses;

h. data collection procedures.

Although routine disclosure of sampling designs is not required, such disclosure should be available on request by interested persons.

As suggested earlier, although these requirements are specifically intended for polls conducted during elections and I would recommend legislation to that end (including appropriate fines for violators), I can see no good reason not to place such disclosure requirements on the publication of all polls. Indeed, I think such requirements would yield significant net benefits (as described above in Arguments Against Banning) for Canadians and the development of democracy in our country.

Probably one consequence of the introduction of the recommended legislation would be a reduction in the amount of published poll results. Relatively incomplete passing references to such results would be effectively prohibited. Editors would either have to provide enough information in their stories to satisfy the requirements of the legislation or pick another story. Although some people will claim this is unnecessary and unwarranted interference with free expression or a free market, I have already explained why I think such claims are unreasonable. Communities have as much right to protect themselves against intellectual pollution as they do against environmental pollution.

REFERENCES

Alwin, D. F., & Campbell, R. T. (1987). Continuity and change in methods of survey data analysis. *Public Opinion Quarterly, 51,* S139-S155.

Andrews, F. M., & Withey, S. B. (1974). Developing measures of perceived life quality: Results from several national surveys. *Social Indicators Research, 1,* 1-26.

Andrews, F. M., & Withey, S. B. (1976). *Social indicators of well-being.* New York: Plenum.

Bailar, B. A., & Rothwell, N. D. (1984). Measuring employment and unemployment. In C. F. Turner & E. Martin (Eds.), *Surveying subjective phenomena* (Vol. 2, pp. 129-142). New York: Russell Sage.

Banning polls a big mistake. (1990, May 4). *Toronto Star,* p. A26.

Beggan, J. K., Messick, D. M., & Allison, S. T. (1988). Social values and egocentric bias: Two tests of the might over morality hypothesis. *Journal of Personality and Social Psychology, 55,* 606-611.

Beniger, J. R. (1987). Toward an old new paradigm: The half-century flirtation with mass society. *Public Opinion Quarterly, 51,* S46-S66.

Boyer, P. (1990). 10 steps to a better election law. *Policy Options Politiques, 11,* 32-34.

Converse, P. E. (1987). Changing conceptions of public opinion in the political process. *Public Opinion Quarterly, 51,* S12-S25.

Converse, J. M., & Schuman, H. (1984). The manner of inquiry: An analysis of survey question form across organizations and over time. In C. F. Turner & E. Martin (Eds.), *Surveying subjective phenomena* (Vol. 2, pp. 283-316). New York: Russell Sage.

Converse, P. E., & Traugott, M. W. (1986). Assessing the accuracy of polls and surveys. *Science, 234,* 1094-1098.

Crespi, I. (1980). The case of presidential popularity. In A. H. Cantril (Ed.), *Polling on the issues* (pp. 28-45). Cabin John, MD: Seven Locks.

Davis, E. E., & Fine-Davis, M. (1978/1979). On the relationship between objective and subjective social indicators: Implications for social planning in Ireland. *Journal of the Statistical and Social Inquiry Society of Ireland, 24,* 91-131.

DeBono, K. G., & Harnish, R. J. (1988). Source expertise, source attractiveness, and the processing of persuasive information: A functional approach. *Journal of Personality and Social Psychology, 55,* 541-546.

DeMaio, T. J. (1984). Social desirability and survey measurement: A review. In C. F. Turner & E. Martin (Eds.), *Surveying subjective phenomena* (Vol. 2, pp. 257-282). New York: Russell Sage.

Frankel, M. R., & Frankel, L. R. (1987). Fifty years of survey sampling in the United States. *Public Opinion Quarterly, 51,* S127-S138.

Germond, J. W. (1980). The impact of polling on journalism. In A. H. Cantril (Ed.), *Polling on the issues* (pp. 20-27). Cabin John, MD: Seven Locks.

Goldfarb, M., & Axworthy, T. (1988). *Marching to a different drummer: An essay on the Liberals and Conservatives in convention.* Toronto: Stoddart.

Gollin, A. E. (1987). Polling and the news media. *Public Opinion Quarterly, 51,* S86-S94.

Groves, R. M. (1987). Research on survey data quality. *Public Opinion Quarterly, 51,* S156-S172.

Hessing, D. J., Elffers, H., & Weigel, R. H. (1988). Exploring the limit of self-reports and reasoned action: An investigation of the psychology of tax evasion behavior. *Journal of Personality and Social Psychology, 54,* 405-413.

Hippler, H.-J., Schwarz, N., & Sudman, S. (Eds.). (1987). *Social information processing and survey methodology.* New York: Springer-Verlag.

Hnatyshyn, R. (1986). *White Paper on election law reform.* Released in June by the Honourable Ray Hnatyshyn, President of the Queen's Privy Council for Canada and Government House Leader.

Holtgraves, T., Srull, T. K., & Socall, D. (1989). Conversation memory: The effects of speaker status on memory for the assertiveness of conversation remarks. *Journal of Personality and Social Psychology, 56,* 149-160.

House of Commons, Canada. (1974, November 29). *Debates.* Ottawa: Queen's Printer.

Hoy, C. (1989). *Margin of error: Pollsters and the manipulation of Canadian politics.* Toronto: Key Porter Books.

Inglehart, R., & Rabier, J.-R. (1986). Aspirations adapt to situations—But why are the Belgians so much happier than the French? A cross-cultural analysis of the subjective quality of life. In F. M. Andrews (Ed.), *Research on the quality of life* (pp. 1-56). Ann Arbor: University of Michigan, Institute for Social Research.

Jacoby, L. L., Kelley, C., Brown, J., & Jasechko, J. (1989). Becoming famous overnight: Limits on the ability to avoid unconscious influences of the past. *Journal of Personality and Social Psychology, 56,* 326-338.

Katz, E. (1987). Communications research since Lazarsfeld. *Public Opinion Quarterly, 51,* S25-S46.

Kozma, A., & Stones, M. J. (1988). Social desirability in measures of subjective well-being: Age comparison. *Social Indicators Research, 20,* 1-14.

Krosnick, J. A., & Schuman, H. (1988). Attitude intensity importance, and certainty and susceptibility to response effects. *Journal of Personality and Social Psychology, 54,* 940-952.

Lee, R. M. (1989). *One hundred monkeys: The triumph of popular wisdom in Canadian politics.* Toronto: Macfarlane Walter & Ross.

MacKuen, M. B. (1984). Reality, the press and citizens' political agendas. In C. F. Turner & E. Martin (Eds.), *Surveying subjective phenomena* (Vol. 2, pp. 443-474). New York: Russell Sage.

Michalos, A. C. (1969). *Principles of logic.* Englewood Cliffs, NJ: Prentice Hall.

Michalos, A. C. (1970a). Cost-benefit versus expected utility acceptance rules. *Theory and Decision, 1,* 61-88.

Michalos, A. C. (1970b). The costs of decision-making. *Public Choice, 4,* 39-51.

Michalos, A. C. (1970c). *Improving your reasoning.* Englewood Cliffs, NJ: Prentice Hall.

Michalos, A. C. (1971). *The Popper-Carnap controversy.* Hague, the Netherlands: Martinus Nijhoff.

Michalos, A. C. (1972). Efficiency and morality. *Journal of Value Inquiry, 6,* 137-143.

Michalos, A. C. (1978). *Foundations of decision-making.* Ottawa: Canadian Library of Philosophy.

Michalos, A. C. (1980a). *North American social report: Vol. 1. Foundations, population and health.* Dordrecht, the Netherlands: D. Reidel.

Michalos, A. C. (1980b). A reconsideration of the idea of a science court. *Philosophy and Technology, 3,* 10-28.

Michalos, A. C. (1981a). *North American social report: Vol. 3. Science, education and recreation.* Dordrecht, the Netherlands: D. Reidel.

Michalos, A. C. (1981b). *North American social report: Vol. 4. Environment, transportation and housing.* Dordrecht, the Netherlands: D. Reidel.

Michalos, A. C. (1981c). Technology assessment, facts and values. *Research in Philosophy and Technology, 4,* 59-81.

Michalos, A. C. (1982). *North American social report: Vol. 5. Economics, religion and morality.* Dordrecht, the Netherlands: D. Reidel.

Michalos, A. C. (1985). Multiple discrepancies theory (MDT). *Social Indicators Research, 16,* 347-413.

Michalos, A. C. (1987). What makes people happy? *Levekårsforskning Konferanserapport* (Proceedings of the Seminar on Welfare Research) (pp. 12-93). Oslo: Norwegian Research Council for Science and the Humanities.

Michalos, A. C. (1988a). A case for a progressive annual net wealth tax. *Public Affairs Quarterly, 2,* 105-140.

Michalos, A. C. (1988b). Integrated development planning using socio-economic and quality-of-life indicators. *Innovative approaches to development planning* (pp. 113-216). Paris: UNESCO.

Michalos, A. C. (1990). The impact of trust on business, international security and the quality of life. *Journal of Business Ethics, 9,* 619-638.

Miller, D. T., & Turnbull, W. (1986). Expectancies and interpersonal process. *Annual Review of Psychology, 37,* 233-256.

Moum, T. (1981). Social inequality, social status, and quality of life. *Psychiatry and Social Science, 1,* 177-195.

Moum, T. (1983, July). *Resignation and quality of life: On the self-regulatory nature of subjective well-being.* Paper presented at the World Conference on Systems, Caracas, Venezuela.

Moum, T. (1988). Yea-saying and mood-of-the-day effects in self-reported quality of life. *Social Indicators Research, 20,* 117-139.

Ottati, V., Fishbein, M., & Middlestadt, S. E. (1988). Determinants of voter's beliefs about the candidates' stands on the issues: The role of evaluative bias heuristics and the candidates' expressed message. *Journal of Personality and Social Psychology, 55,* 517-529.

Roos, J. P. (1988). Behind the happiness barrier. *Social Indicators Research, 20,* 141-163.

Roper, B. W. (1980). The impact of journalism on polling. In A. H. Cantril (Ed.), *Polling on the issues* (pp. 15-19). Cabin John, MD: Seven Locks.

Royal Commission on Electoral Reform and Party Financing, 1990: *Hearings* from various cities.

Schwarz, N. (1984, September). *Informative and directive functions of affective states in information processing.* Paper presented at the 23rd International Congress of Psychology, Acapulco, Mexico.

Smith, T. W. (1978). In search of house effects: A comparison of responses to various questions by different survey organizations. *Public Opinion Quarterly, 42,* 443-463.

Smith, T. W. (1982). House effects and the reproducibility of survey measurements: A comparison of the 1980 GSS and the 1980 American National Election Study. *Public Opinion Quarterly, 46,* 54-68.

Snyder, M. (1984). When belief creates reality. *Advances in Experimental Social Psychology, 18,* 247-305.

Stevens, G. (1990a, March 18). Money's ruining electoral system. *Toronto Star,* p. B3.

Stevens, G. (1990b, May 6). Sorting out bugs in voting system. *Toronto Star,* p. B3.

Strack, F., & Martin, L. L. (1987). Thinking, judging, and communicating: A process account of context effects in attitude surveys. In H.-J. Hippler, N. Schwarz, & S. Sudman (Eds.), *Social information processing and survey methodology* (pp. 123-148). New York: Springer-Verlag.

Sudman, S., & Bradburn, N. M. (1987). The organizational growth of public opinion research in the United States. *Public Opinion Quarterly, 51,* S67-S78.

Turner, C. F. (1984). Why do surveys disagree? Some preliminary hypotheses and some disagreeable examples. In C. F. Turner & E. Martin (Eds.), *Surveying subjective phenomena* (Vol. 2, pp. 159-214). New York: Russell Sage.

Turner, C. F., & Martin, E. (Eds.). (1984). *Surveying subjective phenomena* (Vols. 1 & 2). New York: Russell Sage.

Tversky, A., & Kahneman, D. (1986). Rational choice and the framing of decisions. *Journal of Business, 59,* S251-S278.

Vienneau, D. (1989, June 28). Information chief criticizes ministers. *Toronto Star,* p. A14.

Wedell, D. H., & Parducci, A. (1988). The category effect in social judgment: Experimental ratings of happiness. *Journal of Personality and Social Psychology, 55,* 341-356.

Wood, L. A., & Johnson, J. (1989). Life satisfaction among the rural elderly: What do the numbers mean? *Social Indicators Research, 21,* 379-408.

8

Advertising: Its Logic, Ethics, and Economics

The aim of this chapter is to disclose some of the logical, ethical, and economic features of contemporary advertising in North America. For reasons that are explained later, there appeared to be no satisfactory way to avoid ethics and economics, although the primary focus of this chapter is logic.

After adopting a working definition of *advertising* in the first section, I next show how the theory of public goods plus a few plausible assumptions would lead one to expect some deceptive advertising. Then in the third section, Loto Canada advertising is considered as a case of deceptive advertising with a public sponsor, and in the fourth section subliminal advertising is considered as a particular species of deceptive advertising. Finally, several criticisms of advertising and responses by two contemporary apologists are examined in the fifth section.

A WORKING DEFINITION

According to Littlefield and Kirkpatrick (1970), the authors of a popular contemporary textbook on advertising, "Advertising is *mass communication* of *information* intended to *persuade* buyers so as to *maximize dollar profits*" (p. 100). This definition has a number of

AUTHOR'S NOTE: Adapted from "Advertising: Its Logic, Ethics and Economics" by A. C. Michalos (1980). In *Informal Logic* (pp. 93-111), edited by R. Johnson & A. Blair. Point Reys, CA: Edge Press. Used with permission of the publisher.

I would like to thank Rodrique Chiasson, Acting Director-General of the Research Branch of the CRTC for providing a copy of the Examination File on "Regulation and Policies Proposed Amendment to the Television Broadcasting Regulations," Ottawa Hearing, March 11, 1975.

implications that may not be immediately apparent or acceptable for all purposes. Although it is suitable for my purposes, some of its limitations should be mentioned before proceeding.

First, according to this definition advertisers are interested in communicating messages on a large scale. Although we don't know how big "large" is, it may be assumed, for example, that at least not every display of products for sale will count as advertisement. Second, the immediate aim of the messages according to this definition is to get people to buy things. Thus, so-called social marketing or public service advertising is ignored. For example, Health and Welfare Canada's ads intended to get people to stop smoking and drinking are not covered by this definition. Third, the realization of the immediate aim of advertising is supposed to contribute directly to the final aim, which is the maximization of dollar profits. This apparently presupposes that the individuals or firms sponsoring advertising have as their primary aim the maximization of dollar profits. I suppose many of them have that aim, but there is some evidence that neither maximization generally nor dollar profit maximization in particular are universally accepted goals.

By accepting the Littlefield and Kirkpatrick definition of advertising, I have limited my discussion in some ways and expanded it in others. The limitations have already been indicated. The expansion comes as a result of thinking about advertising in its North American setting as a socioeconomic institution. From this point of view, it is virtually impossible to untangle logical, ethical, and economic issues in a logically tidy fashion. We just have to put up with some fudge.

FROM INFORMATION TO PERSUASION AND DECEPTION

Insofar as ads provide information more or less indiscriminately to great numbers of people, ads may be regarded as public goods. (To simplify things I usually use the single term *goods* as short for *goods and services*. Strictly speaking, ads seem to be typically more like services—e.g., information—than material goods.) There is a substantial body of literature on the theory of public goods. Such goods are supposed to be distinguishable from private goods on the basis of *either* of two characteristics, namely, jointness and nonexclusiveness (Olson, 1969; see also, Olson, 1965). To say that a good is characterized by jointness is roughly to say that using it does not imply using it up. To say that a good is characterized by nonexclusiveness is roughly to say that nonpurchasers cannot be excluded. Information is a perfect example of a public good displaying the character of jointness, and clean air or national defense are examples of public goods displaying nonexclusiveness.

The fundamental problem concerning the provision of public goods is often referred to as the *free-rider problem* (McKean, 1974). Because, without taking special measures, no one in a society can be excluded from public goods displaying nonexclusiveness, there is a temptation for (hypothetically self-serving) citizens to try to pass the costs of such goods on to everyone else. So, for example, Jones will leave his thermostat up because he will be able to enjoy the benefits of a national effort to conserve energy no matter what he does (one person's action has a negligible effect on the total picture), and he won't have to bear the increased costs in chilly discomfort. Similarly, Smith will continue to throw his beer cans out the car window, to stay home on election day, and so on. If the environment is ever cleaned up or good politicians are ever elected, Smith will enjoy the benefits anyhow. Meanwhile, he lets the other people pay the tab. Smith and Jones, then, are free riders.

If free riders are regarded as the fundamental problem for the provision of public goods, coercion is usually regarded as the fundamental solution. People must finally be forced to pay taxes for public safety and fines for public pollution. For failing to be informed about the activities of their political leaders, they pay the price of polluted political processes. Of course in the best of all possible worlds, people would be aware of the nature of public goods, there would be no free riders and no coercion. Part of the task of moralists is to help us get from this world to that other one—without, I would hope, leaving our corporeal bodies behind.

From the theory of public goods and the assumption that advertising involves the distribution of information, one may infer with some plausibility the reason for trying to make ads persuasive. If ad sponsors only distributed information, then, unless their products really were superior to others *and* people could be counted on to prefer superior products more often than inferior products, there would be no reason to suppose that the information would motivate people to buy their products. In fact, many products really are practically indistinguishable from others in their line, such as cigarettes, beer, bicycles, or soap. (Neither producers nor consumers have unlimited discriminatory powers.) So, if ads were only informative, they would probably produce random purchasing of such products. People would be informed that, say, one soap is as good as any other. So there would be no incentive to shop carefully. What's more, there would be no incentive in the form of private profit for producers to advertise. Information about such products would be a clear public good and producers would all tend to take a free ride.

Apparently, then, from the point of view of producers reaping private profits, many ads must be persuasive. However, insofar as products are practically indistinguishable from others in their line, advertisers are left with the logically and morally outrageous task of designing ads to persuade people to differentiate indistinguishables and to prefer one to another! As Rosser Reeves put it: "Our problem is—a client comes into my office and throws two newly-minted half-dollars on my desk and says, 'Mine is the one on the left. You prove it's better'" (quoted in Johnson & Blair, 1977, p. 222).

To avoid misunderstanding, let me emphasize that I am *not* claiming that it is good or smart to accept private enterprise, profit maximization, self-serving behavior, or even advertising itself (Michalos, 1978).[1] What I have tried to do is show that certain assumptions about these things and the theory of public goods lead fairly directly to the conclusion that sometimes (not necessarily always) advertisers are committed to logically and morally bad practices. I have no doubt at all that this fact is probably more or less clear and more or less tolerable to different advertisers. As a class of human beings, I imagine they are no better or worse than the rest of us.

MISLEADING ADS: A CASE STUDY

The previous section may give one the impression that deceptive advertising is only a product of private enterprise. So I would like to review a particular case of such advertising that involves the Canadian government. Although the advertising is sponsored by the government through a Crown Corporation, it is not public service advertising or social marketing.

The amendments to the Combines Investigation Act that became law in December 1975 included several clauses concerning misleading advertising. The new clauses are supposed to "apply to all kinds of serious misrepresentation concerning products or services made to public, rather than merely to published advertisements. Not only the literal meaning of a representation, but also the general impression it conveys is to be taken into account" (Canada Consumer and Corporate Affairs, 1973, p. 2).[2]

When I read the new provisions of the Act, I was impressed by the amount of protection the government was willing to give me. After failing to get the federal government to prosecute itself for patently misleading Loto Canada ads, I was impressed by the amount of deception the government was willing to practice. I can't go into all the details, but the following correspondence will demonstrate some of the logical and moral problems involved with misleading advertising.

The first letter was sent to "Box 99," which is the official complaint address in the Department of Consumer and Corporate Affairs.

July 19, 1977

Box 99
Dept. of Consumer &
Corporate Affairs
Ottawa, Ontario

Sir:

I am writing to appeal to you to put a stop to the seriously misleading advertising of Loto Canada on television. The ads continue to be very attractive and undoubtedly persuasive, but they are clearly giving a distorted picture of reality.

The ads make it seem as if the national lottery presented a good opportunity or chance to increase one's income with a windfall winning ticket. But because it is about 150 times more probable that one will die in an auto accident than that one will hold a winning ticket, the chances of the latter should not be described as good. If they are good, then the others are so much better that it is foolish to buy a ticket. It would seem unlikely that one will be alive long enough to collect it. That of course is false. We are much more secure in our autos than this scenario would suggest. The truth is that it's highly unlikely that any given individual will hold a winning ticket. So it is immoral and should be illegal for our government to create a quite different impression day after day on national television.

The credibility of government information releases is always under some strain in virtually all societies. But with blatantly misleading advertising the tension is needlessly increased. The government cannot expect to be able to con us with phoney ads at one moment and mobilize our support for national unity, belt tightening or other serious problems the next.

At the very least I urge you to see that the odds of winning are always in plain sight wherever lotteries are advertised. Honesty in advertising must be taken seriously.

Sincerely,

Alex C. Michalos

ACM/sdm
cc: Pierre Trudeau
A. Alan Borovoy

I was notified that my letter had been forwarded to another office, and I sent the next letter to that office.

August 30, 1977

Chief of Operations
Marketing Practices Branch
Place du Portage, Phase I
68 Victoria Street
Hull, Quebec

Sir:

Concerning my complaint about Loto Canada TV ads which was forwarded to your office (File No. TP 100.402), I call your attention to the paragraph below from the Combines Investigation Act. I believe the most frequently broadcasted TV ads for Loto Canada violate this section of the Act by not explicitly stating the chances of winning.

Surely the intention of Parliament in this section is to preclude misleading advertising that stimulates people to act in the absence of full knowledge of the likely consequences of their action. The point of the TV ads is precisely to get people to do what Parliament was trying to prevent them from doing, namely, buy on impulse rather than on the basis of a rational calculation of the likely benefits of the purchase. Accordingly, I urge you to do your duty and see that these illegal and immoral ads are stopped.

Combines Investigation Act

Section 37.2(1): No person shall, for the purpose of promoting, directly or indirectly, the sale of a product, or for the purpose of promoting, directly or indirectly, any business interest, conduct any contest, lottery, game of chance or skill, or mixed chance and skill, or otherwise dispose of any product or other benefit by any mode of chance, skill or mixed chance and skill whatever unless
(a) there is adequate and fair disclosure of the number and value of the prizes and the chances of winning in any area to which prizes have been allocated.

Sincerely yours,

Alex C. Michalos

ACM/sdm

I received the following response.

Director of Investigation & Research
Combines Investigation Act
Ottawa-Hull
KIA OC9
October 24, 1977

Dear Mr. Michalos:

Thank you for your letter of October 19, 1977 concerning your earlier complaint against Loto Canada Television advertising.

Section 37.2(1) (a), of the Combines Investigation Act states that in any contest promoting directly or indirectly the sale of a product there must be the following:

"adequate and fair disclosure of the number and approximate value of the prizes and of the area or areas to which they relate and of any fact within the knowledge of the advertiser that affects materially the chances of winning."

With respect to this section of the Act, we have reviewed past and present Loto Canada advertising and we believe that all the requirements of the section have been met. The facts which would materially affect one's chances of winning, i.e., the number of tickets available to be sold and the number and value of the prizes were disclosed. It was also the Director's opinion that adequate and fair disclosure occurred when the above information was made freely available to the public in newspapers and point of purchase display material during the run of the contest.

Should you have any additional questions on this matter please do not hesitate to contact this office.

Yours very truly,

Douglas G. Fraser,
Marketing Practices Branch

DGF/kc

To that I replied:

77 10 31

Douglas G. Fraser
Marketing Practices Branch
Consumer and Corporate Affairs
Ottawa, Ontario

Dear Mr. Fraser:

I am very disappointed by your conclusion regarding Loto Canada advertisements. You apparently believe that if 99 percent of an advertising campaign is misleading but one percent is not, then the campaign is fair. This is outrageous.

Not once has Loto Canada advertised the odds of winning to a national TV audience. Occasionally a TV news reporter will mention the problem. You don't even perceive it as a problem. Posters can be found on most government buildings urging people to buy, but the posters never give the odds. So in most display areas, the odds are not "freely available" as you say. People have to go out of their way to find the odds of winning, but they are bombarded with advertising material urging them to "buy a ticket on their dream."

The advertising is not fair, and you ought to be ashamed of yourself if you are not able to perceive its serious bias and unfairness. We are being systematically misled and encouraged to buy on impulse by Loto Canada and Wintario ads, and it is your responsibility to prevent such things. But you won't. What a sad state of affairs. What a pathetic way to carry out an oath of office or run a government.

Sincerely yours,

Alex C. Michalos

There was no reply to this last letter. I have since written to some MPs and received some sympathetic replies, but there has been no action by the government. If we assume that, for example, Mr. Fraser and others in the Marketing Practices Branch are just ordinary honest civil servants, then it must be granted that they see nothing in Loto Canada advertising that violates the Combines Investigation Act, Sec. 37.2(1) (a). At a minimum that tells us that the determination of misleading advertising is by no means a straightforward issue. I have already suggested what it tells us at a maximum in my last letter.

Since the above letters were written, a battle has raged between provincial and federal governments over the right or wisdom of federal versus provincial lotteries. Both levels of government see the lotteries as good sources of revenue, and both are apparently going to fight to keep the money coming in. There is no noticeable difference in the advertising for the two levels of government.

Given the wide variety of ways to win various sums of money, I now doubt that it will help much to give the odds of winning each sum. What is required is a clearly visible report of the *expected value* of every ticket purchased. If, for example, buyers knew that any ticket had an expected value of 50 cents or whatever and cost a dollar, then they could make an informed choice. Maybe most buyers would be willing to pay for the fun of the gamble. I certainly have no objection to people spending their own money in that way. But at present it's practically impossible to make an informed choice about a lottery ticket's value, and that is intolerable.

SUBLIMINAL ADVERTISING

In the second section it was claimed that people pursuing private profit would often be engaged in deceptive advertising, and in the previous section it was claimed that government agencies also engage in such practices, wittingly or not. In this section I want to address the problem of subliminal advertising. This is the sort of advertising that Key (1973) claimed involved "intuitive or insight logic" (p. 11). It is also the sort Johnson and Blair (1977) seem to have been thinking of when they wrote that

although advertising is an attempt to persuade, the type of persuasion generally used is not *rational*. Instead, advertising attempts to persuade us by appealing to our emotions (our hopes, fears, dreams), to the vulnerable spots in our egos (our desire for status and recognition), by applying pressure to the tender areas of our psyches. . . . In sum, *advertising has a logic of its own*. Thus, learning how to evaluate ads from the standard logical point of view becomes a gratuitous exercise. (p. 218)

Key's (1973) *Subliminal Seduction,* like Vance Packard's (1957) *The Hidden Persuaders* 15 years earlier, stimulated a lot of discussion about advertising tactics. Key refers to subliminal perception as any "sensory inputs into the human nervous system that circumvent or are repressed from conscious awareness" (p. 18). The most famous experimental proof of such perception involves the flashing of brief messages on a screen with a tachistoscope (Arnold, Barnes, & Wong, 1975; Key, 1973). Although subjects typically have no recollection of seeing the messages, certain features of their behavior, attitudes, or beliefs indicate that the messages were received. For example, Key reported that in one experiment

> test groups were shown a sketch of an expressionless face. One group was subliminally exposed to the word *angry* subliminally tachistoscoped (at 1/3000th of a second) over the expressionless face. Another group received the word *happy* over the same face at the subliminal level. Both groups overwhelmingly interpreted the emotional content of the blank face consistent with the subliminal stimuli. (pp. 33-34)

When the Canadian Radio-Television Commission (CRTC) held hearings on subliminal ads in March 1975, no one seemed to have any use for them. The report of the CRTC Research Branch (1975) concluded that: "There is no evidence currently available which indicates that advertisers can effectively use subliminal techniques to sell products because it is not clear what behavioral effects, if any, result from subliminal stimulation" (p. 29).

Mr. K. B. Wong, a research assistant in the School of Business at Queen's University, told the CRTC that "the inability of a researcher to be able to predict how subliminal [stimuli] will be responded to, makes [them], for all practical purposes, very inadequate as a marketing tool" (CRTC, 1975, pp. 446-447). C. R. Thomson, the Counsel for the Association of Canadian Advertisers (ACA), informed the CRTC that his client affirmed "that subliminal advertising techniques are not socially or morally justifiable in any media" (Thomson, personal communication to the CRTC, February 17, 1975, p. 1). And the president of the Canadian Advertising Advisory Board (CAAB) claimed:

> We are unaware of any evidence that the use of such techniques has commercial value in the marketplace. Our objections to the process are based on ethical

grounds. We in the business of advertising agree that advertising as such should be clearly identified and clearly identifiable and heartily support a ban on any explicit representations made in such a way as to escape conscious detection. (R. E. Oliver, personal communication to the CRTC, February 24, 1975, p. 2)

Notwithstanding all these disclaimers, I have the distinct impression that the unwashed orphan that is uniformly turned away from everyone's front door is routinely welcomed at some other entrance. Some of the evidence leading to this impression can only be revealed by examining ads themselves. But remarks like the following from C. R. Thomson for the ACA can hardly be discounted.

Once we accept my basic premise and that is that advertisers are entitled to do more than simply deliver a factual description of their product and service and price; once one acknowledges that *an advertiser is entitled* to appeal for the viewer's demand, *to create demand* for a class of goods and for his goods in particular, once we acknowledge that as being a principle—then *we have got to allow the advertiser to appeal to the conscious and sub-conscious appetites of the viewer.* [italics added] (CRTC, 1975)

Insofar as the logic of advertising is the logic of subliminal perception and "subconscious appetites," I'm inclined to regard the subject as more suitable to empirical investigation than to conceptual analysis. Unfortunately, I just don't know how far the logic of advertising is a matter of such perception and appetites.

It has been suggested that subliminal advertising involves a unique sort of inference or implication relation. Maybe so. But I think what's involved is more a matter of interpretation than inference. Once a particular interpretation has been made of a feature of an ad, the move from that interpretation to the conclusion (practical or cognitive) planned by the advertiser may be a move that's indistinguishable from ordinary inference. The history of attempts to clarify concepts of implication, inference, entailment, and so on is such that I am reluctant to wade into that sea of troubles unless absolutely forced.

At this point I want to set out in a slightly different direction and to consider in detail a set of alleged criticisms of advertising and responses offered to the critics by Littlefield and Kirkpatrick (1970; hereafter LK).

CRITICISM, REPLIES, AND COMMENTS

Before I begin the series of arguments in this section, it may be worthwhile to expand a point that was just barely suggested in the first section. People have traditionally defended free speech or expression on two grounds. For some it has been a matter of moral principle that people ought to be allowed to express their views without fear of reprisals. Although it may be a defeasible moral right, it is nevertheless a fundamental moral right, like the right to life, for example. For others, free expression has been defended as a matter of epistemological good sense. These people are more interested in the pursuit of truth and the avoidance of falsehood than they are in moral principles, and they see the free expression of ideas as a necessary condition of their epistemic aims (Mill, 1859; Trudeau, 1968).[3]

Of course, no one has to choose between these two different grounds for defending free expression, but historically I think people have tended to lean toward one or the other as especially weighty. (If one is primarily interested in the free expression of fictional or visual material—stories, films, paintings, sculptures—then one's defense might run more smoothly from moral grounds, but if one is primarily interested in the free expression of nonfictional or descriptively accurate material, then one's defense might run more smoothly from epistemic grounds.) The point I want to emphasize here, however, is that the two grounds often coalesce. In particular, objections to advertising practices may involve epistemological (or narrowly logical) and moral principles at the same time. Indeed, I suspect that this is typically the case. Hopefully, this will become clearer as the discussion proceeds. Let us turn immediately to a consideration of LK's critique.

1. LK (1970) begin by answering the charge that advertising is often "false, deceptive, and misleading, and that it conceals information which should be revealed and omits limitations and comparative disadvantages of the item advertised." In their view, "There is no justification for false, deceptive, or misleading advertising" (p. 115). They don't deny the charge at all, and they claim that self-regulation and enlightened self-interest (buyers must want to return) tend to minimize such practices. In a very revealing passage LK tell us that: "To tell advertisers to limit themselves to non-emotional, non-persuasive advertising would be to take a step in a direction repugnant to most of us. 'It is not the primary function of advertising to educate or to develop reasoning powers' " (quoted in Smith, 1964, p. 174).[4]

Comment. We have already seen how an advertiser might be led down the garden path to deception. The question is, Are there any good reasons for thinking that there is anything "repugnant" about insisting on "non-persuasive advertising?" Why should LK think that is demanding too much? Presumably they have given their answer to these questions a few pages later. "Persuasion and influence here," LK write, "are just as ethical as in politics, religion, or education" (p. 115). That is, they believe that there is nothing in principle morally wrong with trying to be persuasive as well as informative.

One would like, I suppose, to respond that there is something better about trying to persuade people to vote, worship God, or get an education. But by the time the words are uttered or written, I begin to have second thoughts. A priori I doubt that any old persuasive case made in behalf of any old political, religious, or educational cause must be somehow morally superior to any old case made for any old product or service. There are too many worthless and even dangerous political, religious, and educational causes and too many worthwhile marketed products and services to permit full-scale whitewashes. So I think we have to agree that there is nothing in principle wrong with persuasive advertising, and objectionable cases will have to be tracked down and eliminated one at a time.

2. In response to the charge that "advertising confuses and bewilders more than it helps," LK claim that "differences of opinion are a basic element in our mores and in our norms." Besides, they don't believe anyone can be "objective about his brand any more than can . . . a bridegroom about his bride" (p. 115).

Comment. The latter claim would be self-defeating if it were true, because the claim itself would lack objective persuasiveness. But it's plainly false. Everyone has all sorts of "objective" information about his or her most cherished persons or things. For example, I know the color of my wife's hair and eyes, her height and weight, how she prefers her tea, and so on. Loving someone or something is not the same as being struck dumb. Even the most ardent fans are often prepared to admit that their team doesn't have a hope in hell of winning, and there would be no sense at all in anyone's favoring the underdog unless there were a more or less objective assessment of just who *is* the underdog.

Some years ago David Braybrooke (1967) leveled the charge of confusion against corporations in an excellent article called "Skepticism of Wants, and Certain Subversive Effects of Corporations on American Values." He mentioned, in particular, "the systematic abuse of sexual interests, so that people have their wants for automobiles and all sorts of other things seriously mixed up with their sexual desires" (p. 230). On top of that he claimed that

> corporations not only assist in confusing the public about what it might want, they also obstruct institutional remedies for the lack of information that

leads . . . consumers into misjudgments about wants. . . . How shameful to find, besides the automobile companies dragging their feet about safety standards, the tire companies doing the same thing, the grocers and packagers objecting to truth-in-packaging, the credit firms protesting against truth-in-lending." (pp. 230-231)

Braybrooke's primary concern was as much epistemological as moral. Allegedly incorrigible first-person reports about wants, he argued, could be muddled and in need of revision given the heavy hand of corporate advertising. What's more, it seemed to him (as it does to me) to be morally wrong for corporations to "obstruct institutional remedies" in the ways he mentioned. It is one thing to have differences of opinion, but something else to prevent the unbiased assessment of claims and counterclaims.

3. In response to the charge that advertising is often "vulgar, and in poor taste," LK claim that "advertising has no responsibility to raise consumers' tastes, to preach, to try to elevate." In fact, they insist that a wise advertiser "should determine what your tastes are" and "he should then cater to those tastes" (pp. 116-117).

Comment. I wonder first, just whose responsibility LK suppose it is "to raise consumers' tastes" and "to try to elevate." I suppose they would want to claim that it is the business of teachers, professors, theologians, and moralists "to try to elevate." Advertisers are in a different business, the business of selling products for profit. Therefore, they should have nothing to do with elevating people—unless it's a matter of elevated shoes, airplanes, and so on.

This is a familiar piece of buck-passing that must be met head-on. It is a mistake to think that things like values, norms, and morality must exist in some proper ontological pigeonhole of the universe that one can dip into or avoid pretty much as one pleases. There is no good or evil in the abstract. Good and evil, values if you like, must be attached to things, actions, people, and so on if they are to have any existence at all. Thus, for example, if there is any moral behavior then it will be found by looking at ordinary behavior from a moral point of view. If an advertiser produces ads in which false claims are intentionally made then the advertiser is a liar. All and only people who intentionally make false claims *can* be liars. They will be lying advertisers, lawyers, philosophers, plumbers, housewives, or whatever, but they will be liars all the same. Therefore, and this is the main point, to stop lying when they are practicing their trade, lawyers must stop lying in their work, housewives must stop lying, and so on. There is no other way to make a world without liars.

The mistake involved here seems to be in regarding moral behavior as a special kind of sociological role playing. However, being a morally decent person is not analogous to being a butcher, dentist, or school teacher. It is not another role or alternative hat one slips on now and then. Insofar as analogies help, one may say that being a morally decent person is like being clean in the literal sense of being well-scrubbed. There is no once-in-a-lifetime bath one can take that will keep one clean forever. Every day brings new dirt. However, when one is clean or dirty, one is clean or dirty at dinner, selling shoes, or buying hamburger. Being clean or dirty is not a sociological role in addition to the consumer's role, the farmer's role, and so on. It is an aspect or feature of anyone operating in any of those roles. Just so, being a morally decent person or a person of high moral character is an aspect or feature of a person no matter what his or her sociological role. And it is an aspect that must be forever cultivated.

Insofar as one believes, for instance, that a world without liars is preferable to a world with liars, one ought to recognize one's responsibility for bringing about such a world. People who perform morally good actions are performing public services par excellence (which is not to say that agents receive no private benefits from such actions). Whenever one resists the temptation to lie, for example, one is engaged (in a limited way to be sure) in building a better world. It is the business of advertisers, bakers, and all people in any role whatever "to try to elevate" the world by adopting a moral point of view *in that role.* To say that they might adopt a moral point of view when they are in some other role, like children in Sunday school, is to say that they don't know what it means to adopt a moral point of view or to try to be a morally decent person.

LK's second claim, namely, that advertisers should cater to consumer's tastes, must be understood conditionally to avoid contradicting their first commitment to persuade people to buy products so they can make a profit. Their aim must be to use people's tastes as instruments for manipulating people's consumption habits. Nothing in their position suggests that they would not mold people's tastes to suit their own purposes if they thought they could get away with it. Indeed, just the opposite is true. They are committed to persuading people to buy their products. In LK's own words: "In a sense, demand must be stimulated continuously" (p. 124), whereas "the advertiser's hope is to make prospects dissatisfied with the present status and to keep current customers satisfied" (p. 102). Insofar as anyone has a taste for something that is incompatible with an advertiser's product, the latter must try to alter the taste, the product, or the appearance of the product. Because his primary objective is profit maximization, any of these three alternatives would seem to be live options.

4. Advertisers have been charged with getting "consumers to buy what they (a) do not need, (b) should not have, and (c) cannot afford" (Littlefield & Kirkpatrick, 1970, p. 117). But LK reply that nothing is ever bought that is "not in response to an admission of *need.*" Besides, "who knows what Mrs. Homemaker needs and can afford better than Mrs. H. herself? No one, of course. Just try to get her to buy something that will not (a) protect or (b) enhance her self concept" (p. 117).

Comment. This is an incredible passage, but a fair reflection of LK's position. Roughly speaking, they have only substituted *need* for *want* in the old cliché "We only give the public what it wants."[5] The latter claim was thoroughly discredited by Braybrooke (1967). But what can we make of the suggestion that sellers only give buyers what they need? Does anyone need Hostess Twinkies, Pringles, fat ties, thin ties, short skirts, long skirts, and so on? People have a need for food to live, but for Pringles? For grapefruit with skins that belong on footballs? That can't be true.

LK's claim about the role of the protection and enhancement of one's self-concept in marketing is probably not as outrageous as it may appear. Basically their view seems to be only that people will not pay money to be assaulted in any serious or threatening way. That's weaker than what seems to be claimed in the quotation above, namely, that people will only pay money for things that protect or enhance their self-concept. I doubt that they imagine that, for example, everyone buying bananas, Band-Aids, and buttons is somehow building up his or her self-concept.

5. In response to the charge that advertising helps create a society of "greedy, self-centered individuals who worship materialism," LK (1970) reply that, "The great majority of U.S. consumers believes that each person should expand his needs and then gratify them." What's more, however, they insist that "the purpose and responsibility of advertising are to make ultimate consumers want to consume more" (p. 117).

Comment. The sentence about "the great majority of U.S. consumers" leads me to suspect that LK have a peculiar notion of "needs." They seem to be claiming that one, anyone and everyone, ought to have more needs. For example, I suppose, they would want to say that I ought to need a Cadillac, hair dryer, and over-the-calf socks. (In the latter case I would also need bigger calves—or garters.) On the contrary, I can't think of any good reason for having an obligation to need such things. I even suspect that the idea of obligations to need things is incoherent. So, a fortiori I think the claim that a majority of Americans believes I have such obligations is completely unfounded and farfetched.

The second quotation from LK seems to grant the charge to which they are replying. The responsibility of advertisers, as LK see it, is to make people "want to consume more." It is not claimed, you may notice, that advertisers should try to make us want to consume more *if* that suits our tastes, *if* that's what we want, or *if* that's what we need. The obligation is categorical. The name of their game is "Make people want to consume more." They explicitly claim that "Materialism should not be an end—it should be a means to even better ends" (p. 117). But it's not clear what "better ends" LK might have in mind. Whatever we have, their aim is to make us want more. For advertisers with this view, the best of all possible worlds is one in which all human problems and solutions are manufactured and sold in the marketplace. It is a world in which everyone believes that he or she has some problem that can be solved by buying something that someone else wants to sell. It is a merchandiser's paradise. Indeed, LK suggest that the dream is not too far away.

> Every individual who wants to can be just as individualistic as he or she prefers. And there are enough dollars and enough different goods and services in our affluent society to afford wide ranges of choice. . . . Where else, indeed, in the world can the consumer find the assortment of merchandise and services with which to express his individuality? (p. 118)

How easily they neglect the poor slobs who might want to "express their individuality" without buying something. The very idea of such individuals seems to have escaped these authors completely.

6. It has been charged that advertising constitutes a severe constraint on the content of media that rely on its revenue to stay in business. For example, because advertisers use TV programs as means of getting people to sit still for their ads, controversial programs or programs revealing views about the world that are incompatible with ads are systematically eliminated. LK (1970) reply that "commercial media can be 'free' of government subsidies, 'free' of political control because of dollars from advertisers. . . . Prices of media would have to be higher if there were no advertising" (p. 118).

Comment. Apparently LK grant the charge but believe that constraints by advertisers are less objectionable than constraints by government, and there must be some constraints. Because some Canadian media are not free of government subsidies *or* advertisers, we may have the worst of both worlds. The mind boggles at the prospect of having all media run on the model of *Pravda*, but one can hardly be sanguine about the continuous parade of reminders of yellow teeth, bad breath, smelly armpits, flaky hair, irregular bowel movements, and so on. It seems to me, however, that this is a false dichotomy. CBC radio has no ads but is not constrained by the Canadian government any more than, say, CBS is constrained by the American government. The Trudeau administration has threatened the CBC through the CRTC and otherwise, but the Nixon administration was at least as difficult for CBS. It is also possible to sustain media outlets with private subscriptions, as we do with some journals, radio, and TV stations. Finally, one can always withhold one's support (e.g., change the channel, avoid the product) or take action against offensive outlets (e.g., join citizen action groups opposed to misleading advertising, obscene displays, etc.). Granted that there must be constraints, one doesn't have to be on the receiving end all the time.

7. In response to the charge that ads stress *"insignificant* product details, *minor* product differences, *unimportant* product changes," in a word, trivia, LK (1970) claim that what's minor today may be major tomorrow, that what's minor to you may be major to someone else and that what's perceived as major *becomes* major with increased consumption (pp. 118-119).

Comment. Because ads are often intended to perform the logically impossible task that I earlier described as differentiating indistinguishables, the present charge would seem to be practically a truism. When products are essentially the same, only trivial differences will be discoverable. The point of LK's reply seems to be that if, for example, people are willing to pay two or three times as much for Bayer aspirin as they are for aspirin *simpliciter*, then it is at least misleading to regard the brand name as a trivial feature of the product. But that seems to be irrelevant to the critic's point. The latter seems to be that from the point of view of the effectiveness of the product or that for the sake of which the product is purchased, the brand name is an unimportant feature. (To simplify matters I am ignoring the fact that many drugs are purported to have a 30% placebo effect and that for some people the effectiveness of Bayer aspirin may be greater than the effectiveness of other brands.) Hence, by emphasizing the brand name, advertisers are guilty of trying to make something (significant) out of nothing (significant). Again, that is objectionable on epistemological and moral grounds.

8. It has been charged that advertising wastefully increases the cost of products. But LK (1970) claim that advertising represents "the shortest way to the market," to a mass market at least. It would be far more expensive to try to reach the same number of people with personal selling, house by house, person by person. They also insist that, in theory, effective advertising leads to increased sales volume, which leads to lower per unit costs and the possibility of lower prices (p. 119). They grant, however, that "there is waste in advertising just as there is waste in competition," and then they wax poetic:

> If advertising were outlawed, something would take its place, and that something would most probably be more wasteful and more expensive. Actually, attacks on *advertising* are really attacks on our system and structure of *business*. Advertising is a part of and in harmony with our free enterprise system. Our free enterprise or competitive system is the cause of advertising, not the result. . . . . Abolish advertising because it is wasteful and competitive? Then abolish competition. (pp. 123-124)

Comment. As a former Fuller Brush man, I'm prepared to accept the claim that almost anything is more efficient than door-to-door selling. But personal problems aside, I would accept LK's first claim. Their theoretical defence of advertising is theoretically unexceptional, but not very useful in fact. What we would like to know, but don't, is the relative frequency with which the option of lowering prices is adopted over the option of reinvesting the new profits, distributing them to stockholders and employees, and so on. It would also be useful to know how wasteful advertising practices are, not necessarily in relation to nonadvertising activities but in relation to some hypothetical optimum. (Presumably there is a vast literature on the return-on-the-dollar of various sorts of advertising, although I'm unfamiliar with most of it.)

The most interesting part of LK's remarks in response to the charge of wastefulness is their claim, hardly necessary in this context, that our "competitive system is the cause of advertising." Does competition for market shares entail advertising? Could there be a competitive marketing system without ads? From a logical point of view, of course, the two ideas are separable. We have already contrasted door-to-door marketing with marketing through advertising. In fact many producers simply produce their products and make them available to purchasers without advertising as that term has been defined here, such as farmers in community markets or roadside stands. Unless one loosens up the definition of advertising to include any sort of display of products for sale, it should be possible to easily multiply such examples of nonadvertising marketing.

It is illegal to advertise some services in some areas, although the services themselves are quite legal—legal and medical services, for instance. Although competition is probably far from the minds of many professionals, a spokesman for the Canadian Medical Association once said in a radio interview that one must remember that doctors are small businessmen. (Some of them are relatively big businessmen.)

Granted that competitive marketing does not logically imply advertising, the former seems to be a major contributing factor toward the existence of the latter. After all, it doesn't require much imagination to realize that, for example, if farmer Brown can sell his corn by merely putting it on display in a roadside stand, then he can increase the chances of a sale by increasing the visibility of his stand with big signs, by placing some signs far enough away so people can prepare to stop, and finally by putting "signs" (ads) in news media to get people to make a special trip out to the stand. If they like his corn, maybe they will go for his chickens, too. Maybe people that won't go for the corn will go for the chickens. Given the aim of selling something for profit in a world of scarce resources, it's difficult to imagine anything arising more naturally than advertising. That may be what led LK to see advertising and competition inexorably connected.

It is perhaps worthwhile to add here that I suspect a better case can be made for allowing advertising on the basis of a Principle of Liberty than on the basis of competition. By a "Principle of Liberty" I mean something like the maxim that people ought to be allowed to do whatever they wish as long as it doesn't harm anyone else. Not many people are likely to object to that idea. It follows immediately, then, that insofar as advertising is harmless, it is allowable, and much of it probably is harmless. Perhaps this is the sort of argument LK had in mind when they mentioned "free enterprise" in conjunction with competition. Nevertheless, neither "free enterprise" nor a Principle of Liberty implies advertising.

9. Several charges have been leveled against advertising as a monopolistic force in the marketplace. For example, advertising has been charged with creating barriers to entry for new products or firms, discouraging price competition, and contributing to large-scale economic concentration (Littlefield & Kirkpatrick, 1970). LK's general position with respect to such criticisms is that monopolies came before advertising. Though they don't and shouldn't deny that advertising represents some sort of a barrier to entry, they mention several others that may be at least as significant, for example, "inadequate capital; lack of a full line of products; lack of competence, either manufacturing *or*

marketing, channel difficulties, such as unavailability of essential distributors, or the magnitude of the job of building a dealer organization; patents" (p. 122).

Comment. LK's response is perilously close to claiming that advertising is *not* objectionable because other things *are* objectionable. Whether or not that is their argument, it is obviously unsound. A priori, I suppose that anything that gives one a marketing advantage over competitors might contribute toward monopoly, perfect competition, or something in between, depending on the total distribution of advantages and disadvantages. So it's misleading to claim that any particular marketing advantage, as for example a good advertising scheme, is *on its own* a monopolistic force. In principle such schemes could bring about perfect competition if all other competitors were lucky enough to create equally advantageous schemes. Of course, in fact, some producers, for one reason or another, can mount more successful advertising campaigns than other producers, and the latter have nothing to compensate for their weakness. Some people are economically wiped out in such cases, even though the losers may be more efficient operators than the winners on a dollar-for-dollar or product-for-product basis. That's the sort of thing most small businesspeople, which means most businesspeople, want to see prevented; but it happens. Legislation like the Combines Investigation Act provides some protection against big or unscrupulous operators, but, as suggested earlier in the case of Loto Canada ads, the legislation is not self-implementing.

CONCLUSION

The aim of this investigation was to disclose some of the logical, ethical, and economic features of contemporary advertising in North America. Given such a diffuse goal, it was fairly easy to hit the mark. After adopting a working definition of *advertising*, I showed how the theory of public goods plus a few plausible factual assumptions would lead one to expect some deceptive advertising. Loto Canada advertising was reviewed as a case of deceptive advertising with a public sponsor. Subliminal advertising was briefly reviewed as a particular sort of deceptive advertising. Finally, several criticisms of advertising and responses by Littlefield and Kirkpatrick were examined.

NOTES

1. I have argued against maximization policies and self-serving in Michalos, 1978.

2. Excellent discussions of misleading advertising and the Combines Investigation Act may be found in Thompson, 1977, and in Stanbury, 1977.

3. For an epistemic approach see Mill, 1859, and for a strictly moral approach see the United Nations Universal Declaration of Human Rights or the Canadian Bill of Rights in Trudeau, 1968.

4. For a good analysis of self-regulation in Canada, see Moyer and Banks, 1977.

5. On the differences between needs and wants, see Michalos, 1978.

REFERENCES

Arnold, S. J., Barnes, J. G., & Wong, K. B. (1975, March 11). *Brief to the Canadian Radio-Television Commission on subliminal perception: Implications for regulation* [Mimeo].

Braybrooke, D. (1967). Skepticism of wants, and certain subversive effects of corporations on American values. In S. Hook (Ed.), *Human values and economic policy* (pp. 224-239). New York: New York University Press.

Canada Consumer and Corporate Affairs. (1973). *Proposal for a new competition policy for Canada: First stage.* Ottawa: Queen's Printer.

Canadian Radio-Television Commission. (1975, March 11). *Hearings on proposed amendments to the Television Broadcasting Regulations (Advertising "Subliminal Technique")* [Mimeo].

Canadian Radio-Television Commission, Research Branch. (1975, March). *Subliminal perception and subliminal advertising: An overview* [Mimeo].

Johnson, R. H., & Blair, J. A. (1977). *Logical self-defense.* Toronto: McGraw-Hill Ryerson.

Key, W. B. (1973). *Subliminal seduction.* New York: New American Library.

Littlefield, J. E., & Kirkpatrick, C. A. (1970). *Advertising: Mass communication in marketing.* Boston: Houghton Mifflin.

McKean, R. N. (1974). Collective choice. In J. W. McKie (Ed.), *Social responsibility and the business predicament* (pp. 109-134). Washington, DC: Brookings Institute.

Michalos, A. C. (1978). *Foundations of decision-making.* Ottawa: Canadian Library of Philosophy.

Mill, J. S. (1859). *On liberty.* London: Parker.

Moyer, M. S., & Banks, J. C. (1977). Industry self-regulation: Some lessons from the Canadian advertising industry. In D. N. Thompson (Ed.), *Problems in Canadian marketing* (pp. 185-202). Chicago: American Marketing Association.

Olson, M. (1965). *The logic of collective action.* Cambridge, MA: Harvard University Press.

Olson, M. (1969). The plan and purpose of a social report. *The Public Interest,* p. 94.

Packard, V. (1957). *The hidden persuaders.* New York: David McKay.

Smith, S. V. (1964). Advertising in perspective. In J. W. Towle (Ed.), *Ethics and standards in American business.* Boston: Houghton Mifflin.

Stanbury, W. T. (1977). *Business interests and the reform of Canadian competition policy, 1971-1975.* Toronto: Methuen.

Thompson, D. N. (1977). The Canadian approach to misleading advertising. In D. N. Thompson (Ed.), *Problems in Canadian marketing* (pp. 157-184). Chicago: American Marketing Association.

Trudeau, P. E. (1968). *A Canadian charter of human rights*. Ottawa: Information Canada.

9

A Case Against Tobacco Promotion

For some years many people in the city of Guelph had been trying to convince the rest of the community that a new community facility for the performing arts and other activities should be constructed. In 1992 one of Guelph's biggest employers, Imperial Tobacco Ltd., offered $700,000 to help build what was then called the Guelph Civic Centre in exchange for the city council's agreement to name the Centre's main theater after the du Maurier brand of cigarettes and to display that name on every ticket, notice, and advertisement related to the theater for as long as the facility would exit.

In the interest of bringing some realism to my 1993 winter-term class of 130 students in Business and Professional Ethics, I put the following question to them in their midterm exam.

> Some people think it is morally wrong to accept $700,000 from Imperial Tobacco Ltd. in exchange for naming the Guelph Civic Centre's main theater after du Maurier cigarettes. Some people think not. Make a case for one side, and indicate possible objections and replies to your position.

Shortly after I graded the exam for these students, the city council was going to have its final debate on the question of accepting or rejecting the offer, and some friends asked me to let my views be known. Because it was a very controversial issue and a federal election was just around the corner in which I planned to be a candidate, I was not particularly enthusiastic about getting involved in the debate. As a candidate in the 1988 federal election, I had already alienated some of the roughly 600 unionized employees at Imperial by explaining that, in my view, smoking tobacco was a dangerous and dirty habit that we should all try to eliminate. This time practically all of Guelph's arts community and some of the best working members of my election planning committee were anxious to take the money and run. Of course other members of my committee and many other people were on the other side.

Well, to get right to the bottom line, armed with lots of good ideas from my students and lots of encouragement from my friends, I sent a letter to the city council saying that, all things considered, I would recommend rejecting the offer for the following reasons.

1. The evidence for the harmful effects of tobacco use is beyond reasonable doubt. Lifetime smokers who do not use the product in any particularly extreme way, who are not negligent, and do not have accidents with the product still have a much higher risk than nonsmokers of horrible diseases and deaths as a result of using the product. So far as I know, there is no other product that is sold legally about which this can be said, which makes tobacco quite unique.

2. The expected long-run costs to our community and the human race for continuing its addiction to and dependence on tobacco are greater than the expected long-run benefits. So, as a matter of long-term policy, we should be finding ways to end that addiction and dependence.

3. It is likely that the tobacco industry here will be shrinking significantly in the coming years. Thus, at a minimum we should be trying to make the phasing out of this industry as painless as possible to all concerned. So, for example, instead of accepting the company's contribution to our proposed Civic Centre, we should be encouraging it to increase its investments in retraining its workers so they have a better chance to find alternative employment, in its pension plans for those who will be too old to change jobs, in research and development to find some harmless uses for tobacco products, and in ways to convert their expertise and other resources to sustainable and even growing industries.

4. If we accept the contribution as offered then we will be making it easier for someone in the future to point to Guelph as another example of a community that found it proper to accept such contributions, just as some today use the O'Keefe Centre as an example for us.

5. If we accept the contribution then we will be adding another benefit to the habit of smoking, strengthening the general case in favor of sustaining the habit.

6. Because our governments are clearly trying to phase in their restrictions of tobacco sales to allow a relatively less painful transition to a

tobacco-free society, we would be undermining their efforts if we use the fact that tobacco traffic is still legal as an argument that it is still acceptable.

7. The momentum is currently in favor of restricting and reducing tobacco use. By naming the main theater of our Centre after a tobacco product, we would be boosting the image of the product, arresting that momentum, and displaying insensitivity to those who have fought on the right side of this battle for many years, not to mention those who have suffered ill health or death as a result of using tobacco products.

I have considered the following reasons for accepting the Imperial offer and have found them collectively less persuasive than those above.

1. Some people seem to understand and accept the health risks, while choosing to smoke or chew tobacco.

2. Other companies produce harmful products or are harmful in other ways but we are not rejecting contributions from them.

3. The tobacco industry produces great benefits in the form of pleasure for its consumers, jobs, wages, and salaries for its workers, dividends for its stockholders, taxes for governments and social goods and services paid for out of such taxes, and incomes for the variety of others engaged in some sort of economic exchange with members of the industry.

4. The proposed contribution is a good faith offer by a good local corporate citizen to a community project.

5. Members of our community whose livelihoods depend fairly directly on tobacco sales and whose alternatives are limited will be distressed by our harsh criticism of such sales.

6. Our corporate laws and tax system are designed with the expectation that there will and should be corporate charitable donations. If we reject such donations, then besides losing corporate tax dollars, we will be denying ourselves the benefits designed into the system to compensate for the lost tax dollars.

7. If we reject the contribution, we must either increase our own taxes, increase our loan, find substitute contributions, change our building schedule, or some combination of these tactics. None of these options is particularly attractive.

8. People know about the health problems with tobacco, whether we name the theater after the product or not.

9. The theater would be a great benefit to our community.

At the end of the final debate, the city council voted to accept the company's offer.

A Case for a Progressive Annual Net Wealth Tax

The basic aim of this chapter is to make a case for the introduction of a progressive annual net wealth tax in Canada. I begin (in the first section) with a review of some national public opinion polls indicating the attitudes of Canadians toward taxation and government spending. The second section provides an overview of the distributions of wealth and income and emphasizes the significantly greater inequalities in the former compared to the latter. A progressive annual net wealth tax is briefly described and then proposed as a means to reducing wealth disparities in the third section. In the fourth section I present 19 arguments in favor of such a tax. Following that, in the fifth section I present 31 arguments opposed to a net wealth tax, and I try to show that none of these arguments can be sustained. For reasons explained in some detail in the body of the chapter, the redistribution of wealth should be regarded as a fundamental feature of any national socioeconomic development plan.

AUTHOR'S NOTE: Adapted from "A Case for a Progressive Annual Net Wealth Tax" by A. C. Michalos (1988). In *Public Affairs Quarterly*, *2*, pp. 105-140. Used with permission of Philosophy Documentation Center. An earlier version of this chapter was presented at the Conference on "Women and Economic Equity: The Canadian Context," at Mount Saint Vincent University, Halifax, Nova Scotia, January 23-25, 1987.

Several people have kindly given me helpful suggestions, and I would like to express my thanks to them: G. Bale, F. Cunningham, J. Drewnowski, W. J. Furlong, E. K. Grant, D. Johnston, C. J. Munford, D. C. Poff, M. L. Steele, J. Vanderkamp.

TABLE 10.1 Do You Think Taxes Are Too High or About Right?

	Percentage Answering		
Year	Too High	About Right	Can't Say
1962	47	43	10
1965	49	39	12
1970	75	21	4
1975	66	27	7
1985	69	24	7

SOURCE: The Gallup Report, May 6, 1985. Reprinted with permission of Gallup Canada.

TAXATION

John Kenneth Galbraith (1975) wrote, "Where taxes were concerned, the [American] colonists were exceptionally obdurate; they were opposed to taxation without representation, as greatly remarked, and they were also, a less celebrated quality, opposed to taxation with representation" (p. 57). There is some evidence that Canadians are also not particularly enthusiastic about taxation. Since 1962, on five occasions, the Canadian Institute for Public Opinion (CIPO; Gallup Polls) has put the following question to national samples of Canadians, "Do you think taxes are too high or about right?" On every occasion more people answered "too high" than "about right" (see Table 10.1). (Gallup Polls are typically designed so that reported percentages should be within 4 percentage points of the true percentages 95% of the time. Thus a very conservative interpretation of reported percentages would require differences of about 8 percentage points between two figures to judge that the differences indicate more than mere measurement error. Hence, for example, although in 1962, 47% of respondents answered "too high" and 43% answered "about right," a conservative interpretation would allow that the 4 percentage point difference between these figures might be merely the result of measurement error or, briefly, that the difference was not statistically significant. I generally favor a conservative interpretation of poll results.)

In 1980, 71% of a national sample of Canadians thought that "if the average Canadian felt he or she could get away with it he or she would be likely to attempt [tax] evasion" (reported in Bird, 1980, p. 38). On May 12, 1983, the CIPO released results of asking the following question, "As you may know, the current Federal deficit is approaching 30 billion dollars. Where do you think the government should look for additional funds—Do you think the Federal government should raise

TABLE 10.2 Do You Think the Federal Government's Policies for Tackling the Country's Economic Situation Gives You a Feeling That They Are or Are Not Handling the Situation Properly?

Year	*Yes, Handling Properly*	*Not Handling Properly*	*Don't Know*
1977	28	54	18
1978	27	59	14
1979	27	62	11
1981, Jan.	25	61	14
1981, June	18	67	15
1981, Nov.	20	69	11
1982, June	14	76	9
1983, June	27	61	12
1984, May	23	62	15

Percentage Answering

SOURCE: The Gallup Report, July 19, 1984. Reprinted with permission of Gallup Canada.

taxes, should introduce economy measures or should borrow more money abroad? What should be done first? And in second place?" In first place, 85% of a national sample said, "Introduce economy measures," and in first or second place 92% said, "Introduce economy measures." Three percent favored raising taxes as their first or second choice.

Lest one is inclined to jump to the conclusion that the basis for Canadians' attitudes toward taxation is merely some sort of an innate reluctance to part with their cash, it is worthwhile to notice the results of some other relevant national opinion polls. The CIPO had nine polls that included the question, "Do you think the Federal government's policies for tackling the country's economic situation gives you a feeling that they are or are not handling the situation properly?" In every case, from 1977 to May 1984, most people said they had the feeling that the government was not handling the economic situation properly (see Table 10.2). In 1968, the Federal Task Force on Government Information found that 45% of a national sample of Canadians had "low" or "fairly low" levels of faith in the federal government, and 45% thought it was "inefficient" or "somewhat inefficient" (Michalos, 1980, p. 163). The CIPO reported that 70% of Canadians believed that, "People are asked to make great sacrifices, but government officials themselves live in luxury" (January 2, 1984). Granted that there may be some inclination to hold on to their cash, there is also some suspicion that the federal government (of Liberals or Progressive Conservatives) is not completely in control of its fiscal house.

Taxes are the means of effecting compulsory transfers of assets from the private to the public sector. Although most taxes are called just that (e.g., income taxes and sales taxes), some go by other names, such as premiums for unemployment insurance and social security. Two main principles govern the levying of taxes, namely, that levies should be made according to (a) benefits received or (b) ability to pay. Because many of the benefits received from paying taxes are public goods (e.g., national defense), it is difficult to operate exclusively on this principle. Still, unemployment insurance premiums, for example, are warranted by it. To apply the second principle, some measure of ability to pay must be selected. "Ideally, this measure would reflect the entire welfare which a person can derive from all the options available to him or her, including consumption (present and future), holding of wealth, and the enjoyment of leisure. Unfortunately, such a comprehensive measure is not practicable" (Musgrave & Musgrave, 1984, p. 233). Generally speaking, the measures used are based on income, expenditures, or wealth. Thus, there are income taxes (using income as the measure of the ability to pay), sales taxes (using expenditures), and property taxes (using some wealth as the measure). A tax on incomes is said to be "progressive" if the ratio of the tax to any particular income rises as incomes rise. It is "proportional" if the ratio remains constant for any income changes, and it is "regressive" if the ratio falls as incomes rise. If all other things are equal and a scheme of income taxation is progressive, then the distribution of after-tax incomes will be more equal than the distribution of before-tax incomes. Similarly, a scheme of net wealth taxation that is progressive would leave the distribution of after-tax net wealth more equal than the distribution of before-tax wealth. That is precisely the sort of net wealth tax that is being recommended here.

DISTRIBUTIONS OF WEALTH AND INCOME

Since 1952, Statistics Canada has collected data on the net wealth of Canadians in its Surveys of Consumer Finances. However, as a result of changes in basic definitions and other technicalities, only the survey data from 1970, 1977, and 1984 are reasonably comparable (Statistics Canada, 1986b). The 1970 and 1977 data-sets have been more thoroughly analyzed than the 1984 data-set, but because the figures regarding net wealth are so stable, much of what was found in the earlier surveys is very similar to what has been and probably will be found in the later survey.

The key definitions in these surveys are as follows:

The concept of the wealth of families . . . is rather narrowly defined as the value of total selected assets *less* total debt. . . . Total asset holdings which comprise wealth . . . consist of deposits and savings certificates in chartered banks, trust companies and other institutions, cash on hand, Canada Savings Bonds, other Government of Canada bonds, all other bonds, publicly traded stocks and shares, mortgages, loans to other persons and businesses, amounts (including accrued interest) held in RRSP's [Registered Retirement Savings Plans] and RHOSP's [Registered Home Ownership Savings Plans], other financial assets such as trust funds, cars, market value of owner-occupied homes, equity in vacation homes, other real estate and business/farm/professional interests . . . the value of only one consumer durable good, i.e., cars, has been included in total asset holdings whereas the value of all other consumer durables such as coloured televisions, yachts, sail boats, skidoos and other household furnishings and equipment has been excluded. Also excluded is the value of jewelry, art, stamps, coins, etc.

Total debt, which is subtracted from total asset holdings in order to define the wealth of a family unit, consists of money owed on credit cards, charge accounts and installment debts, bank loans secured by stocks and bonds and household goods, student loans, all other bank loans, loans from sales finance and consumer loan companies, credit unions and caisses populaires, other institutions such as savings banks, life insurance companies, other miscellaneous debts and mortgage debt on the owner-occupied homes. (Statistics Canada, 1979a, pp. 8-9)

The 1977 sample covered about 17,000 households, with some over-sampling of high-income households because "survey data on incomes or other financial items seriously underestimate income or other items at the upper end of the distribution because small samples do not adequately measure the high incomes and because refusal rates may be higher among high income groups or high asset holders" (Statistics Canada, 1979a, p. 11). The overall response rate was 80% and the response rate for the high-income sample was about 45% (Oja, 1983). Details regarding sampling frames, response rates, accuracy of estimates, random and systematic errors, sizes of standard errors, and so on, are given in Statistics Canada (1979a, 1979b, 1980b, 1986b).

Basic results of the 1970, 1977, and 1984 surveys are given in Table 10.3. This table includes detailed breakdowns for individuals living alone (unattached individuals), families of two or more members, and aggregates of families and unattached individuals. In 1984, if all Canadians (unattached individuals and families) were lined up from the very poorest to the very richest and divided into five groups containing 20% (a quintile) of the population in each group, and if the total net wealth of all the units was determined and its distribution among the five

TABLE 10.3 Distribution of Wealth and Income by Quintiles, 1970-1984

Year	Lowest Quintile	Second Quintile	Middle Quintile	Fourth Quintile	Highest Quintile	Highest Decile
Shares of Wealth (%)						
All Units						
1970	−1.0	1.6	8.5	20.1	70.8	53.2
1977	−0.6	2.2	9.4	20.7	68.3	50.7
1984	−0.3	2.4	9.3	19.8	68.9	51.3
Families						
1970	−0.8	3.0	10.1	20.0	67.7	50.8
1977	−0.2	4.2	11.1	20.3	64.6	48.0
1984	0.0	4.3	10.7	19.7	65.2	48.3
Unattached Individuals						
1970	−1.3	0.3	2.9	15.4	82.7	62.4
1977	−1.1	0.4	3.3	16.1	81.3	60.0
1984	−1.1	0.6	4.0	17.6	78.9	59.1
Shares of Income (%)						
All Units						
1971	3.6	10.6	17.6	24.9	43.3	
1973	3.9	10.7	17.6	25.1	42.7	
1977	3.8	10.7	17.9	25.6	42.0	
1979	4.2	10.6	17.6	25.3	42.3	
1980	4.1	10.5	17.7	25.3	42.4	
1981	4.6	10.9	17.6	25.2	41.8	
1982	4.5	10.7	17.3	25.0	42.5	
1983	4.4	10.3	17.1	25.0	43.2	
1984	4.5	10.3	17.1	25.0	43.0	
Families						
1971	5.6	12.6	18.0	23.7	40.0	
1973	6.1	12.9	18.1	23.9	38.9	
1977	5.9	13.1	18.5	24.4	38.0	
1979	6.1	13.0	18.4	24.3	38.3	
1980	6.2	13.0	18.4	24.1	38.4	
1981	6.4	12.9	18.3	24.1	38.4	
1982	6.3	12.6	18.0	24.1	38.9	
1983	6.2	12.3	17.8	24.1	39.5	
1984	6.1	12.3	18.0	24.1	39.5	
Unattached Individuals						
1971	2.9	8.0	14.8	25.8	48.6	
1973	3.2	8.6	15.2	24.9	48.1	
1977	3.8	8.4	15.4	25.8	46.5	
1979	4.6	8.9	15.8	25.1	45.6	
1980	4.5	9.4	15.5	25.7	44.9	
1981	5.0	9.5	15.7	25.1	44.7	
1982	4.9	9.5	15.4	24.9	45.4	
1983	4.8	9.5	14.5	24.2	47.1	
1984	4.9	9.9	15.2	24.6	45.4	

SOURCES: Oja (1983, 1986); Statistics Canada (1984b), p. 155.

groups was calculated, then the result would be as indicated in Table 10.3. The poorest 20% of Canadians (i.e., the lowest quintile) had less than nothing; they were in debt, which is indicated in the table as −0.3% of the net wealth of all units. The next poorest 20% had only 2.4% of the whole pie, and so on. The wealthiest quintile had about 69%, and the wealthiest 10% (decile) had just over half (51%) of the wealth of all Canadians.

For purposes of comparison, Table 10.3 also includes figures regarding the distribution of incomes. The table clearly shows that the 1984 distributions of incomes for all units, families or unattached individuals, were not as unequal or skewed as the distributions of net wealth. For example, considering all units, the poorest quintile had 4.5% and the richest quintile had 43% of the total income of all Canadians.

For a variety of reasons regarding the sample response rates, missing values, imputed values, extreme skewness of the net wealth distribution, and so on, it is difficult to estimate the accuracy of the figures on the basis of which the percentages in Table 10.3 were determined. According to Oja (1983), the 1977 "survey estimates of financial assets and debts may come to 60-70 percent of the true balances of the household sector" (p. 172). Given the likelihood of such substantial underestimations, any differences of one or two percentage points in our figures should be regarded with caution. Thus, it is best to think of the net wealth distributions from 1970 to 1984 as essentially unchanged. Insofar as one is prepared to take the figures at face value, the indicated change of about 2 percentage points in 14 years implies that, if the future were fairly similar to the past, it would take about 70 years to reduce the top decile's wealth 10 percentage points.

Concerning the distributions of income, much more can be said. According to Gillespie (1980a),

> the distribution of income in Canada became considerably less unequal between 1930 and 1951 . . . and remained virtually unchanged between 1951 and 1977. . . . The empirical evidence for the 1970-77 period demonstrates that federal budgets have not substantially altered the economic position of lowest-income families relative to highest-income families. . . . Rather, it seems that federal budgets have provided larger benefits for the latter compared with the former—although both have gained—financed primarily by lower-middle- and upper-middle-income families. (pp. 27, 31)

See also Michalos (1982).

The first time I saw figures concerning the distribution of wealth and income in Canada, I was shocked. Like most other Canadians, I knew that there were people in this country with much less and much more money than I had, and I knew that some of the former were very poor whereas some of the latter were very rich. I naturally wondered how my country compared to similar other countries, for example, the United States and the United Kingdom. Good comparisons were and are very difficult to find. Harrison (1980) presented evidence indicating that the United Kingdom's wealth distribution was skewed much more than that of Canada and the United States, partly as a result of the persistence of large fortunes through inheritance. Although I addressed some of the problems related to poverty and wealth in Canada and the United States in Michalos (1982), I was not able to try to make the case for a net wealth tax that would effectively reduce the great and continuing disparities of wealth and, among other things, provide the revenue to eliminate poverty. It is now time to make that case.

OUTLINE OF THE PROPOSED TAX

More details of the proposal are given below in the course of considering arguments for and against it. However, a brief overview will be useful now. What is being proposed is a progressive annual tax on net wealth that, to some extent, would both supplement and supplant current income, consumption, and wealth taxes. The net wealth tax would be part of a comprehensive tax scheme that would be more efficient to administer and would obtain more revenue more equitably than the current system. The administration of the tax would be combined with the current income tax, and the two kinds of taxes would be calculated together. Thus, the federal government would be primarily responsible for gathering the tax with the cooperation of provincial governments. The revenues obtained would be shared somehow, as current income tax revenues are shared.

Net wealth would be comprehensively defined as what is left over when total debts are subtracted from total assets. The unit of taxation would be individuals or families. Consistent with current income taxes, there would be deductions for dependents and the aged, and exemptions for some housing, household, and personal effects, pension rights, insurance policies, patents, and copyrights. There would be starting and ending points (floors and ceilings) for tax liabilities based on the national distribution of average net wealth holdings, and these points would be periodically adjusted. For example, consider the 1984 distribution of wealth illustrated in Table 10.3. Because the lowest three quintiles' share of the nation's total wealth is far below, the fourth quintile's share is about even with, and the highest quintile's share is far above what it would be in an egalitarian society, a reasonably progressive net wealth tax would have starting points or floors for tax liability set so that no tax would be paid by families in the lowest four quintiles. The 2% or 3% tax levied on families in the highest quintile would be divided so that the wealthiest decile paid more than the second wealthiest decile, and the total revenue would be distributed so that families in the lowest quintile received more than those in the second quintile, and so on. It is likely that the tax would never exceed 5% of any individual's or family's net wealth, and it would most likely be less than 3%.

According to a report of the Organization for Economic Cooperation and Development (OECD, 1979), in 1976 there were 11 member countries with a net wealth tax, namely, Austria, Denmark, Finland, Federal Republic of Germany, Iceland, Ireland, Luxembourg, Netherlands, Norway, Sweden, and Switzerland. Musgrave and Musgrave (1984) claimed that there were 17 countries with such a tax, including the OECD countries, India, and some Latin American countries. The OECD report mentioned above was based on a survey of all member countries regarding the costs and benefits of net wealth taxes with a wide variety of provisions. Several related studies have been carried out by the OECD and should be carefully reviewed by anyone interested in following up my proposal. References may be found in OECD (1979).

ARGUMENTS FOR A NET WEALTH TAX

The following arguments may be offered in support of the establishment of an annual progressive net wealth tax applicable to all Canadians.

1. Net wealth is the best measure of an individual's ability to pay taxes (Bale, 1980; Bird, 1980; Sazama, 1980).

2. Net wealth is much more unequally distributed than income, so a nation that is nominally committed to egalitarianism should be more concerned with the distribution of wealth than of income. In the words of the Ontario Committee on Taxation in 1967, "A democratic society such as ours, espousing political equality for all its citizens, cannot permit undue concentration of wealth in the hands of a few" (quoted in Bale, 1980, p. 48).

3. It is practically impossible for Canadians to focus attention on the existence of the enormous wealth of this country, of the great

disparities in the distribution of that wealth, and of the consequences of such disparities without the official, routine, and public accounting required through an annual tax on net wealth. As indicated above, we have had three roughly comparable surveys examining net wealth, and their results certainly underestimate the real net wealth in this country. Because the Survey of Consumer Finances estimates depend "not only on the willingness of respondents to provide financial data but also on their ability to recall amounts accurately, voluntary cooperation to consult their records, clear understanding of the questions asked and their rapport with the interviewers, etc.," the estimates obtained from such surveys cannot be regarded as adequate for the development of public policy (Statistics Canada, 1979b, p. 50). Furthermore, public policy on such a sensitive matter as the distribution of wealth cannot be allowed to be periodically manipulated by half-baked Royal Commissions like the 1978 Royal Commission on Corporate Concentration. (A rapid review of this Commission's report may be found in Michalos, 1982, pp. 30-34.)

4. It is practically impossible to mobilize interest and support for the initiation of remedial measures to eliminate harmful consequences of significantly unequal distributions of wealth unless there has been relatively continuous monitoring and public discussion. As Sazama ("Panel Discussion," 1980) remarked:

> By talking about net wealth taxation we are raising fundamental issues about how the economic system is organized. To have full popular control of economic power it will be necessary (but not sufficient) to transform private wealth to social wealth. The process of working for a net wealth tax will make those conclusions obvious to more people. (p. 54)

5. The current unequal distribution of net wealth contributes to the unequal distribution in incomes (Michalos, 1982; Ward, 1980).

6. The unequal distribution of net wealth prevents the equalization of opportunities for employment and other necessities of a good life (Bale, 1980; Bird, 1980).

7. The unequal distribution of net wealth creates unequal access to political power. This undermines democracy (Bale, 1980; Bird, 1980; Sazama, 1980; Ward, 1980).

8. The unequal distribution of wealth and incomes must distort markets and economic development in the interests of monopolies and oligopolies, which tend to be characterized by relatively inefficient production and overpricing (Michalos, 1981b, 1982).

9. The current emphasis on income taxes as a source of government revenue places a greater burden on labor than on capital, which therefore requires a net wealth tax to correct the inequity (Bird, 1980; Musgrave & Musgrave, 1984; Ward, 1980).

10. Unlike significantly progressive income taxes that perpetuate current concentrations of wealth by preventing new accumulations, a progressive net wealth tax would reduce the size of and even eliminate some current concentrations (Bale, 1980; Bird, 1980).

11. An appropriately designed net wealth tax would allow the government to reduce income taxes without loss of revenue, and that would allow relatively poorer Canadians to accumulate some wealth and reduce the current wealth disparities.

12. The sum total of net wealth is so much larger than the sum total of annual incomes that the former provides a much larger tax base and a much better source of national revenue. The total estimated net wealth of Canadians in 1977 was about $400 billion, compared to the estimated Gross National Product of about $200 billion (Statistics Canada, 1979b, 1985c). Net wealth in the United States in 1980 was about three times the GNP (Musgrave & Musgrave, 1984).

13. A progressive net wealth tax would have the effect of redistributing the wealth of Canada to the whole community, where it can be more effectively used in the interests of that community. In other words, it would "encourage decision making which is responsible to the community as a whole" rather than that which emphasizes "profits and corporate power" (Canadian Mental Health Association, 1985, p. 82).

14. Current taxes that touch net wealth are notoriously regressive. "For example, the municipal real property tax, in effect a gross wealth tax confined to one kind of asset, is regressive over all income levels. The same is generally true of the provincial retail sales taxes, the federal sales tax and the selective excise taxes" (Bale, 1980, p. 39). To say that these taxes are regressive is to say that they violate the principle of taxation according to ability to pay and that they tend to increase rather than decrease wealth disparities. As a source of revenue, their sustaining virtue is convenience.

15. The making of large fortunes is largely the result of good luck for winners and bad luck for losers, but the making of civilized communities requires reasonable and compassionate alterations in the circumstances resulting from mere luck, which alterations could be initiated by a net wealth tax (Bale, 1980; Bird, 1980; Michalos, 1982). It is perhaps

worthwhile to mention here that even if large fortunes were the result of great skill, hard work, or special virtues of some sort, it would not follow that such fortunes should be preserved. After all, the virtues that allow one to accumulate wealth may be entirely irrelevant to or even incompatible with its wise and compassionate use. Presumably the preservation of civilized communities should take precedence over the preservation of large fortunes no matter how virtuously the latter were made.

16. Optimistically, perhaps, one might expect that the reduction of great disparities in the distribution of net wealth might help reduce envy, greed, selfishness, and competitiveness on the one hand, and encourage sympathy, empathy, compassion, and cooperation on the other hand, as human characteristics and motives of social behavior. Of course, those who are severely taxed might become more envious, greedy, and so on, but because they are fewer in number than the others, there should be a net gain.

17. For political, economic, and moral reasons, it is reasonable to expect Canadians to set their own house in order as part of a global effort to improve the total human condition. Given the relatively greater influence Canadian voters have on their own elected representatives and the relatively greater concern they have for less fortunate fellow citizens, if significant changes cannot be made at home, it is highly unlikely that significant changes can be made in the distribution of wealth from developed to developing or Third World countries.

18. Great disparities in the distribution of net wealth are inefficient and wasteful insofar as they contribute to unemployment and create incentives for people to drop out of a patently unfair race for an acceptable share of the good things in life, which shrinks the size of one important factor of production (i.e., labor) and any output that might have come from it. It was estimated that the "unutilized component of the available labor supply" in Canada in 1982 was about 12% of GNP or $39 billion (Manitoba Political Economy Group, 1985, pp. 36, 41; Michalos, 1982). Obviously, unemployment also tends to increase wealth disparities.

19. People without hope of having socially acceptable means of obtaining a reasonable share of a community's wealth may resort to socially unacceptable means (e.g., property crime); to self-destruction with drugs, alcohol, and more violent forms of self-abuse; or to violent crimes against other members of their families and community (Canadian Mental Health Association, 1985; Michalos, 1980a).

REPLIES TO ARGUMENTS
AGAINST A NET WEALTH TAX

A number of arguments may be and have been raised against the establishment of a tax on net wealth. These will now be presented along with replies that seem sufficient to either destroy or at least seriously undermine them.

1. The sum total of the net wealth of the wealthiest quintile of Canadians is so small that even if it were heavily taxed the revenue would not be sufficient to solve any important problems (Walker, 1980).

Reply. (a) On the contrary, some rough calculations indicate that if only 2% of the net wealth of the wealthiest quintile was taxed, there would be enough revenue to lift all low-income families in Canada out of poverty. Indeed, if the previously mentioned substantial underestimations of net wealth are anywhere near accurate, it would be possible to lift the total low-income population out of poverty without altering the *reported* net wealth of the wealthiest quintile at all! (b) We have already seen that the purposes of a net wealth tax go far beyond the collection of revenue to the prevention of harms such as undermining political democracy, protecting illegitimate special privilege, distorting markets, and social and economic development.

2. The sum total of the net wealth of the wealthiest quintile of Canadians is so big that a tax large enough to break up such concentrations would never be politically feasible or tolerated in this country (Tinker, in "Panel Discussion," 1980, p. 52).

Reply. (a) As indicated above (Outline of the Proposed Tax), no one is recommending a single lump-sum tax on the wealthiest quintile that would rapidly and radically reduce their share of the total wealth in the nation. What is being recommended is an annual progressive tax on net wealth, of less than 5%. (b) It is also recommended that there should be continuous monitoring of national net wealth by percentiles so that the wealth tax can be levied at a rate sufficiently large to guarantee some annual reduction of the current wealth disparities. As a starting point for discussion, one might think of redistributing net wealth from the wealthiest decile to the poorest two or three quintiles at a rate of 1% a year for 10 years, always serving the needs of the poorest quintile first.

3. Insofar as the aim of a net wealth tax is to raise funds to pay for programs to help the needy, the aim can be better served by allowing capital

to flow to its most efficient users, which will finally result in the most rapid growth in output and a bigger pie for everyone (Walker, 1980).

Reply. (a) The size of the economic pie has increased, but there are more Canadians living in poverty and unemployed. In 1973, the GNP was about $120 billion, 12% of the population was living in poverty, and the unemployment rate was 5.6%. In 1984, the GNP was about $420 billion, 18% of the population was living in poverty, and the unemployment rate was 11% (Lindsay & McKie, 1986; Michalos, 1982; National Council of Welfare, 1985). In constant 1971 dollars, the GNP increased 31% from 1973 ($108 billion) to 1984 ($141 billion) (see Statistics Canada, 1985b, 1986a). At the same time, the poverty rate increased 50% and the unemployment rate increased 96%. Hence, increases in the size of the economic pie are not sufficient for the elimination of poverty or unemployment. (b) As already indicated, poverty can be eliminated by redistributing only a fraction of the total net wealth of the richest quintile of Canadians. Hence, any growth in the size of the economic pie is not even necessary to serve the interests of the needy. (c) I am in favor of the most efficient use of all resources and believe that the current practice of allowing capital to flow to the most powerful private corporate or personal hands is much more wasteful than the proposed redistribution (Manitoba Political Economy Group, 1985; Matziorinis, 1980). (d) Evidence from several studies of many other countries indicates a positive correlation between productivity and economic growth on the one hand and relatively less skewed distributions of wealth and greater government spending for social programs on the other (Social Planning Council of Metropolitan Toronto, 1985). For example, Levin (1986) wrote that

> Income and wealth are more evenly distributed in Japan than in the United States, and in Japan as well as in those European countries with a better productivity record than the United States government spending on social programs represents a larger share of gross national product than it does here [i.e., in the United States]. That equality is harmful to growth is an article of faith, not a confirmed hypothesis. (p. 234)

4. A net tax on wealth is essentially a way of destroying wealth (Walker, 1980; Ward, 1980).

Reply. The mere shifting of wealth from rich people to poor people or to the public purse to be used in the interest of the vast majority of Canadians clearly does not destroy wealth (Bird, in "Panel Discussion," 1980).

5. Economic growth requires investment, and investors need the security of large supplies of wealth accumulated through saving and the incentive of the possibility of relatively large profits. Hence, a net wealth tax is bound to undermine saving, investment, and growth (Wagner, 1980; Walker, 1980; Ward, 1980).

Reply. (a) It has already been noted above (Arguments for a Net Wealth Tax, No. 15) that great fortunes are not the result of careful saving but of good luck. (b) The wealthiest quintile has enjoyed about 70% of the net wealth in Canada for more than 30 years (assuming that distributions of net wealth are at least as stable as distributions of income), while investments have gone up and down. (c) It has been demonstrated that special tax incentives given to businesses in the period from 1972 to 1975 yielded net losses to the public purse of from 50% to 80%. Summarizing the results of a comprehensive survey of the impact of tax incentives, Matziorinis (1980) wrote,

> Business investment experience in Canada does not support the hypothesis that tax incentives have been effective in promoting higher levels of invest- ment . . . that the additional investment induced by the measures was only a fraction of their cost . . . [and that] . . . tax incentives seem to have served mainly as an instrument for granting tax relief by lowering the effective corporate income tax rate significantly below the statutory rate. (p. 178)

(d) Similarly, McIntyre (1987) claimed,

> In 1981 [the U.S.] Congress enacted tax breaks that essentially exempted from taxation the profits from new capital investments. The new loopholes were supposed to produce an investment boom, by lowering the cost of capital. But, again, it didn't happen. From 1981 to 1985 the kinds of investment in business equipment that were to be made more attractive grew at only a quarter the rate at which they had grown from 1976 to 1980. Companies did save on taxes but then spent the money on everything but new investment, including increases in dividends, higher executive pay, and a record-breaking wave of giant corporate mergers. (p. 26)

(e) Taking a broader view, Levin (1986) wrote,

> Of course, economic theory tells us that lowering the price of capital services by means of lowering interest rates or taxes will lead to more capital formation. But it remains one of the great puzzles of economic science that, after more than 20 years of careful econometric research, the data simply do not provide strong confirmation for this proposition. And the more complex linkage

between capital taxation and productivity growth is even more difficult to confirm empirically. (p. 491)

(f) It is an incredible oversimplification to suggest that investment decisions are made primarily on the basis of the size of a potential investor's net wealth or of taxes on that wealth. Matziorinis (1980) wrote,

> To attribute a firm's investment decision to tax factors alone is to ignore the relatively greater importance of such factors as the demand for the firm's product in relation to its capacity, the cost and availability of credit to finance the firm's investment, market share and market strategy considerations, capacity constraints, the state of business confidence or a firm's predisposition to invest in light of current and expected business conditions, structural considerations such as the degree of foreign ownership, and the effect of government policies such as the anti-inflation program, among others. (pp. 178-179)

(g) It is a mistake to suppose that only private persons or corporations can accumulate capital and make investments, especially in a country like Canada, which has so many successful Crown Corporations. Hence, it is question-begging in favor of private capital to assert that if private investment were to be reduced then all investment would be reduced (Canadian Union of Public Employees, 1985).

6. Property taxes already tax wealth (Ward, 1980).

Reply. As already indicated above (Arguments for a Net Wealth Tax, No. 14), property taxes reach only one segment of wealth and are highly regressive. The proposed progressive net wealth tax should replace such regressive taxes to some extent.

7. The great disparities in net wealth are finally maintained by the legitimized force of the state in a relatively capitalistic country like Canada. Hence, it is a mistake to imagine that some sort of a tax scheme can alter such disparities (Sazama, 1980).

Reply. If this argument is sound then potential reformers are wasting their time. Because pessimism only leads to despair and inaction, wisdom is on the side of optimism and action.

8. Given the current connections between economic and political power, any new taxes are likely to be designed to continue to favor the rich over the poor (Sazama, in "Panel Discussion," 1980).

Reply. As with the previous objection, it is difficult for a potential reformer to give an entirely satisfactory reply to this sort of radical pessimism or cynicism. Again, one can only say that wisdom is on the side of optimism and action in spite of the unfortunate but real possibility indicated by the pessimists and cynics.

9. Because wealth is equivalent to income insofar as the former can be regarded as potentially generating the latter, income taxes are indirect taxes on net wealth (Fiekowsky, in "Panel Discussion," 1980; Wagner, 1980).

Reply. There is a theoretical equivalence between income and wealth that can be wisely or unwisely applied to the real world. Musgrave and Musgrave (1984) explain the relationship as follows.

> Given *perfect capital markets and assessment procedures,* a 5 percent tax imposed on the value of an asset may readily be translated into an income tax on the income derived from the asset. Suppose that an asset worth $1,000 yields an annual income of $100, in line with a 10 percent market rate of interest. The liability under a 5 percent tax on the asset value is $50. Expressed as a percentage of the asset's income, it equals 50 percent. The 5 percent tax on the asset value (or property tax) is thus equivalent to a 50 percent tax on the property income (or income tax). Putting it more generally, the value of an asset *in a perfect capital market* is given by $Y = iV$, so that $V = Y/i$ where V is its value, Y is its annual income, and i is the market rate of interest obtainable on other investments. If the same yield is to be obtained from a property tax at rate tp and a tax on income therefrom at rate ty, we must have $tp\ Y/i = ty$ or $tp = ity$. [italics added] (p. 470)

The theoretical relationships are instructive. One might prefer a 5% net wealth tax to a 50% income tax generating the same amount of revenue. In fact, in 1966, the Canadian Royal Commission on Taxation was apparently so inclined (OECD, 1979). Nevertheless, it must be remembered that in the real world there are no "perfect capital markets and assessment procedures." In this world wealth is not equivalent to income because

> Capital confers an income independent of the health of the owner and attainable without any current sacrifice of leisure; and, over and above any income derived from it, it gives its possessor independence, security, and the opportunity for advantageous purchase or for a spending spree. These advantages confer additional taxable capacity on the owner of capital. To some extent this additional taxable capacity can be recognised by taxing income

from wealth more heavily than income from work; but this method is imperfect, for it takes no account of the advantages which wealth confers even if it yields no money income and it takes insufficient account of such advantages where the money income yield is low. (OECD, 1979, p. 13)

10. Because physical capital is already taxed twice (i.e., once when it is obtained in the form of earned income and a second time when either the interest it earns as saving is taxed or the profits it earns from investment are taxed) but income is taxed only once, a tax on net wealth would unfairly triple the tax bias against saving, capital formation, and investment (Wagner, 1980).

Reply. The number of times something is taxed is clearly relatively unimportant compared to the amount of the taxes levied. Granting that physical capital is taxed twice, the fact that the distributions of income and wealth have been practically unchanged for 30 years demonstrates the irrelevance of the number of times such capital is taxed.

11. The unequal genetic inheritance of people is partly responsible for the current disparities in wealth, and no fair tax will ever be able to eliminate the existence and unequal consequences of such inheritance (Wagner, 1980; Ward, 1980).

Reply. (a) No one is claiming that all of the consequences of unequal genetic inheritance, whatever they are, should be compensated for by a tax on net wealth. (b) As indicated above (No. 15), there is evidence that large fortunes owe much more to chance than to skill or anything else. (c) It is a mistake to think of the social practice of people leaving wealth to blood relatives as some kind of a biological or, more specifically, genetic phenomenon. (d) Even if biology had some systematic influence on the creation of great wealth, Bale (1980) correctly remarked that "although we can do little about the unequal genetic endowment flowing from the lottery of birth, we can do something about unequal wealth inheritance because such inheritance is entirely a socially created institution" (p. 43).

12. There is no way to measure the degree to which skews in the distribution of wealth are generally harmful because (a) there are too many variables involved to determine causal relations, (b) there are too many value judgments involved, and (c) there is no way to assess and compare how people feel about the alleged impact of wealth disparities. Hence, arguments for a net wealth tax on the grounds of the actual or

potential harmfulness of wealth disparities must be based on mere ideology or faith, or both (Wagner, 1980; Ward, 1980).

Reply. (a) If the argument had merit, it would undermine virtually all economic planning, private and public, because all such planning is based on the assumption that many causal relations can be determined with enough certainty to make them worthwhile. (b) No one knows how many value judgments are involved in the arguments for or against the harmfulness of wealth disparities, the number of judgments is relatively unimportant compared to the kinds, and the variety of kinds is also unknown. (c) For more than a decade psychologists and sociologists have annually published more than 1,100 research studies involving the assessment and comparison of perceived net satisfaction and happiness regarding a wide variety of things (Michalos, 1986). Hence, arguments for a net wealth tax on the grounds of harmfulness may be based on as much evidence, objectivity, science, and reasonable argumentation as arguments against such a tax on such grounds.

13. Economists refer to the question of who pays how much of what tax as the problem of tax incidence. Although there are some settled opinions concerning many issues related to this problem, "controversy and uncertainty still swirl" about the incidence of "sales taxes, corporate profits taxes and . . . property taxes" (Gillespie, 1980b, p. 4). For example, "standard incidence assumptions" allow that half of corporate profits (income) taxes are passed on to consumers (Gillespie, 1980b; Sazama, 1980). However, considering the size and diversity of goods and services produced by multinational firms and conglomerates, the multiplicity of relations among subsidiaries and parents, and the vast opportunities for special pricing and creative accounting, nobody knows how much of the taxes on corporate profits are passed on to consumers. The accepted figure of 50% reflects economists' uncertainty, probably mixed with some optimism regarding the fairness of the system. Because the introduction of a net wealth tax would require the resolution of such very controversial tax incidence issues, it would be wise to avoid introducing such a tax.

Reply. (a) If this argument had any merit, it would undermine virtually all taxation, because one can always find reasons for asserting that there are certain hidden benefits or costs of any tax that significantly alter the apparent incidence. (b) If serious consideration were given to the possibility of introducing a net wealth tax, then there would be improvements in data collection, research, and analysis of all options. So, it is likely that reasonable agreements could be reached concerning outstanding issues of tax incidence.

14. Instead of undertaking the difficult task of introducing a whole new tax, it would be better to continue with the present system and introduce laws that would prevent the possible abuses of great wealth disparities (Piper, in "Panel Discussion," 1980; Wagner, 1980).

Reply. (a) What is being proposed in this objection is precisely what has been tried for years and found inadequate, namely, allowing great disparities and preventing abuses. (b) It is impossible to have great wealth disparities and prevent abuses because there are limits to the world's resources, goods, and services, and typically great accumulations of wealth in one place are possible only by making great withdrawals and leaving poverty in another place (Canadian Conference of Catholic Bishops, 1985; Harrison, 1981; Michalos, 1981b; United Church of Canada, 1985).

15. Those who call for a net wealth tax are motivated by envy, which should not be encouraged or rewarded with success.

Reply. (a) There is no evidence that the motives of those who call for a wealth tax are more or less envious than the motives of anyone else. (b) The arguments presented in favor of such a tax appeal to considerations of justice, morality, and economic efficiency, and these arguments must be regarded as evidence of the motives of the tax proposers. (c) Even if all of those who called for a net wealth tax were motivated by envy (which is highly unlikely), the costs of failing to introduce such a tax and the benefits of introducing it are far more important than any character flaws in the proposers. (d) Anyone who would characterize poor people lacking the necessities of life as merely envious of rich people enjoying luxuries would exhibit callousness, insensitivity, and the lack of fundamental human compassion, which are more serious character flaws that should be condemned.

16. Although there may be great disparities of inherited wealth in some countries, that is not the case in Canada. So, there is no problem here that requires a net wealth tax as a solution (Ward, 1980).

Reply. (a) According to the OECD (1979), "in most countries inheritance is a major source of inequality in the distribution of wealth" (p. 14). (b) The evidence of the studies by Porter (1965), Clement (1975, 1977), and Newman (1975) indicate that there are great disparities of inherited wealth in Canada. (c) Although the origins of great disparities of wealth are important for reasons already indicated, the consequences of such disparities are even more important. Thus, it would be a mistake to ignore the latter as if only the former warranted consideration.

17. Inheritance or so-called death taxes are a kind of net wealth tax, and they have been virtually abandoned in Canada. Their abandonment should be regarded as evidence that they were relatively worthless.

Reply. (a) Canada is almost the only developed country that has abandoned such taxes (Bale, 1980). (b) Although they typically have been designed here so that people with a moderate degree of foresight and some appreciation of estate planning can easily avoid paying such taxes (Ward, 1980), inheritance taxes might be designed to redistribute wealth successfully. (c) There is some evidence that the federal government abandoned such taxes without giving them serious consideration (Bale, 1980). (A more cynical view would be that they were intentionally designed to be ineffective and then abandoned because they were just that.) (d) The specific kind of a tax on net wealth being argued for here is not a single inheritance or death tax but an annual tax requiring annual accounting similar to that involved in income taxes. Again, a single tax package might be designed that efficiently satisfied wealth and income.

18. People who argue for a tax on net wealth would not want such a tax applied to themselves (Ward, 1980).

Reply. (a) There is no evidence that the proposers of a net wealth tax would want themselves excluded from paying such a tax. (b) Because it would be patently unfair, immoral, self-defeating, inconsistent, and apparently irrational to recommend the tax and self-exemption, it is highly unlikely that anyone arguing for the tax would also argue for self-exemption. (c) It is highly likely that anyone who wanted to be exempted from paying such a tax would either never argue for it or else argue against it.

19. A significantly progressive tax on net wealth would discriminate against the very wealthy, and such discrimination would be unjust (Ward, 1980).

Reply. At a minimum, justice requires that people should be taxed in accordance with their ability to pay, which is precisely what is being proposed here. The greater burden falling to the very wealthy is not the result of discrimination but of their greater ability to pay.

20. Insofar as equality of opportunity is an aim of a net wealth tax, that aim can be better served by improvements in the education system and by the elimination of social discrimination (Ward, 1980).

Reply. (a) Several studies have shown that disparities in income and wealth cannot be accounted for by disparities in educational achievement. (b) Great disparities in wealth are at least as much and probably more the cause than the effect of social discrimination (Michalos, 1981a, 1982). (c) All three problems of wealth disparities, inadequate education, and social discrimination merit attention.

21. A tax on net wealth must be unfair because such wealth includes human capital (e.g., native intelligence, personal skills, or attractiveness), which cannot be taxed (Royal Commission on Taxation *Report* [1967] in Bale, 1980; Ward, 1980).

Reply. (a) The fact that all wealth cannot be directly taxed is not a good reason for failing to tax any wealth or for failing to tax a broader range of wealth than is currently taxed (Bale, 1980). (b) The fact that all wealth cannot be taxed makes a net wealth tax similar to practically all other taxes, because it is unlikely that any tax captures everything in fact that it might capture in principle (Bird, in "Panel Discussion," 1980). (c) Human wealth is taxed when it is transformed into income, and a net wealth tax is supposed to supplement rather than supplant income taxes.

22. Insofar as a net wealth tax must include the taxation of homes and property, which are municipally taxed, a wealth tax would create jurisdictional problems (Ward, 1980).

Reply. (a) There are many Canadian precedents regarding problems of jurisdiction and many relatively straightforward solutions; for example, federal and provincial income taxes are easily administered at the same time. (b) Given the regressive nature of municipal property taxes and the progressive nature of the proposed net wealth tax, it is likely that the inclusion of property taxes in a comprehensive tax package would result in a more equitable as well as a more profitable source of revenue. (c) There might even be some administrative cost-saving resulting from the development of a more comprehensive system.

23. Considerable wealth is tied up in things like private homes, automobiles, and various consumer durables (e.g., appliances, stereo sets, and so on), and such wealth does not represent dangerous economic and political power. Hence a net wealth tax would erroneously identify and tax such power (Sazama, in "Panel Discussion," 1980).

Reply. (a) As indicated in the second section (Distributions of Wealth and Income), with the exception of automobiles, consumer durables have been excluded from Statistics Canada's Survey of Consumer Finances, so the measured disparities in wealth have never been based on such things. (b) As indicated earlier in the third section (Outline of the Proposed Tax) and later in my reply to the objection following this one, the proposed tax would include provisions for standard deductions and exemptions regarding basic necessities. (c) When assessments of the significance of wealth are made from the perspective of the total distribution of wealth from the top decile and quintile of wealth holders to the bottom, it will be easier to determine potential and actual dangers. (d) In the absence of routine accounting procedures established through a wealth tax, it has been, is, and will be more difficult to identify any hazards.

24. Net wealth assessment would create too many administrative problems, including those involving the mere discovery of all taxable assets and those involving their evaluation (Bale, 1980; Bird, 1980). For example, jewels, stamps, and works of art can be kept practically anywhere, and the evaluation of such items can be extremely controversial. Although Statistics Canada's Survey of Consumer Finances simply excludes such items, administrators of a tax on net wealth would be obliged to include them. What is worse, it is likely that increases in the administrative problems attached to such a tax would lead directly to increases in government surveillance and litigation.

Reply. (a) Concerning administration, the evidence from the OECD survey is clear and favorable:

> No country with a net wealth tax considered it more difficult to administer than income tax and some specified that it was less so. . . . The view was generally held that the existence of net wealth tax assisted the administration of income tax. The collection of data on wealth enabled investment income to be cross-checked with income-earning assets; the trend in assets-holding might also highlight income discrepancies. (OECD, 1979, p. 127)

(b) As already suggested, several tactics are used to reduce administrative costs. Besides common returns, standard deductions, and exemptions, use is made of evaluations every 3 or 5 years instead of every year for certain items, of average values over several years, of insured instead of actually estimated values, and of values obtained from taxes on capital gains (OECD, 1979). (c) Few countries seemed to be willing or able to provide quantitative estimates of the costs of administration and compliance, but there was no doubt expressed about the benefits of the programs outweighing the costs (OECD, 1979). (d) There probably would be some increase in surveillance and litigation concerning the wealth of the richest decile or quintile in Canada. (e) However, virtually no public program of taxation is perfect; so the decision to have or not have a tax on net wealth must rest on the particular costs and benefits attached to such a tax. (f) Because the number of families and individuals who might require special surveillance or litigation is relatively small and their potential taxable wealth is relatively great, the benefits of the additional administrative problems would be outweighed by their costs. (g) As already suggested, the introduction of a net wealth tax as part of a comprehensive tax package should decrease the total administrative costs, increase the benefits, and make the whole system more efficient than it currently is for most Canadians.

25. Inflation already taxes wealth (Ward, 1980).

Reply. (a) Because the difference between the amount of wealth possessed by the richest and the poorest quintiles has been steadily increasing for many years, inflation must be operating as yet another regressive tax punishing the poor more than the rich. (b) A suitably designed progressive net wealth tax could reduce the inequitable impact of inflation on people with diverse amounts of wealth.

26. A net wealth tax would tend to undermine family businesses, especially small businesses and farms (Ward, 1980).

Reply. (a) In all countries with such a tax, special provisions are made for agricultural property (land, livestock, machinery, forestry, wood-lands), fishing boats, unincorporated and new businesses (OECD, 1979). (b) Because the proposed tax is going to be designed to redistribute wealth from the relatively wealthy to the relatively poor, it would not undermine any small businesses or farms. (c) It would undermine large concentrations of wealth controlled by extended family dynasties.

27. An annual tax on net wealth would provoke the flow of capital out and prohibit the flow of capital into Canada, which would shrink the economic pie and the potential for growth, and incidentally leave relatively less wealth to be distributed to anyone. So, even if the resulting distributions of wealth and incomes were more egalitarian, the country would be relatively worse off with the tax than without it.

Reply. (a) There might be some outflow of capital and some arresting of capital inflow following the introduction of a net wealth tax. However, the unattractive scenario hypothesized as a consequence is based on a very oversimplified view of the nature of the wealth that will be taxed, investment in general and capital flows in particular, and national sovereignty. Each issue will be addressed in turn. (b) More than half of the wealth to be taxed is in relatively fixed assets like buildings and land, which is either difficult or impossible to move (Oja, 1983). (c) There is plenty of theoretical and empirical research on different approaches to the taxation of immovable property. For present purposes, the following remarks are worth quoting from Musgrave and Musgrave (1984):

> Just as an increase in property tax rates may reduce property values and induce capital outflows, so may the provision of additional public services raise values and attract capital inflow. Better schools or municipal services may render the town a more attractive place in which to reside or to operate a business. The improvement raises the demand for housing and structures, leading to higher property values, and thus counteracts the effects of increased property tax rates. Thus, expenditure benefits may be capitalized no less than tax burdens, so that the combined tax and expenditure effects may leave housing values reduced, increased, or unaffected, depending on how the revenue is obtained and what it is used for. (pp. 472-473)

(d) In the case of relatively liquid assets (e.g., cash or bonds), it is virtually always possible for one to find some bank or government some place in the world that would give one a higher rate of return for an investment, but people usually do not rush to make such investments. (e) Many countries, including Canada,

> have used temporary bans or limits on certain financial outflows either when the balance of payments was under downward pressure (Canada, the United States) or to prevent the rapid accumulation of liquid, domestic currency assets held by nonresidents, usually when there has been upward pressure on the exchange rate . . . Japan and the United Kingdom, which even just a few years ago virtually prohibited financial outflows and screened inflows, have now completely liberalised such operations. (OECD, 1982, pp. 58-59)

After a thorough review of capital control practices in OECD countries,

> The main findings . . . suggest that temporary restrictive controls may at times be an appropriate or inevitable response to cope, in the short run, with difficulties created by large destabilizing capital flows (as far as exchange rate, reserves or monetary objectives are concerned) resulting from divergent economic policies and performances among Member countries or from other non-economic factors. (OECD, 1982, p. 60)

(f) Virtually all research and common sense itself indicate that "successful" foreign investors always take more out of a country than they put in. Hence, it is a serious mistake to assume that Canadians would be net losers if new foreign investments are not made here, especially if the investments are made by Americans who have notoriously drained the wealth of this country (Michalos, 1982). (g) Currency exchange rates can be altered to make capital flows more or less attractive (Bird, 1980). (h) More important, because currency exchange rates are typically much greater than any proposed wealth tax rates are likely to be, the former would have much more influence than a wealth tax on capital flows in and out of the country (Matziorinis, 1980). For example, the fact that a Canadian dollar loses about 25% of its buying power by moving to the United States is bound to have much greater influence on its movement than the fact that it is taxed another 2% or 3% in Canada. (i) Economics narrowly and artificially construed aside, serious consideration must be given to the continued erosion of Canada's political sovereignty resulting from efforts "to become more attractive" to very wealthy people whether they are Canadian or not. As short-sighted politicians whittle away at relatively modest health and social security programs, family allowances, unemployment benefits, public housing, educational institutions, research facilities, and so on, the Canadian capacity for autonomous national planning and development is reduced. In the words of the United Auto Workers (1985) Brief to the Macdonald Commission, "at issue is a meaningful democracy and the collective ability to really— rather than just formally—shape our lives" (p. 30).

28. For more than 20 years, nationwide Gallup polls have shown that Canadians regard inflation and unemployment as the most serious problems facing the country (Table 10.4), and disparities in wealth are seldom if ever mentioned. Hence, priority should be given to the reduction of inflation and unemployment, rather than to the introduction of a new tax.

TABLE 10.4 What Do You Think Is the Most Important Problem Facing This Country Today?

| | Percentage Answering | |
Date	Inflation	Unemployment
1963	8	33
1964	3	32
1965	10	14
1966	29	7
1968	38	6
1972	37	34
1973	53	8
1974, April	59	8
1974, October	82	3
1975, July	52	14
1975, November 8	64	8
1976, April	55	12
1976, October 20	50	9
1977, April 13	44	18
1977, July 27	41	28
1978, February 22	38	35
1978, June 17	46	38
1978, October 7	46	30
1979, September 8	50	22
1980, February 6	49	10
1980, August 9	48	16
1981, February 18	55	15
1981, August 22	59	10
1982, January 23	61	12
1982, July 14	54	26
1983, February 7	37	40
1983, July 18	32	47
1983, December 15	33	42
1984, July 9	27	50
1985, January 28	25	56
1985, August 8	21	54
1986, January 13	21	50
1986, July 17	21	44

SOURCES: Michalos (1982), pp. 189-198. Reprinted by permission of Kluwer Academic Publishers; Gallup Poll Releases for the specific dates cited in the table.

Reply. (a) The existence of great disparities in wealth has been cited above (Arguments for a Net Wealth Tax) as one of the fundamental causes of unemployment and inflation, and the introduction of a net wealth tax is being recommended as a necessary part of a solution to the problem of wealth disparities. (b) The most likely reasons for people not citing wealth disparities as the most serious problem facing this country are because people's judgments about national problems are based on the views presented in the corporate-owned and -biased popular press and media (Michalos, 1981a, 1981b), on their personal problems, and on the perceived problems of their neighbors (Michalos, 1986). In all three cases, wealth disparities are relatively invisible compared to unemployment and high prices, just as deadly cancerous growths can be relatively invisible compared to the short-term illnesses and accidental injuries of daily life. (c) Although the Gallup Association is not a public interest research group and has never displayed a great interest in questions related to disparities in wealth, it would be misleading to fail to mention the following polls. In response to the question, "In your opinion, do the courts in this country dispense justice impartially or do they favor the rich and influential?", 60% of a national sample of Canadians said they thought the courts favored the rich and influential (*The Gallup Report*, August 12, 1985). Thirteen years earlier, 72% of those who thought that "some of the laws of Canada . . . favor [a] particular class" mentioned "the upper class, the affluent" as the favored one (February 19, 1972). The same year 54% said they did not think "the big corporations [were] paying their fair share of taxes" (December 2, 1972). As a matter of fact, the relative shares of personal and corporate income taxes in 1972 were similar to those in 1985 (Table 10.5). Seventy-three percent approved of "equalization payments" giving financial assistance to "have not provinces" (May 13, 1972), a figure that later increased to 84% (September 16, 1981). In 1985, 75% approved of increasing Family Allowances, and 69% approved of increasing Old Age Pensions, provided that they were "paid only to families or people who needed them" (January 21, 1985). On the basis of this handful of polls, it is fair to say that Canadians have expressed some concern about some undesirable consequences of wealth disparities, and some willingness to redistribute some wealth from the relatively wealthy to the relatively poor. (d) The best evidence of Canadians' concern with the undesirable consequences of wealth disparities and the need for their reduction may be found in the Briefs presented to the Macdonald Commission, which were gathered together in Drache and Cameron's *The Other Macdonald Report* (1985). These Briefs express the views of a wide variety of Canadians, including "churches, trade unions, women's groups, social agencies and organizations representing Native People, farmers and the disadvantaged." Collectively, Drache and Cameron (1985) refer to this set of people as "the popular sector" (p. ix).

29. Even if a net wealth tax were introduced and additional revenue obtained to create jobs, it is a mistake to think that unemployment can

TABLE 10.5 Personal and Corporate Income Taxes, 1962-1985

Year	Personal Income Taxes (current millions)	Corporate Income Taxes (current millions)	Personal as % of Total	Corporate as % of Total
1962	2,052	1,302	32.8	20.8
1963	2,018	1,298	31.4	20.2
1964	2,168	1,375	31.6	20.1
1965	2,535	1,669	31.9	21.0
1966	2,638	1,759	30.3	20.2
1967	3,050	1,743	28.8	16.4
1968	3,650	1,821	31.1	15.5
1969	4,334	2,213	32.3	16.8
1970	5,588	2,839	35.3	18.0
1971	6,395	2,427	38.4	14.6
1972	7,227	2,396	38.9	12.9
1973	8,378	2,919	39.1	13.6
1974	9,226	3,710	36.8	14.8
1975	11,710	4,836	36.4	15.0
1976	12,709	5,748	36.6	16.6
1977	14,751	5,377	38.5	14.0
1978	13,562	5,828	34.7	14.9
1979	14,788	5,654	34.7	13.3
1980	17,959	6,951	35.1	14.0
1981	21,296	8,130	36.5	13.9
1982	25,232	8,118	34.5	11.1
1983	27,376	7,139	37.6	9.8
1984	29,290	7,286	38.2	9.5
1985	31,080	9,380	37.1	11.2

SOURCES: From Statistics Canada (1965, pp. 7-8); (1970, p. 38); (1975, p. 44); (1977, p. 38); (1980a, p. 40); (1984a, p. 33).

be significantly decreased without concurrent increases in inflation, and the latter hurts everyone.

Reply. (a) As explained in Michalos (1982), the alleged inverse relation between unemployment and inflation is one of nine hypotheses frequently invoked to account for inflation. Although it is theoretically plausible, it is certainly empirically false. Inspection of Table 10.6 reveals that in the period from 1965 to 1985 the alleged inverse relation occurred about 60% of the time for males and females taken together, and about 55% of the time for males and females taken separately. Because the figures for unemployment and inflation would have been expected to rise and fall together or inversely about 50% of the time as a result of mere chance, it is clear that the alleged hypothesis is not only plainly false but pretty worthless for the purposes of scientific explanation and prediction.

TABLE 10.6 Inflation and Unemployment, 1965-1985

Year	Inflation Rate	Unemployment Rate	Male Unemployment Rate	Female Unemployment Rate
1965	2.4	3.9	4.3	2.6
1966	3.7	3.5	3.9	2.6
1967	3.6	4.0	4.5	2.9
1968	4.0	4.8	5.3	3.4
1969	4.6	4.6	5.0	3.6
1970	3.3	5.8	6.4	4.4
1971	2.9	6.3	6.9	5.0
1972	4.8	6.3	6.7	5.3
1973	7.6	5.6	5.7	5.0
1974	10.8	5.4	5.7	4.9
1975	10.8	6.9	6.2	8.1
1976	7.5	7.1	6.3	8.4
1977	8.0	8.1	7.3	9.4
1978	8.9	8.4	7.6	9.6
1979	9.2	7.4	6.6	8.8
1980	10.2	7.5	6.9	8.4
1981	12.5	7.5	7.0	8.3
1982	10.8	11.0	11.1	10.9
1983	5.8	11.9	12.1	11.6
1984	4.4	11.3	11.2	11.4
1985	4.0	10.5	10.3	10.7

SOURCES: From Lindsay & McKie (1986); Michalos (1982): Reprinted by permission of Kluwer Academic Publishers; Statistics Canada (1981, 1985a, 1986a).

(b) Research from many other countries indicates that it is possible to have relatively full employment and low inflation and that Canada's recent record on this score was not as good as that of many developed countries (Social Planning Council of Metropolitan Toronto, 1985). (c) There is good evidence indicating that countries with the best performance record regarding full employment and inflation have made the former their top priority. According to Bellemare (1986), "all countries that attain full employment have made it their primary objective . . . [and] . . . the pursuit of this objective orients the macro-economic, labor-market and regional development policies" (pp. 8-10).

30. Insofar as one of the main reasons for introducing a net wealth tax is to obtain revenue to transfer to those who are relatively poor and needy, some attention must be given to the possibility that recipients will lose some of their incentive to work for a living. In the now familiar scenario, their withdrawal from the labor force would mean the removal of some productive power and its output, which would in turn yield a

smaller total economic pie for everyone. Thus, to prevent the initiation of this whole unfortunate scenario, it would be wise to forget about a net wealth tax.

Reply. (a) An adequate response to this objection should begin by drawing a distinction between poor people who are or are not, in principle at least, in the labor force. Clearly, children, the aged, and the significantly disabled are not under consideration. (b) Concerning the others, although a great deal of research has been devoted toward demonstrating the disincentive effects of relatively moderate programs of social welfare, including unemployment insurance and guaranteed annual incomes, there is still very little evidence of such effects (Michalos, 1982). (c) According to the National Council of Welfare (1985),

> Contrary to what many people believe, most poor families are headed by persons who work or are actively searching for a job. In 1980, 52.4 percent of low-income families were headed by men or women in the labor force, and that percentage increased to 57.8 percent by 1983. In contrast, most poor unattached individuals (64.1 percent in 1983) are not in the labor force. (p. 40)

31. Because corporations have many more assets than families or individuals and the former are already taxed, it is unnecessary to tax the latter and more efficient simply to increase the tax on corporations (Ward, in "Panel Discussion," 1980).

Reply. (a) As already indicated, there are serious problems concerning the taxation of corporations. The most serious problem is the fact that no one knows how much of corporate income taxes are passed on to consumers. Given the opportunities for passing on such taxes that were mentioned earlier when I discussed the "standard incidence assumptions" (No. 13), I suspect that more than half of these taxes are passed on to consumers. If that suspicion is correct, then increases in corporate income taxes would be counterproductive. Obviously, we desperately need better information about how much of these taxes are actually passed on to consumers. Granting this, however, in the short run I still think that corporate income should be taxed more heavily than it is, especially compared to the taxation of individuals. (b) Official statistics show that for more than 20 years corporate income taxes have been relatively smaller than personal income taxes as a percentage of all taxes levied. The figures also show that although the personal income tax share of the total was half again as large as the corporate share in 1962, by 1985 the personal share was more than three times the corporate

TABLE 10.7 National Product and Public Debt, 1965-1985

Year	Gross National Product (current millions)	Net Public Debt (current millions)	Ratio of NPD to GNP
1965	55,364	15,504	.28
1970	85,685	16,943	.20
1971	94,450	17,322	.18
1972	105,234	17,937	.17
1973	123,560	17,456	.14
1974	147,528	18,128	.12
1975	165,343	19,276	.12
1976	191,857	23,296	.12
1977	210,189	29,586	.14
1978	232,211	39,622	.17
1979	264,279	55,806	.21
1980	297,556	68,595	.23
1981	339,797	84,163	.25
1982	358,302	98,758	.28
1983	389,844	122,747	.32
1984	420,870	154,531	.37
1985	474,608	191,448	.40

SOURCES: Michalos (1982): Reprinted by permission of Kluwer Academic Publishers; Statistics Canada (1984a, 1985c, 1986a).

share (Table 10.5). Furthermore, it is worthwhile noticing that though the personal share remained fairly stable from 1975 to 1985, the corporate share steadily decreased and the net public debt significantly increased (Table 10.7). Apparently, then, some of the revenue that governments failed to raise in corporate taxes was raised by borrowing. (Incidentally, the figures in Table 10.7 from 1965 to 1976 show that Keynes was right in claiming that a country can pull itself up by its bootstraps by borrowing and investing in growth. In those years, while the net public debt increased, the GNP increased much faster, with the result that the debt had relatively less significance although it was greater in absolute terms. It is important to keep such things in mind in the presence of people who find the idea of increasing the public debt inherently abhorrent. What is wrong with increasing the public debt is not the extra burden of greater debt but the fact that, as indicated below, to a significant extent the public would be foolishly borrowing from instead of wisely taxing the relatively great wealth-holders.) (c) However, insofar as corporations are the focus of attention, disparities in wealth tend to be depersonalized and the extraordinary power and influence of a relatively few families and individuals tends to be invisible, which invisibility allows them to have even greater influence (Clement, 1975, 1977). According to Coyne (1986),

> In late 1984, . . . close to 80 percent of the companies listed in the Toronto Stock Exchange 300 index were controlled by a single family and/or group. And almost 50% of the value of these companies was controlled by only nine families, notably the Thomsons of Hudson's Bay Company and *Globe and Mail* fame, the two branches of the Bronfman family, Paul Desmarais of Power Corporation, the Reichmann brothers, Conrad Black, and George Weston. . . . Some 60 percent of all of our financial assets are held by five financial service conglomerates and the six large banks. More importantly, several of the financial service conglomerates are each owned by one of the major family dynasties. (p. 15)

(d) Depersonalization is also dangerous because it creates and supports the illusion of relatively "natural" and inevitable forces that are responsible for the political economy here and abroad (Poff, 1985). (e) This illusion tends to serve the interests of those who want to maintain the status quo, including neo-conservative economists who make their living developing and disseminating the illusion in the form of economic science. (f) What is worse, because nobody in particular is responsible for "natural" and inevitable economic forces, it is pointless to ask who benefits and who loses from the current system, and pointless to ask what we can do, what choices can be made, and what actions can be performed to change the status quo in the interests of the vast majority of people. (g) Hence, we are continuously bombarded by a kind of associationist rat-psychologist's rhetoric of the need for "adjustment" and "education for adjustment to a changing world," perhaps the central themes of the Macdonald Commission. It is indeed a pity that long after the battles in the 1940s and 1950s between the associationist and cognitivist psychologists, and the "resounding victory" of the cognitivists (Feather, 1982, p. 3), influential people continue to think and talk about human beings as if they were fairly dull organisms capable only of reacting to circumstances that they cannot create or control. (h) In the end, this refusal to see human beings as human agents robs them of their inclination and their capacity to form their own vision of a good life and to actively pursue its realization. In that end, of course, they have lost their humanity and their very lives.

CONCLUSION

My case for a progressive annual net wealth tax is now complete. It would be redundant and tedious to review the 19 good arguments in favor and the 31 bad arguments opposed to such a tax. It would be remarkable if I managed to address every important consideration and if anyone accepted everything I had to say. That is fair enough. I intended to open discussion, not to close it. According to Thurow (1971), "wealth taxation is a central component in any ideal system of taxation. . . . From both the perspective of potential benefits to be gained and the current costs to be eliminated, wealth taxes merit inclusion in any adequate system of taxes" (pp. 122, 134). A net wealth tax should be regarded as only one feature of a national socioeconomic develop¬ ment plan. Besides recommending a wealth tax to obtain revenue for redistribution, I would favor increased public participation, public planning, and public initiatives in the areas of housing, food, clothing, transportation, education, health, and social services. The aim and net result of the whole plan should be the maximization of human well-being.

REFERENCES

Bale, G. (1980). Taxing wealth: Selecting a strategy. *Canadian Taxation, 2*, 39-48.

Bellemare, D. (1986, November 22). *The birth of a Canadian economy.* Paper presented to Forum 2000: Canada in a Changing World.

Bird, R. M. (1980). Taxing personal wealth. *Canadian Taxation, 2*, 35-38.

Canadian Conference of Catholic Bishops. (1985). Moral vision and political will. In D. Drache & D. Cameron (Eds.), *The other Macdonald report* (pp. 208-213). Toronto: James Lorimer.

Canadian Mental Health Association. (1985). Economic policy and well-being. In D. Drache & D. Cameron (Eds.), *The other Macdonald report* (pp. 80-87). Toronto: James Lorimer.

Canadian Union of Public Employees. (1985). Scapegoating the public sector. In D. Drache & D. Cameron (Eds.), *The other Macdonald report* (pp. 42-48, 196-207). Toronto: James Lorimer.

Clement, W. (1975). *The Canadian corporate elite: An analysis of economic power.* Toronto: McClelland & Stewart.

Clement, W. (1977). *Continental corporate power: Economic elite linkages between Canada and the United States.* Toronto: McClelland & Stewart.

Coyne, D. (1986, April). Corporate over-concentration. *Policy Options Politiques,* pp. 14-17.

Drache, D., & Cameron, D. (1985). Introduction. In D. Drache & D. Cameron (Eds.), *The other Macdonald report* (pp. ix-xxxix). Toronto: James Lorimer.

Feather, N. T. (Ed.). (1982). *Expectations and actions: Expectancy-value models in psychology.* Hillsdale, NJ: Lawrence Erlbaum.

Galbraith, J. K. (1975). *Money: Whence it came, where it went.* New York: Bantam.

Gillespie, W. I. (1980a). Taxes, expenditures and the redistribution of income in Canada 1951-1977. In Economic Council of Canada (Ed.), *Reflections on Canadian incomes* (pp. 27-41). Ottawa: Minister of Supply and Services Canada.

Gillespie, W. I. (1980b). What do we know about tax incidence in Canada? *Canadian Taxation, 2*, 2-7.

Harrison, A. (1980). The distribution of personal wealth in Canada, the U.K. and the U.S.A. In Economic Council of Canada (Ed.), *Reflections on Canadian incomes* (pp. 365-380). Ottawa: Minister of Supply and Services Canada.

Harrison, D. (1981). *The limits of liberalism: The making of Canadian sociology.* Montreal: Black Rose.

Levin, R. C. (1986). Proposals for economic growth. *Science, 234,* 490-491.

Lindsay, C., & McKie, C. (1986, Autumn). Annual review of labour force trends. *Canadian Social Trends,* pp. 2-7.

Manitoba Political Economy Group. (1985). The waste economy. In D. Drache & D. Cameron (Eds.), *The other Macdonald report* (pp. 35-41). Toronto: James Lorimer.

Matziorinis, K. N. (1980). The effectiveness of tax-incentives for capital investment. *Canada Taxation, 2,* 172-179.

McIntyre, R. S. (1987, January). VAT is a bad idea. *The Atlantic Monthly,* pp. 26-28.

Michalos, A. C. (1980). *North American social report: Vol. 2. Crime, justice and politics.* Dordrecht, the Netherlands: D. Reidel.

Michalos, A. C. (1981a). *North American social report: Vol. 3. Science, education and recreation.* Dordrecht, the Netherlands: D. Reidel.

Michalos, A. C. (1981b). *North American social report: Vol. 4. Environment, transportation and housing.* Dordrecht, the Netherlands: D. Reidel.

Michalos, A. C. (1982). *North American social report: Vol. 5. Economics, religion and morality.* Dordrecht, the Netherlands: D. Reidel.

Michalos, A. C. (1986, September). *Integrated development planning using socio-economic and quality of life indicators.* Report written for UNESCO, Division of Study and Planning of Development, Bureau of Studies, Action and Coordination for Development.

Musgrave, R. A., & Musgrave, P. B. (1984). *Public finance in theory and practice.* New York: McGraw-Hill.

National Council of Welfare. (1985). *Poverty profile 1985.* Ottawa: Minister of Supply and Services Canada.

Newman, P. C. (1975). *The Canadian establishment: Vol. 1.* Toronto: McClelland & Stewart.

Organization for Economic Cooperation and Development (OECD). (1979). *The taxation of net wealth, capital transfers and capital gains of individuals.* Paris: Author.

Organization for Economic Cooperation and Development (OECD). (1982). *Controls on international capital movements.* Paris: Author.

Oja, G. (1983). The distribution of wealth in Canada. *Review of Income and Wealth,* Series 29, No. 2, pp. 161-173.

Oja, G. (1986). *Distribution of wealth in Canada 1970-1984.* [Preliminary study, September 1986. Final version to be published by Statistics Canada.]

Panel discussion: Taxation of personal wealth. (1980). *Canadian Taxation, 2,* 49-54. Participants included R. M. Bird, D. A. Ward, G. Bale, M. Wolfson, S. Piper, J. Tinker, P. Setlakwe, S. Fiekowsky, & G. W. Sazama.

Poff, D. C. (1985). Feminism flies too. *Resources for Feminist Research, 14,* 6-9.

Porter, J. (1965). *The vertical mosaic.* Toronto: University of Toronto Press.

Sazama, G. W. (1980). Is the tax system the Robin Hood of our time? *Canadian Taxation, 2,* 16-23.

Social Planning Council of Metropolitan Toronto. (1985). Economic decline in Canada. In D. Drache & D. Cameron (Eds.), *The other Macdonald report* (pp. 3-22, 51-62). Toronto: James Lorimer.

Statistics Canada. (1965). *Federal government finance 1965.* Ottawa: Minister of Supply and Services.

Statistics Canada. (1970). *Federal government finance 1970.* Ottawa: Minister of Supply and Services.

Statistics Canada. (1975). *Federal government finance 1975.* Ottawa: Minister of Supply and Services.

Statistics Canada. (1977). *Federal government finance 1977.* Ottawa: Minister of Supply and Services.

Statistics Canada. (1979a). *The distribution of income and wealth in Canada 1977* (Cat. #13-570). Ottawa: Minister of Supply and Services.

Statistics Canada. (1979b). *Evaluation of data on family assets and debts, 1977.* Ottawa: Minister of Supply and Services.

Statistics Canada. (1980a). *Federal government finance 1980.* Ottawa: Minister of Supply and Services.

Statistics Canada. (1980b). *Incomes, assets and indebtedness of families in Canada 1977* (Cat. #13-572). Ottawa: Minister of Supply and Services.

Statistics Canada. (1981). *Canada year book 1980-81.* Ottawa: Minister of Supply and Services.

Statistics Canada. (1984a). *Federal government finance 1984.* Ottawa: Minister of Supply and Services.

Statistics Canada. (1984b). *Income distribution by size in Canada, 1984.* Ottawa: Minister of Supply and Services.

Statistics Canada. (1985a). *Canada year book 1985.* Ottawa: Minister of Supply and Services.

Statistics Canada. (1985b). *Canadian statistical review* (p. 8). Ottawa: Minister of Supply and Services.

Statistics Canada. (1985c). *National income and expenditure accounts 1970-1984.* Ottawa: Minister of Supply and Services.

Statistics Canada. (1986a, May). *Canadian statistical review* (p. 42). Ottawa: Minister of Supply and Services.

Statistics Canada. (1986b). *The distribution of wealth in Canada 1984* (Cat. #13-580). Ottawa: Minister of Supply and Services Canada.

Thurow, L. C. (1971). *The impact of taxes on the American economy.* New York: Praeger.

United Auto Workers. (1985). Can Canada compete? In D. Drache & D. Cameron (Eds.), *The other Macdonald report* (pp. 23-34, 151-156). Toronto: James Lorimer.

United Church of Canada. (1985). Economic development and social justice. In D. Drache & D. Cameron (Eds.), *The other Macdonald report* (pp. 169-183). Toronto: James Lorimer.

Wagner, R. E. (1980). Sense versus sensibility in the taxation of personal wealth. *Canadian Taxation, 2,* 23-30.

Walker, M. A. (1980). Measuring and coping with a progressive tax system or Robin Hoodery—A Canadian tradition past its prime. *Canadian Taxation, 2,* 8-15.

Ward, D. A. (1980). The case against capital taxes. *Canadian Taxation, 2,* 31-34.

11

The Case Against the North American
Free Trade Agreement

As a candidate in the federal elections of 1988 and 1993 representing the New Democratic Party in the riding of Guelph-Wellington, Ontario, I was deeply involved in the national debates over the Canada-United States Free Trade Agreement (CUSTA) and the North American Free Trade Agreement (NAFTA). In both cases, most of the controversies were related to a handful of fundamental questions that initially provoked some groups with special interests to take action and subsequently led to the formation of coalitions and networks of groups working together. These coalitions were not only able to offer informed criticisms of the assumptions behind the two agreements and the texts of the deals themselves, but they were able to construct viable alternatives (e.g., see Ecumenical Coalition for Economic Justice, 1993, and Action Canada Network, 1993). As one would expect, the alternative agendas offered by the coalitions were typically constructed by combining the agendas of special groups and individuals (e.g., see Barlow & Campbell, 1991; Council of Canadians, 1994; Hurtig, 1991; New Democratic Party, 1993;

AUTHOR'S NOTE: Parts of this chapter were presented to the Sub-Committee on International Trade of the Standing Committee on External Affairs and International Trade, House of Commons, Third Session of the Thirty-Fourth Parliament, December 7, 1992, in Halifax, Nova Scotia, and to the Ontario Cabinet Committee on North American Free Trade, April 2, 1993, in Kitchener, Ontario. The full text of the December 7 presentation may be found in *Hansard, 25*, 109-115.

Watkins, 1993). There was also a Tri-National evaluation of NAFTA combined with aspects of an agenda announced in Mexico City, January 17, 1993, and reproduced in The Development Group for Alternative Policies (GAP) (1993).

In the remainder of this chapter, almost all of the constructive work of all these groups and individuals, as well as that of their counterparts in the United States and Mexico, will be largely ignored. Because proponents of CUSTA and NAFTA often ask opponents for their alternatives, it is worthwhile to have a brief list of references available as a starting point for discussion. Nevertheless, the primary focus here is critical rather than constructive, and it is mainly on NAFTA from a Canadian opponent's point of view. In making the case against NAFTA, my remarks are presented as answers to some of the questions that have been most frequently raised by the other side.

QUESTION 1

Some proponents of NAFTA say that Canadians who oppose it are basically selfish because Mexico will be a major beneficiary of the agreement (Crane, 1993a). That is, there seems to be a moral case in favor of supporting NAFTA in the interest of the poorest member of the agreement. What response can opponents give to this charge?

Answer

There are a few considerations here. Although Mexico may well be the major beneficiary of NAFTA measured in terms of the relative increases in investment there compared to investment in Canada and the United States, there are good reasons for thinking that most Mexicans will probably be worse off with than without NAFTA.

1. One must realize that most of the investment being attracted to Mexico is going into the *maquiladora* region that borders on the United States. Prior to the implementation of NAFTA, in the period from 1985 to 1990, "net new employment creation amounted to only 33,513 jobs in Mexican manufacturing and 242,441 in the *maquiladoras*" (Ecumenical Coalition for Economic Justice, 1991a, p. 4). According to Arregui (1993), in the period from 1981 to 1991, industrial employment in the *maquiladora* regions doubled to 31% of the national total, but the share of the national total decreased from 45% to 34% in the Valley of Mexico.

The *maquiladora* regions of Mexico are special jurisdictions designed to attract foreign investment. In the literature of the United Nations, they are called Free Export Processing Zones (United Nations, 1988). Most of the following descriptive material about such zones comes from this report and Kuznetsov (1991). In the United States, they are often called Enterprise Zones.

By 1985, at least 260 of such zones were identified in various parts of the world. Some have been studied in considerable detail, such as South Korea, Brazil, China, the Philippines, and Malaysia.

Characteristically, such zones offer prospective investors:

1. relief from restrictions on their right to transfer profits and capital to a head office outside the host country
2. relief from duties on equipment and raw materials used in production
3. relief from direct and indirect taxes
4. special credit rates and administrative structures
5. special land rental or sales fees
6. the provision of infrastructures (water and sewage systems, housing, roads, medical and welfare services)
7. relief from environmental pollution laws
8. special labor-relations provisions (bans on trade unions, weaker occupational health and safety regulations, relief from labor laws, including minimum wage and maximum working time laws)

As one might expect, companies interested in taking advantage of such inducements have not been adverse to exploiting such advantages to their fullest. Reports of child labor, long hours, hazardous working environments, and so on have frequently appeared in the press.

What is perhaps equally important but less publicized is the fact that such zones do not produce many of the important benefits that their supporters attribute to them.

According to the United Nations' (1988) report, such zones do create new employment in host countries. However, the employment created has very specific and anomalous characteristics.

Employees are typically females aged 17 to 24 from rural areas, with at best a high school education. They are given minimum training, paid minimum wages, and have relatively short periods of employment with no job security.

Although the employment may involve state-of-the-art, high technology, the latter is not diffused throughout the country as some proponents imagined it might be. On the contrary, part of the motivation for establishing plants in such zones is to prevent the spread of the technology providing companies their competitive edge.

Although the employment generates income for people who might otherwise have none, some studies have shown that, on average, host countries invest as much as 4 dollars for every dollar of foreign investment (Kuznetsov, 1991).

Although employment is created through increased use of local suppliers, studies indicate that transnational companies prefer to deal with each other, using about 10% to 15% of raw materials provided by local suppliers. According to the Ecumenical Coalition for Economic Justice (1991b), only 1.7% of the inputs used by transnational corporations operating in the *maquiladora* regions come from within Mexico.

Sometimes proponents of such zones claim that they must represent favorable options for the people of host countries because, after all, countries keep setting them up and there is virtually an endless supply of willing workers.

Indeed, the streets of most urban areas in Canada and elsewhere are full of homeless, helpless, and hopeless people who would and do sell themselves with equal facility.

Does anyone imagine that in the long run the quality of human existence will be improved by institutionalizing the exploitation of such people?

Though the analogy is pitiful, it seems to me that establishing Free Export Processing Zones is like building new energy-producing incinerators to accommodate the excesses of our wasteful consumer society.

The trouble is, in the case of the zones, human beings are being treated as disposable waste products. Establishing special zones to accommodate such waste practically guarantees that "the poor will always be with us."

According to an article in *USA Today* ("Use Caution," 1992), 37 states have such zones or legislation allowing the development of such zones. They have been proposed as a partial solution to the problem of urban decay. Gorrie (1990) claimed there were 164 "foreign trade zones" in the United States and 7 being promoted for Detroit.

In the presence of CUSTA and NAFTA, it was inevitable that they would be proposed in Canada. In fact, on the day that I made my presentation to the Parliamentary Sub-Committee in Halifax, a group of economists and businesspeople indicated that they had already proposed turning that city into a free trade zone. So far no one has taken the bait.

2. Because the *maquiladora* regions have existed for about 20 years already without significant improvements in the working environment

(Diebel, 1989a), without NAFTA it would be reasonable to predict that there would be no improvement in the future. With NAFTA, however, it is certain that the *maquiladora* conditions will spread to all of Mexico and create enormous pressures to drag down the working conditions of Canadians and Americans to very similar levels. This certainty is the result of a little-known provision in NAFTA (Draft Legal Text, Part II, Chapter 22, Final Provisions, Annex I, Schedule of Mexico, September 8, 1992, pp. I-M-42-43), which, in effect, says that after 8 years from signing the deal, *maquiladora* producers can sell their products anywhere in Mexico. Therefore, anyone interested in competing with these producers for the Mexican market, will have to drive down their costs to the same level, presumably largely by the same means. Thus, the long-run consequences of NAFTA will certainly be, on balance, devastating for Mexican as well as other North American workers.

Because most people reading this chapter will not have access to NAFTA itself, the following quotation from NAFTA Draft Legal Text (1992) may be worthwhile.

> Persons authorized by the Secretaria de Comercio y Fomento Industrial to operate under the "Maquiladora Decree" may not sell to the domestic market more than 50% of the total value of its exports.
> Domestic market may not exceed:
>
> a. during the first year of entry into force of this Agreement, 55% of the total value of its exports;
> b. during the second year . . . 60% . . . ;
> g. during the seventh year . . . 85% . . . ;
> h. from the eighth year after the date of entry into force of this Agreement and thereafter, persons may not be subject to this requirement.

Kopinak (1993) wrote that, "The social costs and disadvantages of the traditional *maquiladoras* are legitimated in Mexican government policy as temporary evils in what is considered an inevitable process of development toward a modern future" (p. 144). However, in the light of the NAFTA provisions just cited, it is clear that such legitimation is quite illegitimate. The fact is that NAFTA has been designed to practically guarantee that "the social costs and disadvantages of the traditional *maquiladoras*" will be permanent for all Mexicans first and later for all their trading partners. Although I have not seen any other references to the provisions cited above, according to Hossie (1993), "A 50-page report on the cities of Reynosa and Matamoros by the Centre for Border Studies and Human Rights Protection says *maquiladoras* . . . will become a standard for Mexican industrial development" (p. A11).

3. Sometimes people recall passages from introductory economics texts that tell us that increases in trade should increase people's standard of living (e.g., McConnell, Brue, & Pope, 1990). In fact, increases in trade do not guarantee increases in standard of living. Mexican trade with the rest of the world has increased in the past decade, but the real wages of Mexicans have decreased. Kopinak (1993) reviewed Mexican studies showing that since their market was opened to more foreign imports in 1982, "exports have doubled" and "imports have at least tripled, . . . leading to a new debt crisis and problems with current accounts" (pp. 150-151). She also noted that "In the last 14 years, the purchasing power accumulated over the previous 55 years has been wiped out and is now half of what it was between 1936 and 1938" (p. 152). Arregui (1993) claimed that as a result of the "fragmentary export industrialization" occurring in Mexico, "In 1991, a given amount of imports cost Mexico twice the volume of exports it had to pay in 1981" (p. 166).

Summarizing several Mexican studies of the impact of the structural adjustment program introduced there in 1982, the Ecumenical Coalition for Economic Justice (1991a) wrote that

- open unemployment has risen from 8.5% to 17.9% of the economically active population;
- real wages have fallen by 60%;
- as many as 10 million children work illegally or subsist as street vendors or window washers;
- per capita consumption of basic foods has fallen 30%;
- prices of corn and beans paid to peasant farmers have fallen by 50% in terms of real purchasing power;
- the share of national income going to salary earners fell from 37.4% in 1981 to 20.3% in 1988 while the owners of capital increased their share from 45.5% to 58.7%. (p. 4)

According to Kalter and Khor (1990), the structural adjustment program was also responsible for reducing the Mexican annual inflation rate of nearly 100% in 1982 to 20% in 1989.

4. Sometimes the same introductory economics textbooks are cited telling us that increases in productivity will lead to increases in Mexicans'

standard of living (McConnell et al., 1990). Again, however, increases in productivity do not guarantee increases in standard of living. For example, Louisiana has higher levels of productivity than Michigan, but Michigan workers have a higher standard of living (Stanford, 1991). Workers at the Ford plant at Hermosillo, Mexico, are at least as productive as Ford workers in Ontario, but the Mexicans still make one seventh of what the Ontarions make (Jackson, 1993).

As we have seen in Canada following implementation of CUSTA, it is possible for exports to rise along with a rise in unemployment and a decline in overall output. For example, examine the figures for the 1989 to 1992 period in the *Bank of Canada Review*—for Merchandise Trade Exports, p. S88, table J1; Annual Unemployment Rate, p. S81, table H5; and Gross Domestic Product at Factor Cost, p. S80, table H4 (Bank of Canada, 1994).

It is also possible for overall output to rise along with rising unemployment, as it has, for example, when capital-intensive manufacturing and farming are substituted for labor-intensive alternatives (Barlow, 1991; Dooley, 1993; Morley, 1992). In fact, many Mexican critics of NAFTA claim that its aim is precisely to implement a model of development that includes relatively high unemployment as a necessary consequence.

> Professor Adolfo Aguilar Zinser of Mexico's National University told a Canadian parliamentary committee, "a very clear, conscious technocratic decision" has been made by Salinas and his advisors to include only half of Mexico's population in a dynamic process of economic growth. The economic model they have chosen means that by the year 2000, fifty million Mexicans would be left to languish as a reserve of cheap labour assuring that wages remain low for years to come. (Ecumenical Coalition for Economic Justice, 1991b, p. 2)

Unlike the critics who object to development models that accept massive numbers of unemployed people as the price of "progress," some critics of the econometric models predicting net job gains from CUSTA and NAFTA point out that the alleged net gains predicted by such models are the result of assuming full employment and balanced trade following implementation of the deals (Stanford, 1992, 1993). Empirical analyses of the performance of OECD countries over the past 20 years shows that almost never happens (Cornwall, 1990). According to Stanford (1993),

> A casual glance at the world economy confirms that neither full employment nor balanced trade can be counted on. Instead, long-run unemployment and

persistent trade imbalances are the norm. Indeed, the two are not unrelated: those countries that have most successfully generated new jobs and/or rising wages are precisely those—such as Japan and Germany—that have generated persistent trade surpluses, thanks to absolute cost competitiveness or other noncomparative advantages in world markets. (p. 94)

Additional criticisms of myths about the virtues of "free trade" compared to "managed trade" may be found in Thurow (1992) and Orr (1992).

5. Addressing the issue of Canadians' moral obligations to the relatively poorer Mexicans, one would have to take some account of the alleged political abuses and violations of human rights, including the unjustified arrest, imprisonment, torture, and murder of critics of current federal government policies like NAFTA. The documentation of such abuses is very extensive. Zinser (1993) claimed that

Mexico today enjoys a unique international status. It is the only remaining single-party authoritarian system that can practice massive electoral fraud and violate human rights without confronting serious recrimination by the international community. . . . [The government's ability to avoid serious criticism] . . . has earned the Mexican regime the distinction of being named "the perfect dictatorship" by Mario Vargas Llosa, Peru's leading literary figure and former presidential candidate. (pp. 211-212)

According to a report of the Action Canada Network (1991),

Electoral fraud is widely reported at all levels. President Carlos Salinas de Gortari himself is alleged to have won the presidency through fraud. On November 20, 1990, 50,000 people demonstrated in Mexico City to demand respect for democratic rights.
 Salinas' party, the Institutional Revolutionary Party (PRI), has ruled Mexico for over 60 years. Main opposition parties are the centre-right National Action Party (PAN) and the newly-formed centre-left Party of the Democratic Revolution (PRD), whose leader, Cuauthemoc Cardenas, is believed to have received the most votes in the 1988 Presidential election.
 At least 80 members of groups and parties opposing the government have been assassinated since Salinas' term began. Many of those killed were members of labour, farm, and indigenous peoples' political organizations.
 Trade unions are effectively suppressed in most cases. The Mexican Workers' Central (CTM), the largest union organization, is tied closely to the government and appears to do little to support workers' rights. (p. 13)

In an interview for the Action Canada Network (1991), Carlos Heredia, an advisor to the Canadian Catholic Organization for Development and

Peace and an employee of a Mexican development organization called "Equipo Pueblo" (the People's Team), summarized the power of "the perfect dictatorship" as follows:

> The way they've managed to control the political situation is that peasants, workers and the popular sector organizations are under the control of the official party through minor concessions. If peasants want credit to work the land, they have to go through the official party to get the credit. If a taxi driver wants a license, he has to do it through the official party. If you're a private entrepreneur and you want to speed up what you're promoting, you have to do it through the official party. Every private or citizens' initiative is channelled through the official party.
>
> We have no independent electoral authority. The elections are fully controlled, from the beginning to the end, by the government and its party. They control voters' lists, they control electoral authorities, they control how the ridings are defined, they control the polls, they control the courts where you take your complaints, and they control the Supreme Court.
>
> So they have the whole electoral process in their hands. That's why, in 1988, despite the fact that Salinas was defeated, he was nominated president.
>
> Since December 1, 1988, 116 members of the Party of the Democratic Revolution, which is the opposition on the centre-left, have been assassinated because of their political involvement.
>
> We have 550 persons that are missing because of their political activism since 1973. Every case is substantiated by documents that tell us how they disappeared. (pp. 17-20)

A fairly detailed report of political abuses in the state of Michoacan may be found in Warnock (1993). On top of all of this,

> The Inter-Church Committee on Human Rights in Latin America cites documentary evidence of 2,476 cases of human rights violations in Mexico over the years 1971-1986. In 1988 and 1989 alone the ICCHRLA reports 22 cases of political killings, 98 cases of torture and 4,837 cases of illegal detentions. (Ecumenical Coalition for Economic Justice, 1991a, p. 16)

Similar reports may be found in Diebel (1993) and Harper (1991). The rebellion of the Zapatista National Liberation Army that began on January 1, 1994, in the southern state of Chiapas was reported to be a direct result of political abuses that reached a crisis with the implementation of NAFTA (Bejar, 1994; Healy, 1994; Nelson, 1994; Roman, 1994; Rumsey, 1994; Taylor del Cid, 1994). According to Roman (1994), following the civil war in 1917,

Article 27 of the new constitution . . . affirmed the primacy of the nation over the land and subsoil rights (oil and minerals) and became the basis for land reform. The traditional Indian form of communal land holding (the *ejido*) . . . protected the community from losing its land and preserved the link between community and land.

The current Salinas administration has changed article 27 to break up *ejido* land into individually-held parcels that can be sold. The NAFTA-linked collapse of corn prices and the legal right and immediate economic necessity of selling off parcels of the *ejidos* means . . . that millions of rural people will be driven off the land to housing and jobs that don't exist. The Zapatistas of Chiapas were correct in relating their struggles to NAFTA. (p. 13)

The problems involved in evaluating such abuses and taking account of their importance in one's overall assessment are familiar and substantial. Whatever one finally concludes regarding one's moral obligations in the light of such alleged abuses, it will probably remain controversial but it should not remain ignored.

6. Finally, although the supporting literature is too vast to be reviewed here, it is worthwhile to mention that one of the main motives for American and Canadian governments wanting to open up the Mexican market is to "help" the Mexican government continue to make payments on its debts to the former governments and commercial banks (Ecumenical Coalition for Economic Justice, 1990; Greider, 1987). At least part of the solution to the Mexican government's threatened defaulting on its international loans in the early 1980s was to roll them over with new payment schedules that require increased exports to pay the additional interest costs, presumably without end. This was and is a fundamental part of the standard "structural adjustment program" (SAP) solution of the International Monetary Fund (IMF). Regarding such SAPs, a 1990 United Nations Children's Fund report claimed that

it is essential to strip away the niceties of economic parlance and say that . . . the developing world's debt, both in the manner in which it was incurred and in the manner in which it is being "adjusted to," . . . is simply an outrage against a large section of humanity. (quoted in Ecumenical Coalition for Economic Justice, 1990, p. 9)

Early in 1994, a U.S.-based group calling itself the "50 Years Is Enough" coalition was formed to lobby against the World Bank and IMF's SAPs (The Development GAP, 1994).

According to Greider (1987), along with other monetary crises in many debtor countries, the Mexican problems were a direct consequence of the increased capital-to-loan ratios required by commercial banks and the tight money policies of the U.S. Federal Reserve addressing the incoherent fiscal policies of the Reagan Administration. Instead of accepting any responsibility for the problems and relieving the victims of their misery by cancelling the debts, the preferred solution merely altered the form of the misery. The moral implications of participating in this solution through NAFTA are considerable.

Hopefully, the following remarks from Greider (1987) will provide some insight into what happened and some incentive to read his whole fascinating book.

> For the previous decade [i.e., 1970s], the leading international banks of the U.S. had pushed for a larger and larger share of [the] global loan market and their capital base had shrunk proportionately. Brazil, Mexico, Argentina, South Korea, the Philippines and Taiwan were the leading borrowers. Collectively, Third World nations had amassed about $400 billion in debts to foreigners, as of 1980, and U.S. banks held about 40 percent of the bank loans.
>
> The nine largest money-center banks were the most aggressive of all. Their risk exposure in less-developed countries had mushroomed to 204 percent of their capital by 1980. In other words, if the Third World nations were to default for some reason, that catastrophe would wipe out—twice over—the capital of the biggest names in American banking.
>
> Mexico's crisis was America's. The two nations were economically intertwined by trade and labor supply much more closely than most U.S. citizens appreciated, but the crucial link was finance. If Mexico went under, so might several of the most celebrated names in American banking. Mexico owed $80 billion to foreign creditors, the largest share to the major American banks. . . . In all, the nine largest money-center banks' exposure in Mexican loans was equal to 44 percent of their capital.
>
> A Mexican default would invite the collapse of the American banking system, starting at the top. Nervous investors and money managers would rush to pull their large deposits out of any banks with heavy exposure on foreign loans, and the panic would spread worldwide—a global "run" on the largest multinational banks.
>
> The United States government could not allow that to happen. (pp. 432-517)

As many financial analysts have affirmed, the international financial and monetary "system" is seriously in need of restructuring (Bienefeld, 1992; Dillon, 1994; Guttmann, 1989). The world cannot continue shifting masses of wealth into the hands of financial institutions run by reckless risk takers protected by government-run deposit insurance agencies, that is, taxpayers.

QUESTION 2

Two former Canadian Ministers of Finance, Michael Wilson (1992) and Mazankowski (Ferguson, 1993), claimed that CUSTA has been a success already because exports to the United States have gone up since January 1989. So we may expect NAFTA to make things even better. If that is true, where is the problem?

Answer

1. If one examines the Canada-to-United States export statistics for the 125 years from 1868 to 1993, one will only find 24 years in which annual exports to the United States from Canada did not increase; that is, 81% of the annual export figures since confederation have been increases. More important, for 46 of the 47 years following World War II (i.e., 98%), Canadian annual exports to the United States have increased (Bank of Canada, 1994, table J3; Census and Statistics Office, 1906; Statistics Canada, 1972, 1991; Urquhart & Buckley, 1965). Thus, because our exports to the United States have increased 81% during the time since confederation and 98% during the time since World War II, it is preposterous to attribute export growth since 1989 to CUSTA. Granting that all the numbers used to reach this conclusion must be subject to a variety of errors (e.g., price inflation and population increases), it is still fair to say that on the basis of the only data we have, export growth to the United States is the natural state of affairs, especially since the war. In the light of this fact, there never was a need for a new trade agreement to get better access to the United States, and the most reasonable alternative to CUSTA and NAFTA so far as Canada-to-United States trade is concerned was business as usual.

Some brief historical remarks about other trade treaties between the two countries may be worthwhile here. In particular, I would mention the two sectorial treaties, the relatively well-known Auto Pact of 1965 and the less well-known Defense Production Sharing Arrangements of 1963, and the two more general agreements, the Reciprocity Treaty of 1854 and the trilateral agreements with Canada, the United States, and Great Britain of 1932 to 1938.

Of the four treaties, the Auto Pact has been most successful for Canada, effectively guaranteeing certain levels of production proportionate to levels of sales of the Big Three American auto producers.

Proponents of the defense treaty hoped to integrate military-related manufacturing in the two countries to such an extent that Canadian production would be massively increased by the levels of production in the United States but, for reasons explained in the following chapter, fortunately that has not happened.

The trilateral agreements were different agreements with the three countries, and I have not been able to make any sort of overall cost-benefit analysis of their results. Kottman (1968) gave a good historical account of these treaties. What struck me as most interesting about the events related to the 1932-1938 agreements was the remarkable impact of the U.S. film industry on the negotiations, and the similarity of this industry's impact on CUSTA and NAFTA. Even though the industry was apparently not able to get everything it wanted in the deals, it had enough clout to prevent passage of the deals if it was not suitably satisfied with their contents (Godfrey, 1992; Hurtig, 1991; Kottman, 1968).

The bilateral treaty of 1854 was examined in some detail by Masters (1963), which is my source for the history that follows. Strictly speaking, the Reciprocity Treaty of 1854 was a treaty between the United States and Great Britain on behalf of the British North American Colonies, because the Dominion of Canada did not exist until 1867.

The provisions of this treaty were in effect about 12 years, from February 1855 to March 1866. Because what we now call Systems of National Accounts were not invented until the late 1930s, accurate measures of the Gross Domestic Products and merchandise trade are not available for that period. However, rough calculations of the export and import figures provided by Masters from official U.S. Senate statistics indicate that the Colonies had a net loss of about $29 million for the 12-year period. Still, it was the Americans who found the exchange insufferable and gave notice of abrogation.

As one would expect, different people had different motives for wanting or not wanting reciprocity. Some thought reciprocity would undermine the activities of Colonists pressing for annexation to the United States. On the contrary, some American congressmen from southern states thought (like contemporary opponents of CUSTA) commercial reciprocity would hasten annexation, and the last thing they wanted to add to the Union was another "two millions of liberty-loving, slavery-hating people." The main political hurdle was finally cleared when Southerners came around to the opposite view.

Although the two countries had formalized a Covenant in 1818 regarding access to the fisheries around the Lower Colonies (Prince Edward Island, Nova Scotia, New Brunswick, and Newfoundland), there continued to be friction. In fact, there was so much friction that in 1852 a small fleet was dispatched to defend British interests. Thus, the very first sentence of the treaty, which is a page long, indicated that its aim was "to avoid further misunderstanding" over the "right of fishing on the coasts of British North America."

Besides indicating the treaty's fundamental aim, the first Article of the six-article treaty called for the creation of a three-person dispute settlement Commission made up of one Representative from each country and an Umpire selected by agreement or by lot.

A second aim of the treaty was the expansion of trade in nonmanufactured raw materials. So the second Article listed items of "growth and produce" that were to be admitted to each country "free of duty."

As straightforward as the language of this Article appeared, one of the first disputes arising from the treaty concerned the American claim that flour made in Canada from American wheat should not be regarded as the "growth and produce" of the Colonies and, therefore, should not be allowed into the United States duty-free.

The similarities between this early dispute and the more recent dispute over the duty-free status of Honda engines are striking (e.g., see Eggertson, 1992; Pritchard, 1992; Saunders, 1992a, 1992b, 1992c).

The fourth Article gave Americans access to the St. Lawrence seaway and "canals in Canada" in exchange for access to Lake Michigan and the promise that the U.S. government will "urge upon the State Governments to secure to the subjects of her Britannic Majesty the use of the several State canals." The latter promise, of course, is similar to the CUSTA provisions regarding admission of Canadian banks to the various States. Again, the Americans got access and Canadians got a promise (CUSTA, Chapter 17).

The treaty was to "remain in force for ten years," after which it could be abrogated on 12-months' notice. However, there was a safety-valve clause allowing each country to temporarily suspend the operations of the third and fourth Articles at any time.

Although the treaty never enjoyed universal acceptance, trade between the two countries expanded in the period of its operation. Unfortunately, there were then, as now, so many factors influencing trade that it is impossible to say exactly which did what. It is certain that, like the populations of both countries, trade had been expanding before the treaty was signed, and it continued to expand after abrogation.

There were great infusions of British capital into the Colonial railways in that period, matched by optimistic government spending. The U.S. Civil War ran from April 1861 to April 1865, temporarily replacing shipments of produce from southern to northern States with shipments from the Colonies to northern States, and increasing the demand for Maritime coal, lumber, and ships. Across the Atlantic, the Crimean War of 1854-1856 forced the British to draw more heavily on agricultural products from the Colonies.

According to Masters and other historians, the most likely main effect of the treaty was to hasten the exchange of goods in conveniently close markets. Most of the duty-free goods exported were of the same sort imported, with different regions simply sending or receiving whatever they had or lacked from their nearest neighbor.

The end came with as much confusion as the beginning and the middle. From the beginning the British recognized that the treaty was inconsistent with the general policy of free trade existing in the Empire. Then, as now, people on the outside clearly perceived the contours and likely consequences of Fortress North America.

The depression of 1857 and the poor harvest of 1858 hurt both sides. Because British manufacturers competed with those in the North, particularly New Yorkers, Great Britain had a bias toward the South. The Yankees could never forget that the British were quick to recognize the southern States as belligerents and then to adopt a policy of neutrality. What's worse, the Colonists did not prevent Confederate assaults on the North via the Colonies.

Even though a great deal of the new money flowing into the Colonies throughout the period of the treaty flowed back into the United States to purchase manufactured products, the Americans complained of great revenue losses from the reduced tariffs. They also complained of revenue losses from the introduction of high tariffs in Canada, instigated by the Association for the Promotion of Canadian Industry. The fact that the American tariffs on manufactured goods were even higher than those of the Canadians was beside the point.

After four reports in the House of Representatives, the Americans gave notice of abrogation in March 1865. Some of those who supported the call for abrogation thought it was the only way to get revisions, but others simply wanted out.

The Colonists immediately sent representatives to England to try to get a renewal. Some thought legislation might be introduced to create the conditions of reciprocity without a formal treaty. Others thought that the pot might be sweetened for the Americans if the Colonies first formed a bigger trading block, a Confederation. Still others, of course, thought that the creation of a bigger trading block would make reciprocity unnecessary. And there were those who immediately looked elsewhere, to Mexico, the Spanish Colonies, and Mediterranean countries.

Presumably if and when the end comes to CUSTA and NAFTA, we can expect a similar period of confusion, a flurry of activity, and a strengthening of Canadian solidarity and sovereignty.

2. Wilson's focus on merchandise exports to the United States was seriously misleading because it failed to consider the trade-off in imports and, more important, failed to consider nonmerchandise transactions in services and investment income. That is, Wilson never considered the total Current Account Balance of Payments with the United States or with the whole world. Considering the bilateral Current Account Balance, it should be noticed that Canada had a surplus each of the 5 years going into CUSTA (i.e., 1984-1988) and a deficit in 4 of the 5 years following the deal (1989-1993) (Statistics Canada, 1994). Considering Canada's Current Account Balance with the whole world, we ran a deficit every year but the first in the 1984 to 1993 period and, beginning with 1989, there was a dramatic leap in the size of our deficits (Bank of Canada, 1994). The fact is that Canada's Current Account Balance of Payments with the whole world has been worse since 1989 than ever before in our history.

3. Wilson never mentioned the fact that there was a significant loss of domestic market share for Canadian producers, requiring a further loss of Canadian jobs and tax revenue. According to Campbell (1992), "A Canadian Manufacturers Association survey in April 1992 found that 44% of the companies have lost market share since 1989" (pp. 10-11). Researchers for the New Democratic Party (1992) claimed that, "Since 1989, Canadian manufacturing jobs have disappeared at four times the rate of U.S. manufacturing job loss" (p. 5).

4. Wilson never mentioned the specific kinds of products that enjoyed export increases. New Democratic Party (1992) researchers claimed that one Statistics Canada report on exports to the United States from Canada in the period 1988 to 1991 showed raw materials exports growing at 23% compared to manufactured goods exports growing at 2%.

In the period 1989 to 1993 there was a notable increase in exports to the United States of crude petroleum, motor vehicles and parts, and construction materials (Bank of Canada, 1994). The increased export of raw materials like crude petroleum was to be expected, because we abandoned the opportunity to require or even encourage by special export taxes any sort of processing of raw crude prior to export (CUSTA, Article 903), leaving increased exports of the raw material as the only means of oil companies increasing their incomes. Selling unprocessed raw materials instead of high-value-added materials is part of the root cause of Canada's underdevelopment (National Advisory Board on Science and Technology, 1991), and both CUSTA and NAFTA exacerbate this problem.

Motor vehicle exports are to some extent still managed by the Canada-U.S. Auto Pact, though NAFTA will weaken the benefits for Canada. Still, any use of motor vehicle trade statistics to make a case for our competitiveness or the virtues of free trade is simply propaganda disguising the fact that such bilateral trade is managed by a cooperative agreement.

Softwood lumber has been a large part of Canadian construction materials exports to the United States for many years and "has been the most contentious dispute in recent Canada-U.S. trade relations" (Sinclair, 1993, p. 195). Given the long history of American demand for this product and the fact that CUSTA Article 2009 explicitly asserts that commerce in this product will be governed by the bilateral Memorandum of Understanding on Softwood Lumber of December 30, 1986, any export increases in softwood lumber cannot be attributed to CUSTA.

5. Finally, Wilson never mentioned the fact that between the implementation of CUSTA in January 1989 to May 1992, the share of Canada's total exports going to the United States increased from 73% to 76% (New Democratic Party, 1992). Wilson could not have known, but it is nevertheless true, that by the end of 1993, the American share of Canadian exports increased to 80% of the total (Bank of Canada, 1994). That means that one effect of the deal was to make us even more dependent on the U.S. market than we were before, which practically everyone in the country agrees is exactly the opposite of the sort of trade development we should be encouraging.

QUESTION 3

Opponents to NAFTA claim it is antidemocratic, that it subverts democracy in general and Canadian sovereignty in particular. What is the evidence for that?

Answer

NAFTA is antidemocratic and subverts democracy and Canadian sovereignty in several ways.

1. It prevents Canadians from buying back key industries to put their ownership in Canadian hands, specifically from requiring "an investor of another party, by reason of its nationality, to sell or otherwise dispose of an investment in the territory of the Party" (NAFTA, Article 1102.4). Foreign ownership implies foreign control at the expense of domestic control through democratic processes (Crane, 1993b).

2. It forces provincial/state and local governments to abide by rules that it had no part in designing. Article 105 says that, "The Parties shall ensure that all necessary measures are taken in order to give effect to the provisions of this Agreement, including their observance, except as otherwise provided in this Agreement, by state and provincial governments." According to Article 201.2, "For purposes of this Agreement, unless otherwise specified, a reference to province or state includes local governments." Article 902.2 asserts that provinces/states must adhere to Articles 904-908 regarding standards and related matters. The government procurement provisions in Chapter 10 apply to federal, provincial/state, and local governments (Article 1002.1). Article 1102.3 says that provinces/states must concur with the investment provisions of Chapter 11. Article 1202.2 asserts that provinces/states will give national treatment to "service providers of another Party" and Article 1407.8 requires similar treatment for providers of financial services.

The province of Ontario (which "alone is the United States' largest trading partner. Not Japan, as one might think, but Ontario"; Rae, 1993) set up a cabinet committee and held provincewide public hearings on NAFTA early in 1993. The province had already been burned by CUSTA when it tried to introduce public auto insurance in 1991 (Ferguson, 1991). Among other things, the final report of the committee affirmed that

NAFTA represents a significant expansion of the FTA [CUSTA] in terms of its direct impacts on provincial jurisdiction.

Ontario would no longer be able to use performance requirements to require local sourcing.

Provincial regulations are specifically not allowed to prefer Canadian goods or services to those produced by the U.S. or Mexico.

Should an Ontario measure fail to comply with the agreement, it could be challenged under the general dispute settlement mechanism, and . . . there is no provision for formal provincial participation in this dispute settlement procedure.

Under NAFTA, the Ontario government would be required to list policies and practices that may be open to challenge under the agreement in order to have them exempted. However, the federal government would have the ultimate responsibility for actually compiling the final list of exemptions "grandparented" under NAFTA. Ontario may therefore lose control over matters that lie within its exclusive jurisdiction.

The Committee considers the impact of NAFTA on provincial government roles, responsibilities and jurisdiction to be a major issue. . . . An agreement which is meant to concern itself with tariff reduction and international trade rules could affect the jurisdiction of the Ontario government and lead to a significant realignment of powers between the provincial and the federal governments. This fact throws into question the constitutional authority of the federal government to implement the agreement. (Government of Ontario, Cabinet Committee, 1993, pp. 32-34)

On October 13, 1993, the Premier of Ontario, Bob Rae, told the Legislature that his government had "decided to challenge NAFTA through a 'legal reference' to the Ontario Court of Appeal." At this time (June 1994), the issue is "still in the hands of lawyers," according to a spokesperson for Ontario's Minister of Intergovernmental Affairs.

3. It establishes a Free Trade Commission to supervise further developments, but the Commission is not elected and although the provinces/states, environmental, citizen, and labor groups have no standing before it, corporate investors and federal governments do have standing (NAFTA, Chapter 20). When there are disputes over international agreements, say, on the environment, the Commission may establish Arbitral Panels at the request of the disputing Parties (Article 2008). Members of the Panels will be selected by the Commission from rosters of people who "have expertise or experience in law, international trade [or] other matters covered by [the] Agreement" (Article 2009.2). Panels "may request a written report of a scientific review board on any factual issue" relevant to a dispute (Article 2015), but "the panel's hearings, deliberations and initial report, and all written submissions to and communications with the panel shall be confidential" (Article 2012). Normally, disputing Parties will accept the final decision of Panels (Article 2018). However, dissenting Parties may suspend benefits of the Agreement, if all else fails (Article 2019).

4. It allows provincial standards and Crown corporations to be challenged regarding the introduction of new or modified "sanitary or phytosanitary measures," though provinces can not challenge the Commission or its rulings (Article 760.2).

5. It locks in the status quo of Crown corporations and public service provisions. Article 1502 is entitled "Monopolies and State Enterprises," whereas Article 1503 is entitled simply "State Enterprises." Accordingly, I suppose 1502 applies to both sorts of entities but 1503 applies only to the latter. According to Article 1502.3(b), "Each Party shall ensure, . . . [that] any government monopoly that it maintains or designates . . . acts solely in accordance with commercial considerations in its purchase or sale of the monopoly good or service in the relevant market, including with regard to price, quality, availability, marketability, transportation and other terms and conditions of purchase or sale."

Those who opposed CUSTA claimed and still claim that Canadian democracy and sovereignty were weakened because the deal would not allow us to have dual pricing of energy and other resources to give domestic producers a competitive advantage, to put performance requirements on foreign investments, to have regional development programs, to have assured and greater access to our own manufacturing markets (e.g., in drugs, films, and books), and to have Crown enterprises designed to serve public purposes (like job creation) rather than mere commercial purposes.

Besides undermining democracy, the NAFTA Article 1502.3(b) weakens Canadian sovereignty even further. In fact, NAFTA was clearly the Mulroney government's third assault on our country's capacity to have public enterprises in the interest of serving public purposes.

Everyone knows that the Mulroney government was committed to the privatization of Crown corporations, like Air Canada and Petro Canada, and I have just remarked on the prohibitions against performance requirements in CUSTA. NAFTA Article 1106 contains a more extensive list of prohibited measures than is contained in the first deal and, more important, this article explicitly applies to investors of "a Party or of a non-Party"; that is, it has implications for would-be participants in the Agreement. Like CUSTA, NAFTA prohibits national content laws requiring transnational corporations to produce a portion of the goods they sell within the country or to purchase inputs or services domestically. To these prohibitions, NAFTA adds new constraints against requiring transnationals to balance their exports and imports, to transfer technology, or to assign world or regional product mandates to their local subsidiaries.

Taken together, these prohibitions would prevent any future government from ever negotiating an agreement like the Auto Pact, requiring companies wishing to sell products in the Canadian market to employ Canadians or use Canadian inputs. Canada could be reduced to a nation of warehouses without a significant manufacturing base.

Whereas the first deal's prohibitions only apply to Canadian and American firms investing in each others' territory, NAFTA measures also apply to companies from outside North America. These expanded terms are aimed at prohibiting Asian or European investors from gaining a privileged position in national markets at the expense of North American firms. For example, NAFTA would prevent Canada, Mexico, or any other country that eventually joins the block from signing a deal with Nissan or Volkswagen offering them access to a national market in return for requiring them to employ Canadians or Mexicans to produce the vehicles.

Thus the Mulroney government, with the help of two other neoconservative governments in the United States and Mexico, crafted a three-wave assault on democracy and national sovereignty. First, public enterprise is to be replaced by private enterprise through an aggressive program of privatization. Then, with CUSTA, governments were prevented from requiring private enterprise to serve public purposes like regional development or job creation. Finally, with NAFTA, governments will be required to make any new public enterprises behave like private enterprises.

With this third assault on public enterprise, these governments sought to guarantee that there will never again be a Crown corporation created and motivated by an interest in serving some great public need, like a national child care program. Enterprises with the noblest motive, the public good, are to be legislated out of existence, giving supremacy to enterprises with the most selfish motive, some private, exclusive good. The fact that two allegedly liberal-leaning governments in Canada and the United States (i.e., Chretien's Liberals and Clinton's Democrats) have ratified NAFTA indicates that current liberalism is not very liberal at all, whether or not it ever was.

6. By eroding the tax base, it erodes the capacity to have social programs. By making it easier for transnational corporations to dictate terms of production and trade, government revenues are bound to suffer. Prior to the implementation of CUSTA, this was predicted by all of its opponents. At this point in time, the correctness of these predictions is beyond doubt (McQuaig, 1993).

The previous two points merit a few more comments. By preventing or limiting our use of Crown corporations and social programs, NAFTA severely limits our capacity to compensate for unacceptable market anomalies, systemic discrimination, and accidents of birth, geography, or demography. It must be remembered that the point of introducing

Crown corporations and social programs is usually to empower relatively powerless people and strengthen our democratic institutions (National Action Committee on the Status of Women, 1993). Public institutions, such as the National Research Council, CBC, Medicare, our system of schools and universities, and so on, create and redistribute new wealth and a better quality of life for all Canadians. The fact that public institutions often create public, rather than merely private, goods and services must be emphasized over and over in the presence of contemporary right-wing propaganda. Constraints on the development of public institutions designed to serve public purposes are fundamentally constraints on the development of democracy, in Canada and elsewhere. (More on the antidemocratic aspects of these deals may be found in Grinspun & Kreklewich, 1994.)

QUESTION 4

Though Canada's former Minister of Finance, Wilson, hailed NAFTA as "the greenest trade deal ever cut," opponents claim it is antienvironment and anticonservation. What is the basis for this complaint?

Answer

There are several reasons for saying that NAFTA is an antienvironmental and anticonservationist document.

1. Although the treaty announces no new environmental standards and no conservationist standards, such as energy efficiency standards, many of its provisions will effectively erode the modest standards already existing and create barriers to the adoption of more progressive ones. What standards it appeals to first are those provided in international treaties, namely, the *Convention on the International Trade in Endangered Species of Wild Fauna and Flora*, the *Montreal Protocol on Substances That Deplete the Ozone Layer*, and the *Basel Convention on the Control of Transboundary Movements of Hazardous Wastes and Their Disposal* (Article 104). Environmentalists around the world agree that such conventions typically represent the least common denominator or most modest standards about which there is international agreement (Canadian Environmental Law Association, 1993). Weak as these conventions are, NAFTA aims even lower by insisting that "In the event of any inconsistency between this Agreement and the specific trade obligations set out in . . . [the three treaties, Parties must choose] . . . the

alternative that is the least inconsistent with the other provisions of this Agreement" (Article 104.1). Because the main objectives of NAFTA are to "eliminate barriers to trade in, and facilitate the cross border movement of goods and services . . . [and] . . . increase substantially investment opportunities," it is clear that this Article was designed to ensure that the cited international treaties would have as little impact as possible on the achievement of those objectives.

Article 755.5 commits each Party to participating "in relevant international and North American standardizing organizations, including the *Codex Alimentarius Commission*, the *International Office of Epizootics*, the *International Plant Protection Convention*, and the *North American Plant Protection Organization*, with a view to promoting the development and periodic review of international standards, guidelines and recommendations." Brief descriptions of the structure and functions of these organizations are given in the Canadian Environmental Law Association (1993), along with the cautionary comment that the Codex Alimentarius Commission "has frequently been criticized by environmental groups in North America for being industry-dominated, and accepting standards lower than many North American ones" (Swenarchuk, 1993a, p. 79). For example, according to the New Democratic Party (1992), the Commission's food standards have been "established through a process dominated by chemical companies and agribusiness. As a result, the Codex allows for residues of pesticides like DDT far in excess of the Canadian standards" (p. 31).

2. Article 754.1 allows a Party to "adopt, maintain or apply any sanitary or phytosanitary measure necessary for the protection of human, animal or plant life or health in its territory, including a measure more stringent than an international standard, guideline or recommendation." The trouble is that by the time one reaches Article 758, this progressive-sounding provision has been hammered into a dangerously regressive piece of legislation. Swenarchuk (1993b) provided a fine detailed analysis of the problems. Briefly, they involve (a) the phrase "in its territory," which was used "in the much criticized GATT [General Agreement on Tariff and Trade] tuna-dolphin ruling, in which the U.S. *Marine Mammals Protection Act* was found incompatible with GATT"; (b) "based on scientific principles" (754.3), which typically cannot be determinative of public policy issues; (c) "based on a risk assessment, as appropriate to the circumstances," which becomes unpacked in Article 757 as requiring that "in establishing its appropriate level of protection regarding the risk associated with the introduction, estab-

lishment or spread of an animal or plant pest or disease, and in assessing such risk, also take into account the . . . economic factors . . . loss of production or sales"; (d) "necessary," which was the thin thread on which Canada hung its case against "a U.S. EPA [Environmental Protection Agency] rule banning the manufacture, importation, processing, and distribution in commerce of most asbestos-containing products"; and (e) "disguised restriction on trade" (754.6), which is practically an open invitation to find what one wants to find in the interest of increasing trade. Summarizing all these problems, Swenarchuk (1993b) wrote that "the wording of the NAFTA which establishes Parties' rights and obligations regarding SPS [Sanitary and Phytosanitary Standards] measures contains considerable uncertainty and in the light of previous trade panel decisions, significant constraints on the rights of Parties to set standards different from international standards" (p. 119).

3. Those who propose more stringent standards must somehow get their case put to the previously discussed Free Trade Commission (Question 3, No. 3), so the latter may appoint a Panel of experts to make a decision according to the principles just described (Nos. 1 & 2). As explained above, neither provinces, local governments, environmental groups, conservationist groups, labor groups, nor individuals have standing before the Commission, and experts from such groups need not be consulted by the Panels. So it is unclear how new and more stringent standards would be established.

4. Some state, provincial, and local laws are initiated to prevent potential harm in the absence of actual harms having already occurred. In such cases, the NAFTA requirement to demonstrate actual harms (No. 2) before establishing more stringent standards would preempt such preventive measures. This requirement directly contradicts the generally accepted precautionary principle of sustainable development. The Ontario Round Table on Environment and Economy expressed the principle thus: "Anticipating and preventing problems are better than trying to react and fix them after they occur" (quoted in Swenarchuk, 1993a, p. 79). According to Greenpeace:

An integral part of the precautionary principle is that the burden of proof should not be on one concerned with the protection of the environment to demonstrate conclusive harm, but rather on the prospective polluter to demonstrate no harm—giving the environment and human health the benefit of the doubt. (quoted in Swenarchuk, 1993a, p. 80)

Authors of the *U.S. Citizen's Analysis of the North American Free Trade Agreement* expressed concern that federal standards like those in the Delaney Clause, "which simply forbids adding carcinogens to processed food," might be challenged (Audley et al., 1992, p. 12).

5. Another consequence of NAFTA's constraining provincial and state government initiatives is that the latter will be prevented from providing their traditional leadership to the international community.

> Advances in green protection strategies now frequently occur in a "leap-frog" fashion. Jurisdictions that establish high standards in a particular area (i.e., Germany on packaging, Ontario on waste management, California on auto standards) provide precedents that environmentalists in other areas then lobby their governments to emulate. International harmonization, by definition, removes the process of continual improvement of standards. (Swenarchuk, 1993a, p. 82)

6. Having no standards to protect the environment and conserve natural resources, the treaty is understandably void of enforcement mechanisms for such purposes. Thus, the U.S. citizen's group charged that

> One of our most basic concerns with the NAFTA is that it lacks any mechanisms to guarantee that an appropriate share of the wealth it may generate will go towards environmental and infrastructural improvement, nor does it commit the three governments to enforce similar environmental, health and safety rules.
>   Interestingly, the Agreement does provide enforcement mechanisms for companies whose intellectual property rights are violated and for investors who believe they have not received the full benefits and protection of the NAFTA's investment section. Thus, we see a serious disparity between the way the economic interests are to be treated, as compared to how the overall public interest is taken care of. (Audley et al., 1992, pp. 8-10).

7. Although NAFTA has no provisions that explicitly allow subsidies for environmental cleansing, conservation, or renewable energy, it does have explicit provisions allowing subsidies for increased exploration and exploitation of fossil fuels, oil, and gas (Article 608.2). These provisions are exactly the opposite of what they would be if the authors of NAFTA were environmentalists or conservationists, and they are clearly incompatible with the sort of sustainable development recommended by the World Commission on Environment and Development (1987). Besides being antithetical to the public interest in sustainable

development, when these provisions are combined with the prohibitions against special export taxes to cover the costs of "increased exploration and exploitation" (Articles 603 & 604), it is clear that not only natural resources are being exploited.

> Selling conventional oil and gas reserves at prices far below their replacement costs subsidizes U.S. consumers. These lower-cost, more accessible and more environmentally benign conventional reserves will have to be replaced by more costly offshore and frontier resources. (Canadian Centre for Policy Alternatives, 1992, p. 19)

8. The proportionality clauses carried forward from CUSTA (Articles 409 & 904) encourage the continuous flow of natural resources without restrictions, which is again completely at odds with principles of sustainable development. In spite of protestations to the contrary from various representatives of the Mulroney government (e.g., Crosbie, 1988), careful analyses have showed that even pure water is included in the proportionality clauses; see, for example, Holm (1988) and Gamble (1988).

NAFTA Article 316 says that, with certain specified exceptions, Parties

> may adopt or maintain a restriction . . . with respect to the export of a good . . . only if . . . the restriction does not reduce the proportion of the total export shipments of the specific good made available to that other Party relative to the total supply of that good of the Party maintaining the restriction as compared to the proportion prevailing in the most recent 36-month period.

Article 605 has similar provisions specifically related to energy and basic petrochemicals.

Even before the implementation of CUSTA and NAFTA, the Mulroney government had seriously undermined Canadian conservationism in the energy field. According to Dillon (1988),

> Canada . . . had restrictions on the export of natural gas since 1907. Between 1959 and 1986, natural gas producers could not export to the U.S. unless they had a 25-year supply of gas available for sale in Canada.
> This "surplus test" was first reduced to 15 years and then eliminated altogether by the Mulroney government. Thanks to this unqualified faith in transnational private enterprise, . . . Canadian governments will have lost the power to assure adequate domestic energy supplies before exports are sanctioned. (p. 49)

9. The global trade envisioned by NAFTA and other international trade treaties is based on a supply of cheap fossil fuel that is probably not sustainable. Given the current traffic in international trade with its characteristic problems securing supplies, problems with periodic massive oil spills, and problems resulting from burning hydrocarbons, it is hard to believe that the current trend toward globalization is sustainable in the long run. Many people have been arguing for some time, with good reasons, that the development model of transnational corporations and the World Bank/IMF is simply counterproductive from the point of view of the long-term sustainable development desired and required by most Third World countries; for example, see the African Alternative Framework in Ecumenical Coalition for Economic Justice (1990). It is also counterproductive for the rest of us, as is argued in the alternative plans cited in the introductory paragraph of this chapter. My point here, however, is that quite apart from the overall social and economic counterproductivity of the globalization-of-trade model of development, the latter is unsustainable from an environmental-conservationist point of view. As Cobb and Daly (1990) put it:

> The quantity of resources required and the quantity of waste produced in [the globalization-of-trade] scenario stagger the imagination. Certainly the global warming and melting of the icecaps will be accelerated, resulting in massive physical dislocations. In reality there is no prospect at all of maintaining or re-achieving good wages by eliminating global unemployment through global industrial growth. (p. 187)

10. NAFTA creates a Catch-22 for conservationists. Conservation must be paid for by governments or industries. If Canadian governments pay, then U.S. industries claim we are giving unfair subsidies; for example, the government of British Columbia backed away from its reforestation subsidies in the face of U.S. complaints that they were unfair (Sinclair, 1993). If we ask our industries to pay, then they claim we are giving them an unfair handicap unless the Americans also make their industries pay. The likely result is that no conservationist measures will be introduced, requiring no payments and guaranteeing an impoverished future for those who come after us.

QUESTION 5

Why do opponents of NAFTA claim it is antilabor?

Answer

There are several reasons for saying NAFTA is antilabor.

1. As in the case of the environment and conservation, although the treaty announces no new minimum labor standards, many of its provisions will effectively erode the modest standards already existing and create barriers to the adoption of more progressive ones. The most dangerous provisions on this score have already been reviewed above regarding the nature and special rules for the operation of *maquiladora* industries and their extension throughout Mexico after 8 years (Question 1, Nos. 1 & 2).

2. It has no labor rights; no rights regarding organizing, collective bargaining, child labor, forced labor, racial or sexual harassment prohibitions.

At many of the public debates on NAFTA, people brought up the "Community Charter of the Fundamental Social Rights of Workers" that was passed by 11 of the 12 members of the European Community in 1992. Because Canadians were having massive public debates on our federal Constitution at the same time we were debating NAFTA, demands were also made to have a Social Charter included in our Constitution. Although no one on my side of the battle would be willing to abandon the idea of a Social Charter, serious criticisms have been raised against the idea of a European-style Social Charter. For example, after remarking that at best the provisions of the European Charter merely have "the status of a political declaration which carries no legal obligations for the signatories," Sanger (1992) endorses the following quotation from Mosley (1990).

> Given the continuing requirement of unanimity in all areas where employee interests are concerned, except occupational safety and health, . . . it is highly probable that the current effort to institutionalize minimum standards in the form of the European Social Charter will be unsuccessful, or result in the lowest common denominator approach. This in fact means creeping "deregulation," as firms are able to escape, or threaten to escape, statutory or collectively agreed to social protection by relocating their operations within the increasingly Europeanized economy. (p. 9)

Hildyard (1993) has similar criticisms.

3. Again, as indicated earlier (Question 3, No. 3; Question 4, No. 3), neither labor unions nor individual workers have any standing before the Free Trade Commission.

4. Because NAFTA's prescribed risk assessment procedure includes balancing economic benefits and costs against those of health and safety (Article 757 and Question 4, No. 2), worker safety may be traded off against high profits.

5. Because greater freedom is given to corporations in the investment provisions of Chapter 11 to move jobs at will, there is less job security for workers, more pressure to depress wages, more pressure to reduce benefits and taxes, and therefore less social security available for workers (Question 3, Nos. 5 & 6). The following quotation from the Canadian Centre for Policy Alternatives (1992) provides an excellent account of the shameless bias built into NAFTA:

> The free movement of labour is ignored. Consider for a moment the difference between two different scenarios. In one, labour is kept immobile, while capital is allowed to flow to wherever it can earn the highest return. This is what the NAFTA is promoting. In the other, *capital* is kept immobile, and *labour* is allowed to move to wherever it can earn the highest wages—that is, to those regions where unions are strongest, where health and environmental legislation is comprehensive, and where social programs are the most developed. Suddenly, in order to attract mobile workers, there is an upward competition between regions to improve the quality of life that they offer—exactly the opposite of the *downward* regional competition that is being unleashed by continental integration in its present form. (p. 92)

6. The NAFTA rules punish people in definite ways who deny expected trade profits to corporations (Chapter 20, Annex 2004), but there are no rules punishing corporations for violating worker rights. The only recognized unfair trade practices are those that destroy expected or real profits, not those that destroy people's lives, the quality of people's lives, or even whole communities. For example, governments must compensate corporations for trade profits lost if Crown corporations are established (Chapters 11 & 20), but there are no required compensations to workers or communities for runaway corporations.

These provisions of NAFTA are similar to those in Chapter 20 of CUSTA, especially Articles 2010 and 2011, which commit the Parties to minimizing the impairment of "reasonably expected" benefits from the deals. Thus, when the United States allocated a billion dollars through its Export Enhancement Program to export subsidies for agricultural products in 1992, many Canadian farmers (among others) called on the government to challenge the Americans on the basis of the CUSTA provisions (Bertin, 1992). Unfortunately, the Mulroney government did not have the stomach for such action, any more than the current Chretien government.

7. NAFTA's Rules of Origin provisions for duty-free goods practically throw away our clothing industry by requiring that Canadian clothing exports must be made from North American textiles and yarns. According to Jack Kivenko, President of the Canadian Apparel Manufacturers Institute, "The Americans made it clear that Canada would have to sacrifice its apparel industry as part of the price to obtain a NAFTA deal" (McKenna, 1992, p. B6). Although American manufacturers typically use yarns made in the United States, 60% of the yarns used by Canadian manufacturers are made abroad. So the deal just gives preference to American over Canadian clothing manufacturers. After noting that employment in the Canadian garment industry had fallen from 95,800 in 1988 to 62,300 in 1992 as a result of CUSTA, the Canadian Centre for Policy Alternatives (1992) wrote that

> NAFTA builds on the model negotiated under the FTA [CUSTA]. . . . Not simply a fabric forward rule of origin, NAFTA incorporates a yarn-forward rule of origin. This means that in order for Canadian-made apparel to be able to access the U.S. or the Mexican market under preferential tariff rates, the garment must be made from North American fabric and spun from North American yarn.
>
>   This is the U.S. model set up to be able to compete in a block with low-cost Asian competitors which have flooded the American markets. NAFTA allows the U.S. to have its own cheap labour source for the final assembling of garments, but still protects its strong domestic textile sector, which is concentrated in the lower-wage, right to work states of the American south. (p. 117)

Again, by moving to a relatively high North American content instead of Canadian content, the deal gives away Canadian jobs in the auto industry. Allowing a high percentage of imports of car parts and cars may be good for profits, but a low percentage of such imports would be better for local jobs.

The former President of the Canadian Auto Workers Union (and current President of the Canadian Labour Congress), Bob White (1992), pointed out that 55% of the Canadian market is held by the Big Three North American producers while the other 45% goes to "imports or very low-content transplants" (p. 1). More important, he remarked that, "If the Big Three got away with the same commitment to Canadian jobs as the Japanese-based multinationals, we'd have about 120,000 fewer jobs here (i.e., employment in the auto industry would fall by about 80%!)."

Accordingly, he recommended "a Canada-U.S.-Mexico sectoral rule of origin of 80%, combined with performance requirements in each country of 65%" (p. 5). Noting also that, "The Europeans have limited Japanese companies to about 12% of their market and have agreed to let this rise to 16% by the end of the decade," he proposed that "the government of Canada introduce quotas to limit the Japanese multinationals' share of our market from offshore to 16%" (pp. 3-4).

The absence of country-by-country content rules in NAFTA makes us more vulnerable to job loss and effectively robs us of "the main policy tool that created and maintained the Canadian auto industry—managed trade for the sector—corporate commitments to Canada in exchange for access" (Canadian Centre for Policy Alternatives, 1992, p. 43).

Interestingly enough, all the while the Americans were engaged in negotiating away vestiges of managed trade built into the Auto Pact, they were and still are trying to negotiate a system of managed trade with the Japanese. Clearly, in spite of the flamboyant rhetoric about the virtues of free trade, the main operative principle seems to be to opt for the system that will do your side the most good. According to Milner (1993),

> referring to U.S. pressure for Japan to meet certain targets on imports, foreign bidding for government contracts, domestic market share allocated to outsiders and other measures designed to rein in the huge Japanese trade surplus, . . . [the former Japanese Prime Minister Kiichi Miyazawa] said "managed trade cannot be done in a country with a market economy, even if you tried. And, of course, it is not good, even as an idea. (p. B1)

On the contrary, Davis (1992) claimed that, like the United States and most other industrial powers, much of Japan's industrial strength was built partly on managed trade.

8. Proponents of the deal talked about adjustment programs for workers losing jobs, but a progressive deal would have protected worker rights and prevented job losses resulting from exploiting the most vulnerable people. It would encourage upward harmonizing of labor standards instead of NAFTA's downward approach. For the record, one of the most cynical acts of our former Prime Minister, Brian Mulroney, was to promise extensive adjustment and retraining programs for workers displaced by CUSTA, and then after the deal was implemented to endorse a report of his hand-picked Advisory Council on Adjustment that asserted that there was no way to determine which jobs disappeared as a result of the deal and no need for new programs anyhow (Diebel, 1989b; "PM Can't Violate," 1989).

9. If one thinks of family farms as relatively labor-intensive enterprises, then the antifamily farm and rural development provisions of NAFTA may also be regarded as antilabor. Examples of provisions that will undermine regional and rural development have already been given above (Nos. 5 & 6; Question 1, Nos. 1, 3, & 4; Question 3, Nos. 1, 2, 5, & 6; Question 4, Nos. 7 & 9). Examples of antifamily farm provisions include those (a) allowing the phasing out of supply management programs that have been essential for Canadian dairy, poultry, and eggs farmers; U.S. dairy, sugar, peanuts, and cotton farmers; and Mexican corn farmers (Chapter 7, Section II, Appendix A, 5-8) and (b) extending patent protection to life forms (Chapter 17), so relatively small farmers will be at greater risk in developing and purchasing seed, which will increase pressure on the continued existence of such farms. Addressing the latter issue, Beth Burrows of the Washington Biotechnology Action Council claimed that

> Life-form patents will result in farmers being denied their traditional rights to save seed [because] planting seeds without paying royalties is making an unauthorized copy of a patented product. Farmers will be forced to pay royalties for every seed and farm animal derived from patented stock, forced to become more dependent on fertilizers, pesticides, herbicides and the machinery made by the same companies who collected the traditional seeds in the first place and now sell back the chemically-dependent derivatives. (Canadian Centre for Policy Alternatives, 1992, p. 40)

The NAFTA econometric model for agriculture is based on cheap prices for farmers, partly on the assumption that cheaper prices for consumers will lead to increases in consumer spending. However, cheaper prices for consumers do not guarantee increases in consumer spending. When Canadian producers moved their operations south to enjoy the benefits of CUSTA, they left many Canadians behind without jobs and with a decreased capacity to consume anything. When relatively small farms are replaced by relatively big ones and many farmers are bankrupt, they are hardly in a position to take advantage of cheap prices. As the relatively small farms disappear, besides losing more control of Canadian food security and production, we will lose viable rural communities. Consequently, more Canadians will migrate to urban areas in search of work, which will make such areas increasingly unlivable and unsustainable. Considering only the massive increases in waste disposal requirements that will follow massive migration to our urban areas, it should be obvious that whatever undermines rural communities will eventually undermine the quality of life of all other communities.

10. Many of the arguments used to show that NAFTA subverts democracy, Canadian sovereignty, environmental protection, and conservation also show that the deal is antilabor because it subverts our capacity to design and implement an industrial strategy. For example, virtually everyone insists that we must develop secondary, high-value-added, high-wage industries based on our natural resources and that the main beneficiaries of such developments would be the people working in those industries (National Advisory Board on Science and Technology, 1991). Thus, because most of the provisions listed in the previous comment (No. 9) severely limit our capacity to develop such industries, they effectively destroy the possibility of having such beneficiaries.

11. The CUSTA (Article 2005) and NAFTA (Article 2107 & Annex 2106) provisions that allow American producers of films, records, books, tapes, and magazines ("cultural industries") to demand compensation if Canadians move to take back their own markets may also be regarded as antilabor.

I believe that someone once wrote a book citing something like 160 different definitions of culture. So one should not expect easy communication in this area. In my view, however, the word *culture* has a broad meaning, designating all those institutions, artifacts, practices, beliefs, and attitudes that give a community of people their distinctive ways of living, being, and doing. In the view of the authors of the two trade deals, the word *culture* has a narrow meaning, designating primarily artistic creations like literature, film, drama, and music.

In both deals, so-called cultural industries in the narrow sense of the term are allegedly excluded from consideration, though in fact subsidies to such industries may be attacked with countervailing duties in other industries. So even in the narrow sense of the term, culture is on the table in both deals.

At any rate, what I want to stress here is that from the point of view of a broad definition of *culture*, both deals directly threaten Canadian culture and a wide variety of jobs connected to culture. When a deal is made that affects people's jobs, businesses, incomes, social security, lifestyle, and even whole communities, the government and the Prime Minister in particular must not pretend that it is merely "a commercial deal cancellable on six months notice." Ways of making a living are also ways of living. For people living in rural communities and fishing villages, farming and fishing are commercial and cultural industries. And the same may be said for virtually all of our industries. So, insofar as the trade deals restructure our commercial industries, they will also restructure our culture. More precisely, they will remake Canada in the image of the United States, through a process that has clearly been accelerated since January 1989.

Regarding culture in the narrow sense, it must be remembered that

> 97 per cent of films shown in Canada are foreign, largely American; 96 per cent of TV drama is foreign, largely American; 90 per cent of record and tape sales are foreign, largely American; 76 per cent of books purchased in Canada are foreign, largely American; 75 per cent of magazines are foreign, largely American. That adds up to about 80 per cent total American cultural domination. (Fraser, 1991, p. A23)

The fact that only 3% of screen time in Canadian theaters is devoted to Canadian films means that nearly all of the money made in such theaters is made by foreign producers, mainly American. Under such circumstances, it is practically impossible to develop a strong film industry generating great wealth and jobs. By agreeing to the provisions of the "cultural industries" of these deals, we simply agreed to refrain from creating wealth and jobs in these industries. In effect, we capped the satisfaction of our labor needs and industrial growth potential to benefit the American industries. Interestingly enough, in NAFTA the Mexicans were guaranteed 30% of the screen time in their theaters (I-M-15). (The May 1994 issue of The Canadian Forum ["Ginn and Tonic," 1994] contains a good overview of the recent furor over what that magazine's editor, Duncan Cameron, called the Liberals's disgraceful abandonment of "the idea of building a Canadian-owned book-publishing sector.")

QUESTION 6

In October 1992, Bill Clinton made a campaign pledge to insist on "parallel agreements" that would protect the concerns of environmentalists, conservationists, and labor unions, and in August 1993 such side deals were in fact agreed to by the three governments. So, have the objections listed in response to the previous two questions (4 and 5) lost their force?

Answer

After reading careful analyses of the side deals, I believe the objections listed above have not been undermined at all by these deals. The main analyses of these deals that I have relied on were written by Stanford,

Elwell, and Sinclair (1993), Robinson (1993), and Makuch and Sinclair (1993). There is no point in reproducing these analyses, but it will be useful to present some of their overall summary comments to support my position after some additional comments of my own.

Throughout the 1993 federal election campaign, candidates from the Liberal Party promised that they would reduce or remove the harmful effects of CUSTA by renegotiating that agreement with the United States, and that they would not implement NAFTA unless the side agreements lived up to their expectations. When the current Liberal Minister of International Trade was the trade critic for the Liberals in opposition, he said,

> The best Canadians have been offered by this [Mulroney] government are bald platitudes about how free trade with Mexico naturally will lead to more jobs in Canada, better opportunities for Canadians and greater investment in Canadian industry. . . . This abiding faith in the market's invisible hand has not proved sufficient over the past three years (under the FTA [CUSTA]) and there is certainly no reason to think that it will prove any more adequate today as we face a North American free trade agreement. (Ferguson & McCarthy, 1992, p. A11)

After the Liberals won the election, the Prime Minister and the President had some discussions and Canadians were informed that the Liberal Party's promise had been kept, although nothing at all had been changed in CUSTA, NAFTA, or the side deals. Apparently "promise keeping" has a special meaning for politicians.

Regarding the renegotiation of CUSTA, opponents claimed and still do claim that NAFTA constitutes a renegotiation of CUSTA, and Canadians lost even more.

For example, one reason Liberals called for renegotiation was to revise the subsidies code of CUSTA. CUSTA recognizes only two kinds of subsidies as acceptable, namely, for oil and gas exploration and exploitation (Article 906), and for military purposes (Article 2003). In effect, CUSTA recognizes U.S.-style development, insofar as the United States uses military industry as its chief development tool. However, in CUSTA the two Parties agreed to take 7 years to work out a new subsidies code (Article 1906), but in NAFTA they agreed to abandon that commitment (Article 1907.2a; Winham, 1992). New codes might be developed through GATT, but in NAFTA we agreed to let the current U.S.-style code continue indefinitely. So, the Liberal issue of renegotiating the CUSTA subsidies code was addressed in NAFTA and settled in favor of the American position.

A second example concerns the Liberals' claim to have wanted to renegotiate to get more control over Canadian energy and other resources. Again, a renegotiation took place with NAFTA, and again we gave up still more to the Americans. As indicated above, the detailed investment chapter (Chapter 11) in NAFTA puts more limits on our ability to manage our resource development, prohibiting performance requirements, content requirements, processing requirements, export/import balancing, and so on. This chapter guarantees that there can be no managed trade in, for example, land transportation; there can be no more Auto Pacts, which has been so successful for us. So, again the Liberal issue of renegotiating the CUSTA energy provisions was addressed in NAFTA and settled in favor of the American position.

Regarding the so-called parallel agreements, to begin with, it is important to be clear about just what is intended. Prior to seeing the final text of the deals, our former Minister of Finance was the clearest proponent of side deals, and his position was that such deals would be in principle acceptable only if they were completely consistent with NAFTA. Put another way, he was willing to add things to NAFTA that were consistent with its provisions, but he was not willing to consider anything inconsistent with NAFTA. Thus, in his view, NAFTA may have some errors of omission, but there is nothing already included in the Agreement that ought to be excluded. This was also the view of the U.S. trade negotiator, Mickey Kantor (Saunders, 1993).

Obviously people who think (as I do) that NAFTA includes provisions that are antidemocratic, antilabor, and antienvironment/anticonservation could not be expected to endorse parallel agreements based on the premise that all of NAFTA's objectional provisions must be accepted precisely as they are, without any revisions or deletions. To enter into negotiations over side deals with such constraints would be either foolish or deceptive, or both. Taking the Minister at his word, opponents of NAFTA were sure that no side deals could be constructed that would satisfy his demands and ours, and still be logically coherent. In May 1993, 80 Canadian environmental groups issued a press release affirming their view that in the presence of the full force of NAFTA, parallel side deals of the sort being considered would be useless (Robinson, 1993; see also Swenarchuk, 1993b). As it turned out, the opponents were certainly right. Following the final agreements on the side deals, Robinson (1993) correctly asserted that

> The NAFTA will enhance capital mobility, reduce state regulatory capacities, and intensify the market pressures that generated the economic and social trends of the 1980s. . . . The NAFTA, with or without the side deals that have

just been completed, will carry North America further down the undesirable road it travelled in the 1980s, and at an accelerating pace. . . . In the process, the NAFTA will further dim economic development and democratic prospects in all three countries. (p. 47)

Summarizing their views on the labor side deal, Stanford et al. (1993) wrote that

> The proposed North American Agreement on Labour Cooperation (NAALC) is, as its title suggests, essentially a cooperation agreement. The NAALC does not adopt agreed basic labour rights and standards, such as those defined through the International Labour Organization (ILO) conventions. The NAALC does not define minimum standards. It merely pledges the three parties to ensure the effective enforcement of their own labour laws.
>
> Nothing in the side deal requires the parties to change their existing labour laws or standards. Each government's right to set its own standards and levels of protection as it sees fit is explicitly recognized. This is made clearest in a footnote to defining technical labour standards which states that "for greater certainty, the setting of all standards and levels in respect of minimum wages and labour protections for children and young persons by each Party shall not be subject to obligations under this Agreement." Nothing in the labour side-deal prevents governments from changing, or even lowering, existing levels of protection. (p. 56)

Just to make sure the vital point is not missed, a few pages after the comment that the "NAALC does not adopt agreed basic labour rights and standards," these authors asserted that "fundamental worker rights such as the right to organize, right to collective bargaining, freedom of association and the right to strike cannot be reviewed or disputed under the NAALC" (p. 61). If one wanted to cut the heart out of the international labor union movement, one could not find a better place to stick the knife than in just this set of worker rights. Again, compare this to the protection NAFTA gives to the rights of investors and corporate holders of intellectual property. Because the rights of the latter are protected by international treaty, they cannot be bargained away when conflicts of interest arise with labor groups. On the contrary, because the rights of working people are not protected by international treaty, they are exposed to total annihilation through relentless competition with the earth's most vulnerable unemployed and underemployed masses.

Robinson (1993) goes even farther in condemning the NAALC for being weaker than current American regulations. In particular, after explaining some of the strengths of Article 301 of the U.S. Omnibus Trade Act of 1988 (which everyone outside of the United States correctly regards as patently protectionist), he wrote that

Whatever the final story on Article 301, in exchange for giving up its GSP-related leverage [Generalized System of Preferences Act of 1986], the United States would get instruments that are significantly less powerful in four ways. First, the type of government fines found in the side-deals are less effective than trade sanctions for the purposes that a social dimension is intended to serve. . . . The fines that would be imposed under the side-deals will not fall on the corporations that actually violate the laws. Instead they will fall on national governments [i.e., tax payers].

Second, . . . American laws reference internationally recognized rights and standards that cannot be unilaterally weakened by an offending regime. By contrast, the effectiveness of the NAFTA side-deals system depends on the good will of the regimes that it is supposed to regulate.

Third, the existing U.S. law covers basic worker rights, while these are excluded from the ambit of the labour side-deals. Finally, even if the NAFTA side-deal provisions were equally resistant to evasion by authoritarian fiat, and better targeted on corporate offenders, the process by which fines are brought to bear on offenders is more cumbersome under the NAFTA.

Thus, it appears that the side deals reduce the U.S. government's capacity to use its most powerful and legitimate instrument—access to the American consumer market—for the non-violent promotion of international worker rights and labour standards. The same argument holds for Canada, of course, if it develops similar or better domestic trade law provisions. (pp. 44-45)

The Development GAP (1994) reported that 31 environmental groups from Canada, the United States, and Mexico provided the North American Commission for Environmental Cooperation (NACEC), which was established by NAFTA's side deal on the environment, with recommendations for improving its proposed structure and functions. Many of the recommendations were based on the analyses provided by Makuch and Sinclair (1993). Summarizing their views on the NACEC, they wrote that

The central mandate of the "Commission for Environmental Cooperation" is to facilitate study and cooperation on North American environmental issues. It may also review a narrow set of circumstances in which NAFTA countries fail, on a persistent basis, to enforce a small number of their environmental laws. The review process is complicated, lengthy and secretive, leaving substantial doubts as to whether it will ever serve the environment.

Detailed analysis of the text of the ESA [Environmental Side Agreement] and relevant NAFTA provisions yields the conclusion that the ESA will do nothing to mitigate or eliminate the environmental abuses of NAFTA.

If NAFTA's environmentally damaging provisions are to be corrected, then as a first step, the ESA must override these provisions. Unfortunately, it does not do so.

The dispute resolution process . . . takes place behind closed doors and permits only NAFTA Parties (not provincial governments or citizens) to participate. It is to be conducted in the absence of proper legal procedures and without adequate opportunities to collect evidence or call expert witnesses. The evidentiary requirements which must be met in order to successfully penalise a government for not enforcing its environmental laws appear to be insurmountable.

The critical environmental impacts of resource management and conservation issues have been placed outside the reach of the dispute resolution and enforcement provisions of the ESA.

This exemption sets a dismal precedent for other international environmental agreements. Natural resources are renewable only if they are properly managed. The resource exclusion embraces an untenable definition of environmental law. It is a concession to short-term commercial interests, rebuffing public concerns about unsustainable resource exploitation.

The environmental side deal will not redress NAFTA's erosion of environmental standards and resource conservation. . . . In many ways, it represents a significant step backwards. (pp. i-ii, 42-44)

If these authors are right, as I believe they are and you can judge for yourself by reading their monographs, they raise the question: Who really benefits from the side deals and at whose expense? The answer is as clear as it could possibly be: The same people who benefit from CUSTA and NAFTA, namely, transnational corporations and investors, or briefly, capital at the expense of labor and everyone else. (For similar views, see Chomsky, 1993; Cobb & Daly, 1990; Crane, 1993b.)

QUESTION 7

Proponents claimed that NAFTA is about liberalizing trade, but opponents claim the deal is fundamentally a protectionist treaty, protecting American transnational corporations and investors in Fortress North America. What is the basis for the opponents' claim?

Answer

1. The trilateral deal NAFTA is explicitly given precedence over the multilateral deal GATT (Article 103), unless there is specific notice to the contrary. That is one reason why Europeans and Asians correctly regard the deal as creating a trading bloc, Fortress North America (Day, 1993; Fagan, 1992; Terry, 1991).

Given the number of international trade treaties that have been initiated since the Second World War and the likelihood that such treaties would continue to be made, the World Bank sponsored a conference in April 1992 on the impact of such treaties on trade and related matters. According to De Melo and Panagariya (1992) participants at the conference "disagreed on whether regionalism will help or hinder multilateralism. But they agreed that this time, it is here to stay, so steps must be taken to ensure that the world does not divide up into inward-looking trading blocs" (p. 37). NAFTA seems to be a major step in the opposite direction.

It is worthwhile noting that although the GATT has been effective in lowering tariffs since 1947, there is considerable evidence that nontariff barriers (NTBs) have been erected to provide roughly similar levels of protection. According to Laird and Yeats (1989), for all developed countries,

Overall, the percentage of manufactured products affected by nontariff barriers rose from 5 percent in 1966 to 51 percent in 1986. . . . The share of developed country imports affected by NTBs nearly doubled over the 20-year period from about 25 percent in 1966 to 48 percent in 1986. (p. 13)

2. The chapters on investment (11) and intellectual property (17) give more protection to investors and transnational corporations than any other international treaty in existence. The real winners in this deal, besides the oil and gas industry, are the pharmaceutical manufacturers, biotechnologists, and computer software makers. The big losers are consumers, inventors, and the poor. The aim of these chapters is to prevent communities from controlling their own economic development in the interests of those communities.

The extra protection given by Canada's Bill C-91 to transnational pharmaceutical manufacturers provides a good case study of NAFTA's impact. The provisions of Bill C-91 were largely designed by the Pharmaceutical Manufacturers Association of Canada (PMAC) (Diebel, 1992), which represents 67 drug (mainly brand-name) manufacturers, about 18% of which are Canadian-owned. The PMAC regarded C-91 as a model for intellectual property rights and eventually hoped to have it accepted worldwide.

There was a furious battle over C-91, with the Canadian Drug Manufacturers Association (CDMA), representing 19 Canadian-owned drug (generic) manufacturers, all of the provincial health ministers except Quebec's, and probably most Canadians lined up against the Mulroney government and the PMAC.

From the opponents' point of view, the protection of intellectual property rights was not at the center of the controversy. The fundamental issues concerned and still do concern the Canadian drug producers' access to the Canadian market, the avarice of multinational drug companies, and appropriate attitudes toward medical products. I will briefly comment on each issue in turn.

Canada's Patent Act prior to 1987 already provided a full 20 years of patent protection for medicines that are actually invented and developed in Canada.

The battle over C-91 was really about how much protection Canadians should give to foreign multinational companies over products developed elsewhere and marketed here. In other words, the battle was over how long Canadian manufacturers should be prevented from access to Canadian markets. Foreign producers already control more than 90% of Canada's drug market. The effect of the 20-year rule may increase that share to 98%.

As suggested above (Question 5, No. 11), Canadian producers have a long tradition of fighting for access to their own markets, especially in the arts, films, recordings, videos, magazines, and books. Passage of C-91 may have ended the drug battle in favor of foreign multinational producers, although the current Liberal government promised to review the impact of this Bill and the CDMA are pressing the government to keep its promise.

For Third World countries, C-91 represents the sort of law that not only prevents them from access to their own markets but also virtually assures them of a continued state of relatively lower development and dependence on the more developed world. From the Third World point of view, passage of C-91 must have looked like a final closing of the ranks of the developed countries against the less developed countries.

Proponents claim that brand-name manufacturers need the additional protection that C-91 offers to carry on research and development (R & D) in a competitive market. Table 11.1 listing the average annual rate of return on equity before taxes for the drug industry compared to all other industries in the period 1972 to 1987 indicates that the drug industry is among the most profitable of all industries in Canada. In view of the numbers in this table, I think it is fair to say that the drug manufacturers' demand for increased protection indicates their insatiable greed rather than any sort of need.

The pharmaceutical industry has a long history of problems with alleged overpricing in Canada and the United States, some of which is summarized in Michalos (1980). Quite apart from the battles over the likely consequences of NAFTA, a report written for the U.S. House of Representatives Energy and Commerce Committee recently found unac-

TABLE 11.1 Rate of Return on Equity Before Taxes, 1972-1987

Year	Drug Industry %	All Industry %	Rank Among 87 Industries
1972	24.7	14.1	8
1973	24.3	19.7	17
1974	27.4	22.8	19
1975	25.0	17.8	12
1976	22.7	15.8	15
1977	21.4	14.7	16
1978	22.7	17.4	20
1979	28.3	21.9	17
1980	30.1	20.1	10
1981	31.0	17.4	6
1982	30.0	5.4	7
1983	33.9	9.9	3
1984	40.3	15.7	2
1985	41.1	12.7	3
1986	45.5	14.9	1
1987	42.2	16.2	1

SOURCE: From *Pharmaceuticals, Patents and Politics: Canada and Bill C-22* (p. 3), by J. Lexchin (1992). Ottawa: Canadian Centre for Policy Alternatives. Reprinted with permission.

ceptably high levels of profit-making in this industry (Guyatt, 1993; "U.S. Drug Firms," 1993).

The third issue concerns what one might call an appropriate attitude toward medical products. Defenders of C-91 assume that trade in pharmaceuticals is like any other commercial trade, although it is much more profitable. However, people on my side believe that just as special considerations must be given to the production of hardware for purposes of military and environmental defense, so must they be given to the production of medicines. It was precisely this belief that led to the introduction of compulsory licensing here in 1969, and to the introduction of our national hospital and health insurance programs before that.

Apart from these fundamental issues, opponents also have much less confidence than proponents do in the Patent Medicine Prices Review Board. The trouble is, first, that it is unlikely that the government will monitor prices, and so on, forever.

Second, the more our market is controlled by foreigners, the less control we have over information relevant to their operation and therefore, the less well informed we can be regarding any judgments made about those operations. As it is, 90% of the research data on new drugs that is used by government regulators comes from the industry, which cannot be regarded as an unbiased source (Taylor, 1992).

So, third, any alleged monitoring of such companies becomes more and more difficult and of dubious value.

So, fourth, in the long run the companies will have a much freer hand at determining what investments, jobs, and innovations occur where.

And finally, Canadians will become like any Third World country, dependent on the largesse and good will of such companies not only for the means to make a decent living, but for life-preserving and -enhancing medicine.

3. According to Cadsby and Woodside (1993),

> In one sense, rules of origin are always protectionist, reflecting the fact that the very notion of a free trade area is itself protectionist in discriminating against products of non-member countries. However, rules of origin may also be constructed and manipulated to maintain disguised protectionist barriers between the members of the free trade area itself.
>
> Both the FTA [CUSTA] and the NAFTA contain rules of origin which are protectionist in one or both of these ways. (pp. 451-452)

Referring to the yarn-forward rule of origin mentioned above (Question 5, No. 7), Cadsby and Woodside (1993) claim that "It is a very stringent and highly protectionist requirement. In practical terms, it also discriminates against the Canadian apparel industry" (p. 454).

4. The Structural Adjustment Policies of the World Bank are designed into NAFTA, so that adherence to those policies is a necessary condition of admission to Fortress North America. Giving additional protection to transnational patent holders, insisting on shifting from sustainable agriculture or manufacturing to cash cropping and other export-oriented production, reducing real wages, and government services are all good means of protecting banker's loans above everything else. Thus, the Canadian Centre for Policy Alternatives (1992) claimed that, combined with President George Bush's Enterprise for the Americas Initiative, NAFTA's "true agenda" was clear, namely, "the recolonization of Latin America as a source of cheap labour, raw materials and markets for U.S. corporations. The implicit threat is that if countries do not accept all [the SAP] conditions they will be frozen out of the U.S. market" (pp. 98-101).

5. Strong patent protection prevents dissemination of technology and more rapid development of Third World countries. Eliminating compulsory licensing prevents countries from insisting that patented

products be marketed in the interests of community development (Ecumenical Coalition for Economic Justice, 1992).

6. Finally, by protecting transnational corporations from special taxes and community development while allowing them to have market shares, NAFTA allows these corporations to take a free ride on indigenous people's needs to develop their own regions. As indicated above, CUSTA and NAFTA effectively eliminate the possibility of having Crown corporations established for the sole purpose of serving the public interest above any private interests. In this sense, the treaties protect private power and interests against any incompatible public interest.

REFERENCES

Action Canada Network. (1991). Fortress North America. *Action Dossier, 29*, pp. 1-43.
Action Canada Network. (1993). Setting a people's agenda. *Action Dossier, 39*, pp. 1-60.
Arregui, E. V. (1993). Industrial restructuring in Mexico during the 1980s. In R. Grinspun & M. A. Cameron (Eds.), *The political economy of North American free trade* (pp. 163-175). Montreal: McGill-Queen's University Press.
Audley, J., et al. (1992). *U.S. citizen's analysis of the North American Free Trade Agreement.* Washington, DC: The Development GAP.
Bank of Canada. (1994). *Bank of Canada review.* Ottawa: Author.
Barlow, M. (1991, October 25). Mexicans will pay the price. *Globe and Mail*, p. A21.
Barlow, M., & Campbell, B. (1991). *Take back the nation.* Toronto: Key Porter.
Bejar, A. A. (1994). Zapatistas rock a leaky boat. *Canadian Dimension, 28*, 11-12.
Bertin, O. (1992, September 3). U.S. antes $1-billion in trade war with EC. *Globe and Mail*, pp. B1, B2.
Bienefeld, M. (1992). Financial deregulation: Disarming the nation state. *Studies in Political Economy, 37*, 31-58.
Cadsby, C. B., & Woodside, K. (1993). The effects of the North American Free Trade Agreement on the Canada-United States trade relationship. *Canadian Public Policy, 19*, 450-462.
Campbell, B. (1992). *A critique of "The Global Trade Challenge," A Tory trade tabloid.* Ottawa: Canadian Centre for Policy Alternatives.
Canada Department of External Affairs. (1987). *The Canada-U.S. free trade agreement* (CUSTA). Canada: Author.
Canadian Centre for Policy Alternatives. (1992). *Which way for the Americas: Analysis of NAFTA proposals and the impact on Canada.* Ottawa: Author.
Canadian Environmental Law Association. (Ed.). (1993). *The environmental implications of trade agreements.* Toronto: Queen's Printer for Ontario.
Census and Statistics Office. (1906). *The Canada year book 1905.* Ottawa: Author.
Chomsky, N. (1993, April 13). A new deal for the new imperial age. *Toronto Star*, p. A15.
Cobb, J. B., & Daly, H. E. (1990). Free trade versus community: Social and environmental consequences of free trade in a world with capital mobility and overpopulated

regions. *Population and Environment: A Journal of Interdisciplinary Studies*, *11*, 175-191.

Cornwall, J. (1990). *The theory of economic breakdown: An institutional-analytical approach*. Cambridge, UK: Basil Blackwell.

Council of Canadians. (1994, Winter). A citizens' agenda for Canada. *Canadian Perspectives*, pp. 1-23.

Crane, D. (1993a, January 18). Selling Canada bit by bit. *Toronto Star*, p. A13.

Crane, D. (1993b, March 20). Punishing Mexican shortcomings only slows down modernization. *Toronto Star*, p. D2.

Crosbie, J. C. (1988, June 17). There will be no sell-out of our water. *Toronto Star*, p. A22.

Davis, B. (1992, July 25). Protectionist air shrouds pending pact. *Globe and Mail*, pp. B1, B12.

Day, M. (1993, March 22). Why Asia is casting a wary eye at NAFTA. *Globe and Mail*, p. A13.

De Melo, J., & Panagariya, A. (1992). The new regionalism. *Finance and Development*, *29*, 37-40.

The Development GAP. (1993). Tri-national consultation on the North American free trade agreement, January 15-17, 1993, Mexico City, D.F., Mexico. *Naftathoughts*, *3*, 1, 3-5.

The Development GAP. (1994). Campaign launched on World Bank, IMF. *Naftathoughts*, *4*, 6-8.

Diebel, L. (1989a, March 29). Panel rejects special help for jobs lost over free trade. *Toronto Star*, p. A3.

Diebel, L. (1989b, April 2). Mexico's cheaper labor paying off big for bosses. *Toronto Star*, p. B6.

Diebel, L. (1992, December 6). How U.S. drug lobby put new patent law atop Canada's agenda. *Toronto Star*, pp. A1, A7.

Diebel, L. (1993, March 17). "Courageous" Mexicans dying over trade pact Barrett says. *Toronto Star*, p. A10.

Dillon, J. (1988). A continental energy policy. *Facts*, *10*, 47-50.

Dillon, J. (1994). Monopolizing money. *Canadian Forum*, *73*, 8-12.

Dooley, R. (1993, March 4). NAFTA is no big deal for farmers in Mexico. *Guelph Mercury*, p. A5.

Ecumenical Coalition for Economic Justice. (1990). *Recolonization or liberation: The bonds of structural adjustment and struggles for emancipation*. Toronto: Author.

Ecumenical Coalition for Economic Justice. (1991a). Ethical reflections on North American economic integration. *Economic Justice Report*, *2*(3), 1-16.

Ecumenical Coalition for Economic Justice. (1991b). Free trade will not help Mexico's poor. *Economic Justice Report*, *2*(2), 1-4.

Ecumenical Coalition for Economic Justice. (1992). NAFTA: A new economic constitution for North America. *Economic Justice Report*, *3*(3), 1-5.

Ecumenical Coalition for Economic Justice. (1993). 51 alternatives to NAFTA. *Economic Justice Report*, *4*(1), 1-12.

Eggertson, L. (1992, March 26). Canada, U.S. agree on Honda content issue. *Globe and Mail*, p. B6.

Fagan, D. (1992, June 10). Japanese assert NAFTA pact will violate GATT. *Globe and Mail*, p. B10.

Ferguson, D., & McCarthy, S. (1992, March 24). Premiers tackling PM on free trade. *Toronto Star*, pp. A1, A11.

Ferguson, J. (1991, August 19). Trade envoy slams NDP insurance plan. *Toronto Star*, p. A1.

Ferguson, J. (1993, February 19). Free trade agreement hailed as exports surge. *Toronto Star*, pp. A1, A30.

Fraser, S. (1991, November 28). No more Rambo-ization. *Toronto Star*, p. A23.

Gamble, D. J. (1988, August). *Water exports and free trade: A summary analysis with a critique.* Paper presented to the Canadian Bar Association National Convention, Montreal.

Ginn and tonic: A symposium on the sale of Ginn Publishing. (1994, May). *Canadian Forum*, pp. 12-20.

Godfrey, S. (1992, March 28). Behind the big screen. *Globe and Mail*, pp. A1, A6.

Gorrie, P. (1990, April 4). U.S. zones offer a break to Canadian firms. *Toronto Star*, p. E3.

Government of Ontario, Cabinet Committee on the North American Free Trade Agreement. (1993). *Final report.* Toronto: Queen's Printer for Ontario.

Greider, W. (1987). *Secrets of the temple: How the Federal Reserve runs the country.* New York: Simon & Schuster.

Grinspun, R., & Kreklewich, R. (1994). Consolidating neoliberal reforms: "Free trade" as a conditioning framework. *Studies in Political Economy, 43,* 33-62.

Guttmann, R. (Ed.). (1989). *Reforming money and finance: Institutions and markets in flux.* Armonk, NY: M. E. Sharpe.

Guyatt, G. (1993, January 14). Higher costs for health care, higher profit for industry. *Globe and Mail*, p. A19.

Harper, T. (1991, April 14). Salinas's free trade trip wasn't all smooth sailing. *Toronto Star*, p. B4.

Healy, T. (1994). The land belongs to those who work it. *Canadian Dimension, 28,* 5-7.

Hildyard, N. (1993). Maastricht: The protectionism of free trade. *Ecologist, 23,* 45-51.

Holm, W. (1988). *Water and free trade: The Mulroney government's agenda for Canada's most precious resource.* Toronto: James Lorimer.

Hossie, L. (1993, March 12). NAFTA will fuel Mexican ills, study says. *Globe and Mail*, p. A11.

Hurtig, M. (1991). *The betrayal of Canada.* Toronto: Stoddart.

Jackson, A. (1993). NAFTA and the myth of a win-win. *Policy Options, 13,* 24-28.

Kalter, E., & Khor, H. E. (1990). Mexico's experience with adjustment. *Finance and Development, 27,* 22-25.

Kopinak, K. (1993). The maquiladorization of the Mexican economy. In R. Grinspun & M. A. Cameron (Eds.), *The political economy of North American free trade* (pp. 141-161). Montreal: McGill-Queen's University Press.

Kottman, R. N. (1968). *Reciprocity and the North Atlantic triangle 1932-1938.* Ithaca, NY: Cornell University Press.

Kuznetsov, A. (1991). Free economic zones. *Social Sciences Quarterly Review, 22,* 123-137.

Laird, S., & Yeats, A. (1989). Nontariff barriers of developed countries, 1966-86. *Finance and Development, 26,* 12-13.

Lexchin, J. (1992). *Pharmaceuticals, patents and politics: Canada and Bill C-22.* Ottawa: Canadian Centre for Policy Alternatives.

Makuch, Z., & Sinclair, S. (1993). *The environmental implications of the NAFTA environmental side agreement.* Toronto: Canadian Environmental Law Association.

Masters, D. C. (1963). *The reciprocity treaty of 1854.* Toronto: McClelland & Stewart.

McConnell, C. R., Brue, S. L., & Pope, W. H. (1990). *Economics: Principles, problems and policies* (5th Canadian ed.). Toronto: McGraw-Hill Ryerson.

McKenna, B. (1992, August 13). Deal fails to fit clothing firms. *Globe and Mail*, p. B6.

McQuaig, L. (1993). *The wealthy banker's wife: The assault on equality in Canada.* Toronto: Penguin.

Michalos, A. C. (1980). *North American social report: A comparative study of the quality of life in Canada and the USA from 1964 to 1974: Vol. 1. Foundations, population and health.* Dordrecht, the Netherlands: D. Reidel.

Milner, B. (1993, June 12). Japanese PM rejects demand for managed trade. *Globe and Mail,* p. B1.

Morley, D. (1992, August 24). More hard times for Mexico's poor? *Globe and Mail,* p. A21.

Mosley, H. (1990). The social dimension of European integration. *International Labour Review, 129,* 153-154.

National Action Committee on the Status of Women (NAC). (1993). *NAC brief to the Sub-Committee on International Trade.* Toronto: Author.

National Advisory Board on Science and Technology. (1991). *Science and technology, innovation and national prosperity: The need for Canada to change course.* Ottawa: Committee on National Science and Technology Priorities.

Nelson, J. (1994). The Zapatistas versus the spin-doctors. *Canadian Forum, 72,* 18-25.

New Democratic Party. (1992). *Notes on NAFTA.* Ottawa: Author.

New Democratic Party. (1993). *Strategy for a full-employment economy.* Ottawa: Author.

North American free trade agreement: Draft legal text (Parts I & II). (1992, September 8).

Orr, J. L. (1992, July/August). Canada's free trade dilemma: Renegotiate or abrogate? *New Federation, 3,* 33-37.

PM can't violate pledge to workers. (1989, March 30). *Toronto Star,* p. A26.

Pritchard, T. (1992, March 9). Honda's Ohio plant "kicked in the butt." *Globe and Mail,* p. B1.

Rae, B. (1993). [A major NAFTA speech by Premier Bob Rae, March 17, Hamilton, Ontario.]

Robinson, I. (1993). *North American trade as if democracy mattered.* Ottawa: Canadian Centre for Policy Alternatives.

Roman, R. (1994). The Mexican rebellion and NAFTA. *Peace Magazine, 10*(2), 12-14.

Rumsey, S. (1994). Chiapas journal. *Canadian Forum, 72,* 26-27.

Sanger, M. (1992). *Free trade and workers' rights: The European Social Charter.* Ottawa: Canadian Centre for Policy Alternatives.

Saunders, J. (1992a, March 3). Customs, Honda collide over duties. *Globe and Mail,* p. A1.

Saunders, J. (1992b, March 4). Japan takes backseat in dispute. *Globe and Mail,* p. B1.

Saunders, J. (1992c, March 14). Honda decision leaves bureaucracy buffs guessing. *Globe and Mail,* p. B1.

Saunders, J. (1993, March 12). U.S. politicians warn NAFTA in danger. *Globe and Mail,* pp. B1, B4.

Sinclair, S. (1993). The use of U.S. trade remedy laws: Case study of the softwood lumber disputes. In Canadian Environmental Law Association (Ed.), *The environmental implications of trade agreements* (pp. 195-221). Toronto: Queen's Printer for Ontario.

Stanford, J. (1991). *Going south: Cheap labour as an unfair subsidy in North American free trade.* Ottawa: Canadian Centre for Policy Alternatives.

Stanford, J. (1992, April). *C.G.E. models of North American free trade: A critique of methods and assumptions.* Testimony to the United States International Trade Commission Public Hearing on Economy-Wide Modelling of the Economic Implications of Free Trade, Investigation No. 332-317.

Stanford, J. (1993). Continental economic integration: Modelling the impact on labor. *Annals of the American Academy of Political and Social Science, 526,* 92-110.

Stanford, J., Elwell, C., & Sinclair, S. (1993). *Social dumping under North American free trade.* Ottawa: Canadian Centre for Policy Alternatives.

Statistics Canada. (1972). *Canada year book.* Ottawa: Minister of Supply and Services.

Statistics Canada. (1991). *Canada's balance of international payments* (Cat. #76-001) March. Ottawa: Minister of Supply and Services.

Statistics Canada. (1994, March). *Canada's balance of international payments* (Cat. #76-001). Ottawa: Minister of Supply and Services.

Swenarchuk, M. (1993a). The environmental implications of NAFTA: A legal analysis. In Canadian Environmental Law Commission (Ed.), *The environmental implications of trade agreements* (pp. 101-131). Toronto: Queen's Printer for Ontario.

Swenarchuk, M. (1993b). The environment and international trade agreements: An overview. In Canadian Environmental Law Commission (Ed.), *The environmental implications of trade agreements* (pp. 64-100). Toronto: Queen's Printer for Ontario.

Taylor, P. (1992, January 21). Drug approval process flawed, regulators say. *Globe and Mail*, pp. A1, A2.

Taylor del Cid, A. (1994). Race hatred and class warfare in Mexico's south. *Canadian Dimension, 28*, 8-10.

Terry, E. (1991, December 24). Stakes are high in battle to shape Asian bloc. *Globe and Mail*, p. B9.

Thurow, L. (1992). *Head to head: The coming economic battle among Japan, Europe, and America.* New York: William Morrow.

United Nations. (1988). *Transnational corporations and world development.* New York: Author.

Urquhart, M. C., & Buckley, K. A. H. (1965). *Historical statistics of Canada.* Cambridge, UK: Cambridge University Press.

U.S. drug firms' profits under fire. (1993, February 26). *Toronto Star*, p. D4.

Use caution in weighing "enterprise zone" ideas. (1992, May 15). *USA Today*, p. 8A.

Warnock, J. W. (1993, August). Mexico—Michoacan struggles for democracy. *Canadian Dimension*, pp. 33-35.

Watkins, M. (1993). An alternative trade and development model for Canada. In R. Grinspun & M. A. Cameron (Eds.), *The political economy of North American free trade* (pp. 125-137). Montreal: McGill-Queen's University Press.

White, R. (1992, February 11). *Notes for an address on the Canadian auto industry: Time for action.* Speech given to the Financial Post Conference, Toronto Hilton Hotel, pp. 1-33.

Wilson, M. (1992, January 9). Free trade: Looking at the bright side. *Globe and Mail*, p. A15.

Winham, G. R. (1992). Dispute settlement (Chapter 19) in the Canada-U.S. Free Trade Agreement (FTA) and the North American Free Trade Agreement (NAFTA). Testimony before the Sub-Committee on International Trade, Canadian House of Commons, Chateau Halifax, Halifax, Nova Scotia, December 7, 1992.

World Commission on Environment and Development. (1987). *Our common future.* Oxford, UK: Oxford University Press.

Zinser, A. A. (1993). Authoritarianism and North American free trade: The debate in Mexico. In R. Grinspun & M. A. Cameron (Eds.), *The political economy of North American free trade* (pp. 205-216). Montreal: McGill-Queen's University Press.

12

Militarism and the Quality of Life

In 1978, the United Nations General Assembly endorsed the Final Document of the first Special Session on Disarmament calling for the commission of a group of governmental experts to examine the relationships between disarmament and development. Twenty-seven experts were selected from every continent, with Inga Thorsson designated as Chairperson. The group's official report was submitted to the U.N. Secretary-General in October 1981. The report included nine recommendations, and this chapter is a relatively limited attempt to respond to the following two:

> The Group recommends that all governments, but particularly those of the major military powers, should prepare assessments of the nature and magnitude of the short- and long-term economic and social costs attributable to their military preparations, so that the general public can be informed of them.

> The Group recommends that governments urgently undertake studies to identify and to publicise the benefits that would be derived from the reallocation of military resources in a balanced and verifiable manner, to address economic and social problems at the national level, and to contribute towards reducing the gap in income that currently divides the industrialised nations from the developing world and establishing a new international economic order. (Sanger, 1982, p. 107)

AUTHOR'S NOTE: Adapted from *Militarism and the Quality of Life* by A. C. Michalos (1989). Toronto: Science for Peace/Samuel Stevens. Used with permission of the publisher.

In the first section I present an overview of some social indicators for Canada and the United States covering the years from about 1963 to 1983. Following this, in the second section I review Canadian federal government expenditures in general for the period from 1974 to 1986. The third section summarizes available information on the Canadian arms industry, including production and export figures. In the fourth section I present 15 arguments against the Canadian production and export of military arms broadly construed. After that, in the fifth section, I consider 16 arguments in favor of the production and export of arms and offer critical replies to each of them. Insofar as my arguments are sound, a case should have been made for resisting the current federal government's proposed increases in the production and export of arms, and for beginning to scale down current militaristic activities.

AN OVERVIEW FOR CANADA AND
THE UNITED STATES OF AMERICA

Some of the groundwork for the present investigation was prepared in my *North American Social Report* (Michalos, 1980a, 1980b, 1981a, 1981b, 1982). In that work I compared the quality of life of Canadians and Americans in the period 1964 to 1974 in the areas of population structure; mortality, morbidity, and health care; criminal justice; politics; science and technology; education; recreation; natural environment and resources; transportation; communication; housing; economics; religion; and morality and social customs. Broadly speaking, three conclusions were reached. First: "On the basis of an examination of over 135 social indicators and over 1659 indicator values, it seems fair to say that the quality of life in the 1964-74 period was comparatively or relatively higher in Canada than in the United States." Second: "If one looks at the first and last recorded stock values for the usable indicators for each country independently of the other country, [one finds that] . . . both countries improved in more ways than they deteriorated." Third, considering the responses of national probability samples of Canadians and Americans to more than 117 Gallup Poll questions: "The countries were more similar in the 1963-8 period than in the 1969-75 period." In short: "Taking the results of my analyses of nonindependent paths [social indicator trends] and opinion poll responses together, it seems fair to say that the countries tended to be or become dissimilar in more ways than they tended to be or become similar" (Michalos, 1982, pp. 171-174). Regarding the specific item of military expenditures, "In

TABLE 12.1 Ranking Canada and the United States Among 142 Countries on Military and Social Indicators, 1984

Indicator	Canada	United States
Military:		
Expenditures per capita (–)	22	8
Expenditures per soldier (–)	6	4
Expenditures per square km (–)	89	24
Average social economic standing (+)	3	4
GNP per capita (+)	10	6
Education:		
Public expenditures per capita (+)	3	7
School-age population per teacher (+)	7	20
Percentage school-age population in school (+)	3	6
Percentage women in university enrollment (+)	13	16
Literacy rate (+)	5	5
Health:		
Public expenditures per capita (+)	6	8
Population per physician (–)	24	22
Infant mortality rate (–)	9	18
Life expectancy (+)	4	8
Nutrition:		
Calorie supply per capita (+)	17	5
Calories as percent of requirements (+)	26	10
Percentage of population having safe water (+)	1	1
Number of preferable rankings*		
Negative	4	1
Positive	5	3
Total	9	4

SOURCE: Reproduced, with permission, from *World Military and Social Expenditures 1987* (pp. 46-47), by R. L. Sivard (1987). Copyright © 1987 by World Priorities, Inc., Washington, DC. [Sivard's text gives specific definitions of indicators and their sources.]
NOTE: * Excluding the indicator for average socioeconomic standing, and two indicators with tie scores.

the 1965-74 period American military expenditures as a percent of GNP were always two to four times higher than their Canadian counterparts. . . . In the final year the American figure stood at 6% of the GNP, compared to 2% for Canada" (Michalos, 1980b, p. 176).

Although I planned to update all my numbers to 1984 and later, other projects always got in the way. However, Table 12.1 summarizes the results of comparing the rank-order values of Canada and the United States among 142 countries on 13 indicators for 1984, based on Sivard (1987) [Plus signs (+) in Table 12.1 designate positive indicators and minus signs (–) designate negative indicators].

Canada's rank-orders were preferable to those of the United States on 9 of the 13 indicators. According to Sivard's aggregation procedures,

TABLE 12.2 Federal Government and Defense Expenditures (current millions)

Year Ended March 31	—Expenditures—		Column 2/1 (%)
	1 Total	2 Defense	
1974	22,839	2,232	9.8
1975	29,245	2,512	8.6
1976	33,978	2,974	8.8
1977	39,011	3,371	8.6
1978	42,882	3,771	8.8
1979	46,539	4,108	8.8
1980	50,416	4,391	8.7
1981	58,066	5,077	8.7
1982	67,674	6,028	8.9
1983	88,521	6,938	7.8
1984	96,610	7,843	8.1
1985	109,215	8,762	8.0
1986	111,227	9,094	8.2
1987	116,389	9,993	9.0
1988	125,535	10,769	9.0

SOURCES: From Government of Canada, Minister of Finance (1978, 1982, 1986, 1988).

Canada was better off than the United States in "socioeconomic stand-ing" generally and in military expenditures. These are the most recent figures available, and I suppose the assessments would not have changed much by today. Assuming that government expenditures for social and economic purposes contribute more to a good quality of life than government expenditures for military purposes, the numbers in Table 12.1 suggest that Canadians have been able to make a more favorable trade-off on this score than Americans.

CANADIAN FEDERAL GOVERNMENT EXPENDITURES

Table 12.2 lists the Canadian federal government's total and defense expenditures for the period 1974 to 1988 in millions of current Canadian dollars.

In the final year, defense expenditures were estimated to be nearly $11 billion or 9% of total government expenditures. There has been a steady increase in defense expenditures as a percentage of total expen-ditures since the 1984 federal election of a Progressive Conservative government. The 1987 figure is a bit above the 15-year average of 8.7%. However, according to the Tories' White Paper on defense policy,

Challenge and Commitment: A Defence Policy for Canada (Canada, Department of National Defence, 1987): "The Government is committed to a base rate of annual real growth in the defence budget of two per cent per year after inflation, for the [coming] fifteen-year planning period" (p. 67). At the same time: "After 1986-7, the budget states that operating costs in all federal departments will not be permitted to rise by more than 2 percent in nominal terms each year, which, after inflation, is a real cut of 2 percent" (Prince, 1986, p. 39). If the defense budget does increase at the projected rate, then in 10 years it will be about 10.5% of total federal government expenditures, which would be roughly its 1972 rate. Putting the 2% real growth rate for defense spending together with the 2% real cut rate for all other federal departments, by 1998 the defense budget would be about 12.5% of the total, or roughly what it was in 1970 (Treddenick, 1984).

Table 12.3 puts defense shares of the total federal government expenditures in the context of the shares of 16 other functional areas and a residual "others."

Because Statistics Canada's accounting procedures are not exactly the same as those of the federal government, there is roughly a percentage point difference between the figures published by the two agencies. On average, for example, the defense share according to Statistics Canada was about 7.6% rather than 8.7%. The Statistics Canada figures are preferable for present purposes because the 16 functional areas are more detailed and easier to identify than their counterparts in successive federal budgets.

Inspection of the figures in Table 12.3 shows that the defense share of the total expenditures is typically greater than 13 of the 16 substantive functional areas. Only Old Age Security payments, Unemployment Insurance payments, and national debt charges tend to take bigger slices of the total pie. While the shares of Old Age Security and Unemployment Insurance payments typically run from 1 to 3 percentage points above the defense share, the national debt share tends to run about twice as high as that of defense. At a minimum what these figures suggest is that Canada's defense expenditures constitute a significant share of the total federal government expenditures and raise provocative questions regarding the actual versus a more desirable distribution. Because most of this chapter consists of specific arguments for less spending on the production and export of military arms broadly construed and of replies to arguments for more spending on such things, much more will be said about diverse trade-offs as our discussion proceeds.

TABLE 12.3 Federal Government Expenditures by Function (in percentages)

Year Ended March 31	1	2	3	4	5	6	7	8	9
1974	8.8	5.7	7.3	8.0	1.1	12.5	8.9	4.1	3.4
1975	7.4	5.5	7.1	7.4	1.3	11.1	8.1	5.9	3.1
1976	7.2	5.1	6.7	7.5	1.6	10.7	9.0	5.3	4.0
1977	7.8	5.6	6.7	8.0	2.0	10.5	8.9	4.8	4.7
1978	7.9	5.6	6.4	6.8	2.3	10.6	9.5	4.6	4.0
1979	8.1	5.5	6.5	7.6	2.6	10.1	9.3	4.1	3.9
1980	7.7	5.1	5.7	7.3	2.9	11.1	7.2	3.0	3.4
1981	7.3	5.1	6.3	6.5	3.1	10.9	7.0	2.7	3.3
1982	7.4	5.1	5.2	6.0	3.2	10.8	7.0	2.6	3.3
1983	7.2	4.7	3.0	5.0	3.3	10.4	10.8	2.4	3.5
1984	7.6	4.8	3.1	6.1	3.6	10.2	9.9	2.3	4.1
1985	7.5	4.7	3.3	6.3	3.8	10.0	9.1	2.1	4.0
1986	7.4	4.8	3.0	6.1	4.2	10.7	8.9	2.2	3.9

Column Codes

1 National Defense
2 General
3 Transport and Communication
4 Health
5 Canada Pension Plan

6 Old Age Security
7 Unemployment Insurance
8 Family Allowance
9 Assistance to Disabled

Year Ended March 31	10	11	12	13	14	15	16	17	18
1974	3.8	1.0	0.6	1.8	1.2	7.8	1.5	7.1	15.4
1975	3.3	0.9	0.7	1.9	1.1	8.7	1.6	7.4	17.5
1976	3.2	0.8	0.9	2.0	1.4	7.3	1.4	7.7	18.2
1977	3.3	0.7	1.2	1.9	1.0	8.3	1.4	7.1	16.1
1978	4.2	0.7	1.1	2.4	1.6	7.6	1.5	7.7	15.5
1979	4.4	0.8	1.3	1.9	1.4	6.7	1.5	9.3	15.0
1980	4.2	0.6	1.4	1.8	1.6	7.2	1.7	10.1	18.0
1981	3.7	0.5	1.5	1.6	1.6	6.5	2.1	10.8	19.5
1982	3.4	0.4	1.4	1.6	1.4	6.7	1.9	14.2	18.4
1983	3.1	0.5	1.9	1.7	1.2	6.7	3.1	13.3	18.2
1984	3.5	0.5	1.6	1.7	1.2	6.4	3.1	12.9	17.4
1985	3.4	0.4	1.8	1.8	1.0	6.0	2.5	14.7	17.7
1986	3.4	0.4	1.3	1.8	0.9	5.8	2.8	17.0	15.4

Column Codes

10 Education
11 Environment
12 Housing
13 Foreign Aid and Affairs
14 Research Establishments

15 Transfers to Other Levels of Government
16 Transfers to Its Own Enterprises
17 Debt Charges
18 All Other Expenditures

SOURCES: From Statistics Canada (1976, pp. 44-45); (1979, pp. 40-41); (1982, pp. 40-41); (1985, pp. 41-42).

THE CANADIAN ARMS INDUSTRY

Because there is no generally accepted definition of *military arms* broadly or narrowly construed, there is bound to be some controversy about any alleged measured level of production or export of such things. The estimates given here are taken mainly from Treddenick (1987) and Regehr (1987). According to Treddenick (1987), "the defence industrial base is that part of the nation's economy providing goods and services required to support military activities" (p. 24). Granting that the definition is very broad, it becomes more useful when it is operationalized by identifying "the defence industrial base in terms of current demands placed on Canadian industry resulting from expenditures for domestic defence procurement and for exports." The latter account comes very close to Regehr's (1987) when he writes: "For purposes of implementing control measures, the Canadian government should define a military commodity as a commodity purchased by a military force or agency" (p. 212). Presumably, both authors would exclude some items like food and housing supplies, and both would include not only weapons but "the support facilities and equipment that make weapons usable" (Regehr, 1987, p. 70; Treddenick, 1986, pp. 35-36). Treddenick specifies a "narrow industrial base" within the broader sector, which includes "industries producing specialized military equipment." Operationally, the narrow industrial base includes manufacturers of aircraft and parts, motor vehicles, shipbuilding, communications equipment, and some chemicals insofar as the products are sold to military agencies. Applying these rough definitions and some appropriate caveats, he reaches the following conclusions:

> If economic significance means the amount of economic activity generated in the defence industries, then by comparison to total economic activity in Canada, the defence industrial base must be judged to be insignificant. Total defence production accounts for considerably less than one per cent of both gross domestic product and total employment. When the narrow defence industrial base alone is considered, these contributions fall to about one-third of a percentage point in each case. Defence production is also not significant in any single provincial economy. Only in Nova Scotia and New Brunswick does employment generated by defence production approximate one per cent of total provincial employment, in most provinces it is considerably less. Defence production must also be considered insignificant in terms of international trade. Defence exports, net of re-exports, currently account for less than one per cent of total merchandise exports while defence imports, including indirect imports, account for just over two per cent of total merchandise imports. Finally, because of its comparatively low level and because it is

TABLE 12.4 Canadian Military Exports 1959-1986 (current millions; percentages are in parentheses)

	Destination			
Years	United States	Europe	Other	Total
1959-1969	2,419 (79)	440 (14)	207 (7)	3,066
1970	227 (67)	41 (12)	69 (20)	337
1971	216 (64)	67 (20)	53 (16)	336
1972	175 (58)	74 (24)	52 (17)	300
1973	199 (64)	73 (23)	38 (12)	309
1974	150 (54)	46 (16)	85 (30)	281
1975	189 (67)	59 (21)	34 (12)	282
1976	191 (57)	113 (34)	32 (9)	336
1977	314 (57)	76 (14)	164 (30)	554
1978	267 (55)	130 (27)	88 (18)	485
1979	368 (65)	146 (26)	55 (10)	568
1980	482 (67)	142 (20)	98 (14)	722
1981	827 (72)	149 (13)	175 (15)	1,151
1982	1,028 (72)	158 (11)	248 (17)	1,434
1983	1,207 (81)	129 (9)	145 (10)	1,481
1984	1,361 (78)	243 (14)	150 (8)	1,754
1985	1,644 (86)	154 (8)	105 (5)	1,903
1986	947 (68)	196 (14)	245 (18)	1,388
Total	12,211 (73)	2,436 (15)	2,043 (12)	16,687

SOURCES: From *Arms Canada* (p. 17), by E. Regehr (1987). Toronto: James Lorimer and Company Limited; "Canadian Military Industry Update," by K. Epps (1987a), *The Ploughshares Monitor, 8*, p. 12. Reprinted with permission of James Lorimer and Company Limited and Project Ploughshares.

difficult to make a theoretical case for its transferability to the civilian sector, defence research and development must also be considered insignificant relative to overall economic activity. . . . The relatively small size of the Canadian defence industrial base makes it extremely difficult to see it as the mainstay of the capitalist system in Canada, in either the Marxian or the Galbraithian sense. (Treddenick, 1987, pp. 50-51)

Table 12.4 and Figure 12.1 provide a longer and more detailed view of Canadian military exports since 1959. The bottom line of Table 12.4 shows that about 73% of our exports have gone to the United States, 14.6% to Europe, and 12% to other places, mainly in the Third World.

Although we have just seen that Treddenick would be one of the last people to exaggerate the economic significance of the Canadian arms industry, he remarks that, "Not only have total exports consistently exceeded domestic demand by large amounts, but exports to the United States alone have done so. . . . This export dependence of the defence industries, and particularly the dependence on a single country, is the outstanding economic feature of the Canadian defence industrial base" (Treddenick, 1987, p. 31).

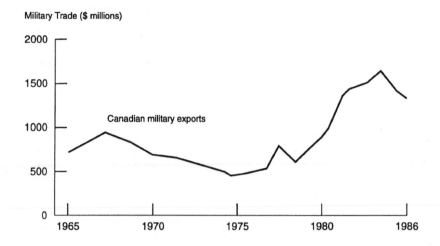

Figure 12.1. Canadian Military Exports in Current Dollars

SOURCES: From *Arms Canada* (p. 18), by E. Regehr (1987). Toronto: James Lorimer and Company Limited; "Canadian Military Industry Update," by K. Epps (1987a), *The Ploughshares Monitor, 8*, p. 12. Reprinted with permission of James Lorimer and Company Limited and Project Ploughshares.

ARGUMENTS AGAINST PRODUCING AND EXPORTING ARMS

The following arguments may be offered by Canadians against the production and export of military arms broadly construed.

1. Any resources that are used for the production and export of arms cannot be used for the production and export of such necessities as food, water, clothing, shelter, medical care, and education. Because the latter are more life sustaining than the former, they should not be traded for the former (Regehr, 1987; Wallace-Deering, 1986).

Addressing the issue of the relation between the international arms race and the underdevelopment of much of the world, Miller (1986) wrote,

> By massive increases in his military budget, [President Ronald Reagan] has driven up American deficits and with them real interest rates, thereby adding to the debt-servicing burden of the developing world. With Third World debts now approximating $900 billion, any increase in interest rates adds billions of dollars to these debts. In addition, high interest rates drain capital from the nations of the developing world at a time when they desperately need it for their own development plans. And so, ironically, those nations which can least afford it find themselves helping to finance the American military build-up. (p. 126)

Sanger (1982) noted that developing countries

are doubly vulnerable. They suffer when the effect of military spending in the industrialised countries aggravates the economic problems in the developed world, because they can then expect a slower flow of development aid, investment capital and technological know-how, as well as less quickly expanding markets for their exports. . . . And the developing countries suffer also when their own military expenditures affect plans for their economic and social expansion. (p. 46)

Additional corroborative details regarding the relation between the arms race and underdevelopment may be found in the Thorsson Report (United Nations, Expert Group, 1981); United Nations, Panel (1986); Perry (1986); Sivard (1986); and Gumbleton (1986).

2. Even if one ignores issues related to the export of arms, any resources that are used for the production of arms to be deployed by Canadian forces cannot be used for such necessities as food, clothing, shelter, medical care, education, and other social services. According to Werlin (1986), since the Mulroney government came to office in 1984,

Transfer payments from Ottawa to the provinces for health care and education have been reduced, unemployment insurance benefits have been cut back, public housing subsidies, environmental protection programs, and support for cultural activities (most importantly the Canadian Broadcasting Corporation) have all been reduced. Increases in the defence budget [averaging 6% a year for the rest of the decade] have quite simply been made by reducing the budget for public services. (pp. 96-97)

Thus, in the interest of promoting life-sustaining programs and expenditures, increases in the production of arms should at least be kept below increases in other government programs and expenditures.

3. The availability of arms increases the inclination to resort to and the ability to use violent means to make social and political changes, and decreases the inclination to resort to and the ability to use nonviolent means. Again, because the latter are more life sustaining, they should be given priority over the former (Regehr, 1987).

Adeniji (1987) made the connections quite clear in the following passage.

There have been more than 150 wars since 1945 fought in the developing countries, resulting in more deaths than in the Second World War. The number of countries that have been involved in these wars—about 80—is an indication of disarray in the present security system as far as the third world is concerned. Internal conflicts caused by the neglect of the non-military aspects of security, regional distrust arising from territorial claims and other political factors are inflamed by the ready availability of arms for cash or in return for ideological solidarity. . . . Through arms supplies, ideological battles are introduced into otherwise purely local disputes and solutions are rendered difficult. (p. 105)

Wilson (1986) touched another aspect of the problem when she wrote that

The massive allocation of human and material resources to military research and development (fifty percent of all natural scientists work directly or indirectly for military purposes) has distorted the developed world's perception of what is socially useful and necessary, . . . [and] . . . international institutions, because of our inability to renew or reform them, have been paralyzed by the military build-up and lack of trust between countries. (pp. 140-144)

Epps (1987b) reports on increases in Canadian National Defence contracts to university-based researchers under the Mulroney government. In Epps (1987a), former Defence Minister Perrin Beatty is quoted as saying that, "The Department of National Defence has seen steadily increasing funds for research and development-directed contracts in Canadian industry. . . . In the last ten years the expansion has been almost sevenfold" (p. 10).

4. Because Canada's biggest trading partner is the United States and about half of our manufacturing industry (not merely our arms industry) consists of American subsidiaries, much of our production and export is designed to American specifications, requirements, and interests. Thus, much of what our arms industry produces and exports is designed to satisfy demands resulting from an American cold war vision of international Soviet threats to peace. Insofar as this is a biased vision and relatively dangerous for the continued existence of life on the planet, it would be wise to reduce all activities based on this vision, including all activities related to the production and export of arms (DeRoo, 1986; Regehr, 1987).

Galbraith (1986) provocatively and succinctly gave the following account of the origin and nature of the cold war bias:

The Soviet Union is indispensable to the American military power. Fear of the Soviet Union and tension in our relations directly and overtly serve our military power; any relaxation of tension would damage the resources it commands. From this comes the great fact of our time; tension is actually cultivated to support the military power. . . . And in a world where military intelligence and enemy intention are extensively in the hands of the military, it would be astonishing were they not made to serve that tension. We accept this fact extensively—and, at budget time, very visibly. . . . The concept of one superpower's relentless will to dominate the world serves the military designs of the other superpower. The hard fact of universal retreat must be kept subordinate to that need. (p. 107)

Pentz (1986) takes a similar line.

5. To increase Canada's "capacity to assess and pursue independent and innovative foreign policy and defence options," we ought to decrease opportunities for the United States to influence our decision-making processes. Reductions in the integration of Canadian and American arms industries would significantly decrease such opportunities and they should therefore be undertaken (DeRoo, 1986; Regehr, 1987; Werlin, 1986). According to Treddenick (1986),

To confirm that military expenditures have an opportunity cost is not an argument against them; nor is the discovery that this opportunity cost is very high. Cost is only one-half of the equation, and probably the less important half. . . . The other half of the equation must come to grips with the much more intractable problem of determining how a nation's preferences for military security are formed—how it perceives threats to its interests and how it sees its own particular role in the world. (pp. 38-39)

6. Because Canada and the United States agreed to have a rough balance of arms trade through the 1963 Defense Production Sharing Arrangements (DPSA), Canada cannot expect long-run economic gains from arms trade with the United States. Continued increases in the production and export of arms must rely on overseas markets. Because Europeans tend to insist on exchanges similar to those of the DPSA, the most promising markets are those of the Third World. However, if we increase sales of arms to Third World countries then we will also increase the carnage of wars, economic dependence, and distorted social development. It has been estimated that as many as 20 million people have died in the 150 wars mentioned earlier (Regehr, 1987). Besides contributing to the massacre, increases in the importation of weapons create foreign exchange shortages that relatively poor countries try to alleviate through greater exploitation of their natural resources for export. Thus they develop dependent subsidiary economies incapable of indigenous innovation that might allow them economic independence

in the long run. Distorted economies, then, contribute directly to distorted social development, because the greatest burden of government expenditures must be devoted to international debt services rather than to social services (Regehr, 1987). In many ways, as Regehr explains, if Canadians increase their traffic in arms to Third World countries, we will inevitably reproduce some of the debilitating effects on them that trade with the United States has on us (for a more detailed analysis of this point see Michalos, 1982).

7. Increases in the production and export of arms to Third World countries would increase the militarization of those countries, not only by increasing the amount of military hardware at their disposal but by encouraging any tendencies they might have toward authoritative and centralized political decision making (Sivard, 1986). "The military," Regehr (1987) writes, "represents . . . an . . . organizational structure, with a high degree of centralization and hierarchy. The emphasis is on command and subordination, on discipline rather than creativity, with alternative thinking and approaches frequently defined as 'subversive' " (p. 14). Because increases in the militarization of Third World countries tend to undermine their democratic institutions and participative decision making, such increases ought to be resisted. As Kelly (1986) wrote,

> Both our struggle against the arms race, and our struggle for human rights in all parts of the world must be fought simultaneously. . . . It is wrong to say that human rights must be a condition for disarmament; and it is wrong to say that human rights will be the consequence of disarmament. Both must take place together, as part of a single process, the making of a democratic peace—a peace that will not be oppressive. (p. 221)

8. Increases in the production and export of arms will tend to increase the number of people in Canada whose livelihoods depend on militarization. Moreover, it is likely that most (certainly not all) people whose livelihoods depend on militarization will be relatively uncritical of militarization. Because militarization is inconsistent with our democratic institutions, inclinations, and practices, the latter would be undermined by increases in the production and export of arms. Hence, increases in the production and export of arms ought to be resisted in the interest of protecting our own democratic institutions, inclinations, and practices.

9. Because the arms industry tends to be highly specialized and concentrated, labor and material costs tend to be relatively high. As

indicated in my reply to Argument No. 11 below, the arms industry tends to be characterized by relatively low productivity. The combination of these characteristics implies that increases in arms production have inflationary effects as costs outrun productivity gains. Werlin (1986) notes that arms production is inflationary because it generates "spendable income without at the same time enlarging the supply of goods available in the market place" (p. 98). Hence, in the interest of reducing inflation, increases in the production and export of arms ought to be resisted (Melman, 1984; Regehr, 1987; Sanger, 1982).

10. It has been estimated that if 1% of the more than 50,000 nuclear weapons currently stockpiled by the United States and the former U.S.S.R. were exploded, there would be a nuclear winter of from 6 months to 3 years that most people on the planet could not survive. Because increases in the production and export of arms raise the likelihood of wars and because any wars could accidentally initiate a global nuclear war leading to a nuclear winter, increases in the production and export of arms ought to be resisted (Pentz, 1986).

In the discussion after the presentation of his paper at the 1986 Vancouver Symposium, Pentz (1986) said he would make the following

> list of possible scenarios for the privilege of unleashing Armageddon. First on my list is that one side would incorrectly perceive the other side's intentions and capabilities. We are in a chronically dangerous situation at present, because both sides constantly apply, or misapply, worst-case analysis. . . . The second most likely cause of nuclear war is an accident . . . of the kind involving a simple failure of systems. . . . Murphy's Law likes complex systems. The third most likely cause is an unpremeditated escalation of a small, local conflict. The fourth cause—which I don't believe can be eliminated—is madness in high places. (p. 301)

Similar lists of possibilities may be found in Garcia-Robles (1987) and El-Shafei (1987).

11. Because some increases in the Canadian production and export of arms will be connected to the U.S. Strategic Defense Initiative (SDI) and the latter is seriously defective technologically, militarily, and politically, we should at least resist any increases with such connections (Sivard 1986; Tsipis, 1986). Tsipis concluded his review of SDI with the pronouncement that it is "voodoo science," and according to Nadis (1988), "In October of 1986, a poll found that 98 percent of the members

of the [U.S.] National Academy of Sciences in fields most relevant to SDI research believed that SDI could not provide an effective defense of the U.S. civilian population" (p. 23).

12. Because Canada is a relatively small country with a relatively small military establishment and presence in the world, we have the opportunity to initiate changes in our defense policies without creating significant shocks or threats to other countries. New Zealand has denied nuclear-armed American warships the right to enter its ports and has established Nuclear-Weapons-Free Zones (NWFZs) covering more than 65% of its population. Anderton (1986) suggested that a basic premise of such actions is simply that "small nations must take a stand for peace themselves, if they hope to influence big nations" (p. 193). Thus, Canada might undertake a gradual phasing out of all arms manufacturing that is not directly connected to the particular needs of our own defense policies, assuming that the latter may be specified relatively independently of the policies of the American establishment. As of August 1987, there were more than 166 NWFZs in Canada, including the cities of Toronto, Vancouver, Hamilton, and Regina, and the provinces of Manitoba, Ontario, and the Northwest Territories (Davies & Marchant, 1986; Gaundun, 1987). The New Democratic Party has proposed that Canada join its Nordic neighbors (Norway, Denmark, Sweden, Finland, Greenland, and Iceland) in declaring all our countries a NWFZ, which would be an important building-block for an Arctic common security system (New Democratic Party of Canada, 1988).

The United Nations report on Unilateral Nuclear Disarmament Measures (1985) argued for a gradual reduction in arms patterned after the historical trend of gradual increases. Thus, the "de-escalation and reversal" of the arms race

> could be facilitated by unilateral initiatives of States aimed at reducing the level of international tension, gradually creating an atmosphere of mutual trust and confidence and in general improving the environment for negotiations on arms limitation and disarmament. . . . The scope of unilateral initiatives . . . could include reductions in military expenditures, reductions in the number of troops, cuts in the number of certain types of weapons or even their elimination, moratoria and freezes, policies of no-first-use of nuclear weapons, establishment of nuclear-weapon-free zones and a wide variety of restraints in military programmes. (p. 1)

13. The biggest threats to international security in the future are scarcities of raw materials, environmental degradation, declining eco-

nomic growth, and the severely unequal distribution of the world's wealth. Because increases in the production and export of arms contributes nothing and even decreases resources available to address these problems, in the interest of increasing international security, we ought to reduce expenditures on the former in favor of expenditures on the larger threats (Creighton, 1987; Sanger, 1982; United Nations, Panel, 1986). (Several attempts to construct broader, basically nonmilitaristic and globally realistic views about the nature of international security may be found in United Nations, Department for Disarmament Affairs, 1987.)

14. Because the need for arms is largely in the eye of the beholder, one ought to be skeptical about any alleged need calling for increases in the production and export of arms. Treddenick (1987) gives about 10 reasons for defense spending tending to become a bottomless pit, but the following remarks seem to capture a main source of the problem:

> As an economic good satisfying human wants, defence, at least in peacetime, is an abstract concept, one which is technically complex and generally not well understood by the public. It cannot be measured in any objective sense. Whether defence is adequately provided for, or whether the composition of defence spending, including the equipment mix, is appropriate is a matter of perceptions about intentions and relative force sizes, training, tactics, morale and so on. It is therefore impossible to say that there is too much or too little defence spending, or to say that there are too many tanks or too many ships in the same way that it is possible to say that there is too much of other types of goods. The relationship between spending on defence, including how it is spent, and how much defence capability is actually achieved is therefore highly ambiguous. This ambiguity can make defence planning a challenging occupation, but at the same time it provides economic policy makers with an expenditure instrument of a flexibility unmatched by other forms of government expenditure. (pp. 15-18)

Adeniji (1987) takes a similar line.

15. There is some evidence from a national opinion poll taken in October 1987 that most Canadians would prefer to see less emphasis on a militaristic approach to international security, which would imply less emphasis on the production and export of arms. The survey was sponsored by the North-South Institute in Ottawa, and the sponsors' analysts summarized their view of their findings as follows:

> The Canadian public seems to be on a completely different wavelength from its government in what it sees as the main threats to Canadian security and

what should be done about them. In 1987 the government allowed a Defence White Paper to be seen to speak for Canadian security policy, and the Department of National Defence to be seen to shape Canada's views on peace and war. In the year that ended with Mr. Gorbachev in Washington signing the INF Treaty [banning missiles of immediate range from Europe], NSI's [the North-South Institute's] survey shows most Canadians implicitly rejecting both the Cold War diagnoses and prescriptions of the Defence White Paper tabled by Mr. Beatty [who was then Minister of National Defence] in June.

   Canadians themselves have a different and much wider agenda for enhancing international security, including environmental, health, developmental and ethical/political goals. In the maintenance of peace, they seem likely to see Canada's best contribution in more arms control and disarmament efforts, international cooperation, conflict resolution and peacekeeping, rather than in the build-up of arms. Even among various international purposes—quite apart from needs at home—most Canadians resoundingly reject increased defence spending as a priority. (North-South Institute, 1988, p. 2)

Regarding the last quoted sentence, given the survey question "If one wanted to increase Canada's influence internationally, which do you think would be most effective?" 6.2% answered "Increase the size of our armed forces," 10.4% said "Spend more on aid for developing countries," 31.5% said "We should speak out more often on international issues," and 48.7% said "Put more emphasis on our economic and trade power." Given the question, "If the Canadian government had an additional sum of money to spend for international activities next year, which of the following options would you choose?" 5.0% said "Expand services at Canadian embassies and consulates abroad," 18.8% favored "More equipment and personnel for Canada's national defence," 28.7% favored "Expanded aid programs to Third World countries," and 44.4% wanted "Programs to increase our overseas trade" (North-South Institute, 1988, pp. 4, 12).

According to Lambert (1987), "Polls by Angus Reid and Goldfarb . . . show the majority of Canadians opposed to cruise testing, opposed to the purchase of nuclear submarines, and in favor of making Canada a nuclear weapons free zone" (p. 24).

ARGUMENTS FOR PRODUCING AND EXPORTING ARMS

In this section I review arguments that may be offered by Canadians in favor of the production and export of military arms, and I try to show that every one of them is defective.

1. Because sovereign nations have a right to defend themselves, they must have the right to purchase arms. The latter is plainly useless unless someone, at least some nation, has the right to produce and sell arms. There is no good reason to suppose that only this or that particular nation has a right to produce and sell arms. Thus, Canada or any other sovereign nation apparently has the right to produce and sell arms (Regehr, 1987). (To avoid confusion, it may be worthwhile to point out that Regehr is a staunch opponent of militarism but he has provided an excellent review of many of the arguments for both sides of the issue.)

Reply. Even if it is granted that in principle any nation has the right to produce and sell arms, it does not follow that in fact it is wise or morally right for every nation to engage in such activities. Presumably, the argument presupposes an "if all other things are roughly equal" caveat. Without such a caveat, the argument might be used to justify the production and export of arms even in situations in which such activities prevented the production of such necessities as food and shelter. As already explained, there are many situations in which just such trade-offs are made and the existence of these cases shows the inherent limitations of the rights argument.

2. Because governments in particular have a responsibility to protect their territories and citizens, they must have a responsibility to provide arms as required for this task. Such a responsibility might be impossible to fulfill without military arms. Thus, governments must have the right to purchase arms, which again implies the right of someone to produce and sell them (Regehr, 1987).

Reply. The reply to Argument No. 1 is applicable to this one as well.

3. As a member of the 16-nation North Atlantic Treaty Organization (NATO), Canada has an obligation to "contribute its fair share to the common defence." Its contribution might be made by purchasing, producing, or selling arms or any combination of these three, and Canada apparently has a right to fulfill its obligations to the alliance in any of these three ways (Canada, Department of National Defence, 1987; Regehr, 1987).

Reply. Granting that Canada has a right to fulfill its obligations in any of these three ways, one might argue that the production and export of arms ought to be abandoned in favor of meeting our obligations only by purchasing arms from others. One might be led to this conclusion as a result of being persuaded by the positive arguments presented above against the production and export of arms. Because the adoption of this policy would increase the costs of arms procurement in several ways, it might lead to an overall reduction in military hardware that would also be an attractive consequence for people taking this line. I think the costs of adopting this approach to meeting our obligations to the NATO alliance would outweigh the benefits. We would become even more dependent on the United States than we are now, with all of the problems such dependency entails.

In my view, the appropriate response to this NATO obligations argument is withdrawal from the alliance. A thorough defense of this view would require a lengthy discussion, which would be out of place here. Briefly, however, I think that this alliance, like the seven-nation Warsaw Treaty, is an anachronism. For Canada, NATO is a very expensive anachronism, because it carries a price tag of more than a billion dollars a year to keep our one brigade in Europe. As the New Democratic Party's defense critic (Blackburn, 1987) wrote in response to the Tories' Defence White Paper: "It is simply expensive symbolism" (p. 6). Even if we stay in NATO, there is no good reason to maintain this expense.

The alliances may have made sense in the 1950s, but they have increasingly become part of the problem of international insecurity rather than part of the solution. The policies of each alliance are dominated by the biased views of the United States and the former U.S.S.R., views that are effectively sensitive to East-West problems as defined by the superpowers and relatively blind to North-South problems as defined by the other 136 or so nonaligned nations on earth (Regehr, 1987). According to Sivard (1986), the United States and the former U.S.S.R.

> have less than 11 percent of the world population but in 1985 they accounted for 23 percent of the world's armed forces, 60 percent of the military expenditures, more than 80 percent of the weapons research, and 97 percent of all nuclear warheads and bombs. . . . Distrust between the two countries has been fanned by exaggerated fantasies on both sides and by careless rhetoric of political and military leaders. (p. 9)

There is no evidence that Canada has had and will have more influence on the United States inside than it would have outside NATO, but it is certainly the case that Canada's membership in the alliance adds legitimacy to United States' policies pursued through the alliance. Virtually every arms-escalating defense initiative Canada has entertained in the past 20 years, if not longer, has been justified by our alleged obligations to NATO, such as renewing the North American Aerospace Defense Agreement (NORAD); deploying and increasing the number of Canadian troops and military hardware in Europe; testing cruise missiles over Alberta; allowing low-level flights of bombers over Labrador; having B-52 flight training over British Columbia, Alberta, and Ontario; the preposterous proposal of purchasing nuclear submarines (to participate in the U.S. Navy's Forward Maritime Strategy); and allowing Canadian companies to participate in Star Wars research. Thus, in the interest of freeing Canada from its obligations to an anachronistic and dangerously biased alliance, and of strengthening such multilateral organizations as the United Nations, we ought to withdraw from NATO. (The current federal government, like the one before it, is committed to the alliance, as is clear from Canada, Department of National Defence, 1987. For brief but devastating critiques of the latter document, see Creighton, 1987; Epstein, 1987; Robinson, 1987a, 1987b.)

4. Because we have a right to fulfill our obligations of alliances by producing and selling arms, and it is profitable to do so, it is prudent to do so (Regehr, 1987). In the words of our Department of National Defence (1987), "Canadian defence spending contributes significantly to the maintenance of a robust and flexible economic environment. Defence purchases contribute to the development of internationally competitive Canadian industries" (p. 84).

Reply. For reasons already given and others yet to be presented, it cannot be granted that it is profitable and prudent to produce and sell arms, all things considered. However, even if it were granted, as in other classical cases of prisoners' dilemmas and the "tragedy of the commons," actions that are apparently reasonable from an individual's point of view narrowly construed may turn out to be disastrous given similar actions by many other individuals. Regehr (1987) pointed out that the result of such prudential reasoning is "an international arms trade that is out of control and serves as the pre-eminent vehicle for the militarization of the planet" (p. 10). What is worse, of course, is the fact mentioned above, namely, that the arms have been used to kill more than 20 million people. Furthermore, "the intermingling of military and economic considerations may blunt the nation's sensitivity to the arms race with the result that incentives to search for ways to reduce armament expenditures may be submerged" (Treddenick, 1985, p. 91). The latter consideration is obviously applicable to all of the economic arguments for increases in the production and export of arms.

5. Because the production and export of arms to members of the NATO alliance allows us to increase standardization and create valuable economies of scale, it should be encouraged (Regehr, 1987).

Reply. The reduction of the cost of producing anything that is morally, legally, and rationally acceptable is generally laudable. As indicated in the previous section, however, there are good reasons for thinking that increases in the production and export of arms are not morally or rationally acceptable.

6. Because the Canadian production and export of arms is such a small percentage of the world's total, it is relatively insignificant to particular recipients and to the general world supply of arms. Besides, as indicated above in The Canadian Arms Industry, the share of Canada's own economy devoted to armaments is also very small. So, nationally and internationally it has relatively little economic, moral, or political significance (Regehr, 1987).

Reply. Regarding the international aspect of this argument, Regehr (1987) responded as follows:

> Canada's share of annual arms sales to the Third World is about 1 per cent. Since 1945 arms transfers have provided the fuel for more than 100 wars in the Third World, producing more than 20 million military and civilian combat deaths. One per cent of those deaths amounts to 200,000—about twice the number of Canadians who have lost their lives as the result of war during this century. (p. 20)

Assuming that non-Canadian lives are worth as much as Canadian lives, and that an economically, morally, and politically significant number of the latter were lost in wars, it must be granted that the estimated 200,000 lives lost in Third World wars are also significant.

Regarding the national aspect of the argument, suppose that Treddenick's estimates are accurate and about half of 1% of the Canadian GNP is involved in arms production. In 1986 that would have been half of 1% of at least $500 billion or roughly $2.5 billion dollars. Two and a half billion dollars that year would have matched the federal government's expenditures for Family Allowances and for Research and Development (R & D) in the natural sciences. It would have been 6 times the federal government's expenditure on the environment, 13 times the expenditure for R & D in the social sciences, and 3 times the expenditure on recreation and leisure. It would have just about matched the country's expenses on community colleges, and it would have added another 22,676 new or renovated housing units to the 56,689 units funded by the federal government in 1986 (Statistics Canada, 1987a, 1987b). Clearly, because it would be unreasonable to dismiss all these national expenditures as economically, morally, and politically insignificant, it must be granted that the sixth argument is unsound.

7. The greater a nation's military strength, the greater its influence in negotiations with other nations. Because the production and sale of new arms strengthens Canada, it also increases our ability to influence other nations in the removal of all arms (Regehr, 1987).

Reply. It seems unlikely that Canada's military strength and influence based on it could be significantly increased without increasing defense expenditures beyond a point that would be acceptable even to most Canadian Cold Warriors. The people who are inclined to favor increases in our military strength tend to be the same people who favor keeping us in NATO, where we would always be dominated by the United States and the United Kingdom. Though increases in military strength are apparently not sufficient to guarantee greater influence internationally, such increases are probably not even necessary. Even relatively small and militarily weak countries are able to have significant impacts in the various international organizations of the United Nations system, and the latter in turn have significant impacts on the so-called superpowers. Although one could always haggle about the meaning of *significant impacts* and *influence* in this context, I think those who would argue that the various organizations in the United Nations system (e.g., the World Health Organization, International Labor Office, UNESCO, etc.) are uniformly insignificant or powerless would find the historical record overwhelmingly against them.

8. The more arms a nation has, the less likely it is that they will be used. Because the production and sale of arms is a necessary condition of nations having arms, the former contributes to global stability and peace (Canada, Department of National Defence, 1987; Regehr, 1987).

Reply. This argument is based on the Roman dictum that says, "If you would have peace, prepare for war." It seems to have led and to lead directly to increases in the production and export of arms around the world, and consequently, to a highly insecure system of international security (Adamichin, 1987; Carroll, 1986; Cassese, 1987; Corradini, 1987;

Robinson, 1987b; Sanger, 1982). According to Sivard (1986), as the weapons of the United States and the former U.S.S.R. become more sophisticated, "The incentive grows to be the first to use the weapons, to destroy as much as possible of the enemy's nuclear forces before they can be fired. The chances of miscalculation, the fragility of 'deterrence,' increase in proportion to the rise in numbers and the advance in technology" (p. 14).

Although increases in the numbers of nuclear weapons have not led to a nuclear war, there is a correlation between increases in the numbers of conventional weapons in Third World countries and wars (Regehr, 1975). There are also many hypothetical scenarios leading from conventional wars to a nuclear war, for example, in Greene, Percival, and Ridge (1985). Thus, in the interests of creating a more secure system of international security and reducing the numbers of wars in Third World countries, increases in the production and export of arms should be resisted (Werlin, 1986).

9. The production and export of arms should be encouraged because it will improve Canada's balance of payments, for example, especially with regard to the 1963 DPSA with the United States and with the repatriation of petrodollars (Regehr, 1987).

Reply. Because Canada and the United States agreed to have a rough balance of arms trade through the DPSA, it is impossible for us to have a significant "balance of payment surplus or a net gain in jobs" in the long run in this area. Roughly speaking, every dollar spent in Canada by the United States must be matched by a dollar spent in the United States by Canada. So, there should be no balance of payments advantage in arms trade with our biggest trading partner. In spite of DPSA, Werlin (1986) claimed that "arms spending in Canada is a major factor contributing to our trade deficit in manufactured goods" (p. 99). Watkins (1984) claimed that when American subsidiaries in Canada sell arms to the United States, part of the former's profits are given back to their American parent firms, and "there's no question that there's a net drain on the balance of payments that results from that." Besides, he claimed that because "foreign subsidiaries in Canada have a much higher tendency to import machinery and parts than do domestic, Canadian firms," that also has a negative effect on our balance of payments (p. 16).

10. The production and export of arms should be encouraged because it will create employment (Canada, Department of National Defence, 1987; Regehr, 1987).

TABLE 12.5 Jobs Created by Spending One Billion Dollars (1983 dollars)

1983-1984 DND spending	22,000
Road and highway construction	37,000
Residential construction	38,000
Consumer spending	39,000
Hospital services	51,000
Education and related services	54,000
Radio and TV broadcasting	55,000
Urban transit systems	87,000
Post Office	90,000

SOURCE: From "Military Spending," by T. Sanger (1986, January-February), *The Facts*, 8(1). Ottawa: Canadian Union of Public Employees. Reprinted with permission.

Reply. Our reply to this argument was already suggested in our reply to Argument No. 9. Regehr (1987) says:

> If military exports must, in the long run, be matched by military imports, then for every job that is created through exports, another job is lost by virtue of the reciprocal imports. Because a major part of Canada's capital defence budget is not spent in this country, Canadian military spending creates jobs in the United States, and to some extent in Europe, but not in Canada. (p. 175)

Second, because investments in the arms industry typically produce fewer jobs per dollar than investments in most other industries (Table 12.5), any new government investments in job creation ought to give priority to the latter over the arms industry (Regehr, 1987).

Furthermore, as Sanger (1982) explained,

> military activities can be regarded as contributing to structural unemployment. [Because] . . . military procurement crowds out capital investment in key civilian sectors, . . . the countries which take on the heaviest burden of military expenditure tend to suffer a progressive decline in their international competitiveness as traders in civilian goods. They lose export markets, and even some of their domestic production is displaced by imports. Thus, a large military establishment begins to undermine the capacity of a country's economy to generate new employment over the long term. (p. 40)

Hence, in the interest of increasing our capacity to create new jobs in Canada, we should withdraw from the DPSA and shift our investments to peaceful Canadian enterprises with relatively strong job creation possibilities. Additional references and arguments concerning the relatively limited job creation capacity of arms production may be found in Treddenick (1986) and Melman (1984).

11. The production of arms should be encouraged because it will generate technological spin-offs leading to increases in productivity (Regehr, 1987).

Reply. On the contrary, increases in the production and export of arms ought to be resisted in Canada because they would retard commercial industrial innovation and civilian productivity.

> Through an analysis of seventeen noncommunist industrialized countries over a period of two decades, the U.S. Council on Economic Priorities confirmed the observation that superior technological and industrial developments take place when the focus is on production for civilian use. Those economies with less emphasis on military production experienced faster growth and had a better job creation record. (Regehr, 1987, p. 165)

Figure 12.2 illustrates the inverse relationship between military expenditures as a percentage of GNP and annual rates of manufacturing productivity growth for 10 countries. Sivard (1986) wrote that

> Since 1977, when WMSE [World Military and Social Expenditures] first illustrated this negative correlation, the pattern has not changed. Among major industrial countries, the highest rates of military expenditures are associated with low growth in productivity, as in USSR, US, and UK. In contrast, Japan with a very low military burden, has a good investment record, an exceptional 9 percent average gain in productivity, low unemployment, and a highly favorable competitive position in international markets—the very goals that debtors are searching for. (p. 20)

Sanger (1982) also cited evidence produced for the Thorsson Group showing that "military expenditure had a 'very negative effect' on the gross formation of private fixed capital and an indirectly negative influence on economic growth" (pp. 37, 48-52). As more research and development funds are poured into the aerospace and electronics sectors of the economy, which are especially important to the military establishment,

> older basic industries, such as steel, automobiles, railroads, machinery and metal-working, are suffering from technological stagnation. This in turn causes lower productivity and a loss of competitiveness in those industries. . . . The situation is then often aggravated by a flight of capital to other countries, because investment at home has become unattractive. (Sanger, 1982, p. 39)

A review of additional arguments along these lines may be found in Treddenick (1986).

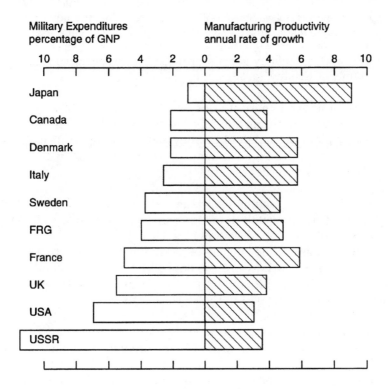

Figure 12.2. Military Burden and Productivity, 1960-1984

SOURCE: Reproduced, with permission, from *World Military and Social Expenditures 1986* (p. 20), by R. L. Sivard (1986). Copyright © 1986 by World Priorities, Inc., Washington, DC.

12. Because the export of arms helps to keep Canadian producers commercially viable and available as suppliers of our own military needs, such exports should be encouraged (Regehr, 1987).

Reply. This argument is based on a questionable assumption, namely, that the manufacture of arms should be a commercially viable enterprise. On the contrary, one could take the view that the manufacture of arms should be a government sponsored, nonprofit, public enterprise. The only arms produced or exported would be those required by Canadian forces in their routine air and sea surveillance, patrolling, and peacekeeping activities. As Regehr (1987) writes,

According to this assumption, military production is not a commercial activity like other commercial endeavours (just as prescription and other restricted drugs do not operate under usual market conditions). Thus, commercial viability is not a central question. This view of military production prevails in wartime, when military needs are defined without reference to economic opportunity or viability. (p. 68)

13. Insofar as the export of arms tends to lead to further exports of replacement parts, training and repair services, and some influence on the strategic planning and public policy making of importing countries, such exports ought to be encouraged in order to strengthen Canada's international position (Regehr, 1987).

Reply. This is an argument for the use of the same devious and dangerous influence-pedaling tactics employed by the world's major arms merchants. If Canada adopted such a policy, it would be yet another "clear case of the keepers of peace having turned freebooters" (Rasgotra, 1987, p. 136). Even if we ended up with a greater amount of international influence, it could serve no worthwhile purpose because we would have become part of the world's arms problem.

14. If Canada does not produce enough arms to appear as if it could defend itself or, minimally, as if it could provide adequate levels of surveillance for its northern borders, then the United States will probably become more active in the north. Because it is prudent to defend ourselves and our sovereignty against such increases of American activity around our northern borders, it is prudent to produce enough arms to perform this task. Producing arms for export, as indicated above, simply allows us to reduce the cost of such production (Regehr, 1987).

Reply. This argument reveals Canada's precarious position regarding cooperation with the United States. It may be safely assumed that the Americans are going to be militarily active in the north for some years, with or without the cooperation of Canada. It may also be assumed that any perceived or actual lack of cooperation by Canada would create some friction and tension between the two countries, which both countries would like to avoid. Thus, the same assumptions that led us to accept the 1957 NORAD agreement giving the United States free access to Canadian airspace could lead us to a "maritime NORAD" giving the Americans free access to our coastal waters, including the Northwest Passage through our Arctic islands (Dyer, 1988, p. 4). In both cases cooperation implies a shared vision of a Soviet threat and an escalation of arms.

As one might expect given my view of NATO and NORAD, I think it is imperative that Canadians simply refuse to go along in order to get along with the American military establishment. We should not allow ourselves to be increasingly militarized in the interest of feeding American paranoia or an irrational "military-industrial complex." As Blackburn (1987) wrote,

> We can contribute to stability and defence by putting in place surveillance, warning, and interception systems that would guarantee that no first-strike across Canadian territory could go undetected. The North American Aerospace Defence Agreement should be replaced with an agreement with the United States under which Canada would assume total responsibility for the conventional defence of its portion of the northern half of North America. (p. 11)

Presumably, the last quoted sentence is simply a diplomatic way of telling one's neighbors to mind their own business. At the same time, we should initiate multilateral discussions in the United Nations with an aim to designing an international Arctic surveillance system that would give both the United States and the former U.S.S.R. guaranteed protection against any undetected first-strike operations.

15. Given the continuous development of sophisticated contemporary arms technology around the world, it is practically impossible for Canada to avoid relatively permanent arms research and development without losing some competitive advantage. Thus, if we must have some arms research and development, we might as well try to offset its cost with exports (Regehr, 1987).

Reply. This argument is based on the assumption that marginal technological improvements are militarily significant, which is unbelievable given the current levels of conventional and nuclear arms around the world. The argument also seems to assume that there could be something like a technological final solution that would guarantee military superiority to its inventor and that would justify continuing massive R & D expenditures in search of it. Again, this assumption is unwarranted for the same reason as the first. The technological arms race presupposed by this argument ended some years ago, and everybody lost. The great task before us now is to design political institutions that will make the world secure from a military disaster.

16. Caldicott (1986) presented the following argument as representative of the view of the U.S.-based Committee on the Present Danger: "You

can't trust the Russians because they cheat on treaties. If the Soviets cheat on treaties, you can't have arms control, and if you can't have arms control, nuclear war becomes inevitable. If nuclear war is inevitable, then America has to prepare to fight and win a nuclear war" (p. 312). For our purposes, one would add: If America has to prepare to fight and win a nuclear war, then so does Canada.

Reply. If we ignore the assumption that the Soviets are any less trustworthy than the Americans, the Committee's last premise is a non sequitur. If nuclear war is inevitable then so is nuclear winter, in which most of the people of the northern hemisphere will die (Caldicott, 1986; Greene et al., 1985). The one great fact to be remembered about so-called nuclear war is that it is virtual suicide for people living in the northern hemisphere. For these people it may be assumed that there will be practically no winners or losers. It does not matter where the bombs go off first or who has more to explode. For these people there is an open question regarding what, if anything, they rationally or morally ought to do now. Quite apart from the prospect of nuclear war, we all know we are going to die sooner or later and that fact does not seem to imply any particular course of action. Different people cope with mortality in different ways. On the other hand, for those of us who do not believe that war is inevitable, it seems both reasonable and morally responsible to try to find ways to decrease its likelihood. Decreasing the production and export of arms is certainly one way.

If we ignore nuclear weapons and the possibility of a nuclear war, it is worthwhile to consider a war fought only with conventional weapons and the consequences of exploding nuclear reactors. Clearly, in any war between members of NATO and the Warsaw Pact, some nuclear reactors would be destroyed. Depending on how reactors were damaged, there would be relatively localized blow-ups, massive meltdowns, and middle-sized messes. When the reactor at Chernobyl blew its top, agricultural land, people, and animals were poisoned thousands of miles away in Sweden and the United Kingdom. No one knew exactly how much radioactive fallout would be produced by the explosion, how far the winds would carry it, in what direction and with what consequences in human casualties in the long and short run. There are about 370 operating nuclear reactors in the world now, most of which are in Europe and North America. In a war any of these might be damaged by a variety of means. In the past, people dropped bombs, killed "enemies," negotiated peace with survivors, and went home. But even if only conventional weapons were used in a war between East and West, the destruction of some of our vast numbers of nuclear reactors would guarantee that there would be deadly radioactive material carried by the winds, groundwater movements, and other natural water cycles to millions of people in North America and Europe no matter where the explosions occur. The "victors" might have no homes to go to. Even if one assumes that a war between East and West with only conventional weapons is inevitable, it does not follow that Canada ought to be increasing its production and export of arms. The predictable catastrophic consequences of such a war still leave an open question regarding what, if anything, one rationally or morally ought to do. On the other hand, the best course of action for the rest of us is still to try to decrease the likelihood of such a war by decreasing the production and export of arms.

CONCLUSION

The UNESCO Charter reminds us that "Since wars begin in the minds of men, it is in the minds of men that the defence of peace must be constructed" (UNESCO, 1989, p. 5). I am enough of a feminist to believe that even if the original authors of that sentence understood the term *men* in its generic sense, it has special reference to males. We are the ones typically socialized to be competitive, aggressive, out of touch with our feelings, and all too often arrogantly defensive of our own ignorance. So, I hope that men especially will give serious consideration to this chapter.

As I remarked at the beginning, insofar as my arguments are sound, a case should have been made for resisting the current federal government's proposed increases in the production and export of arms, and for beginning to scale down Canada's current militaristic activities. I have not recommended total disarmament or the gradual phasing out of our military establishment. On the contrary, I have suggested that the latter has a legitimate role to play both nationally and internationally with such things as routine surveillance, disaster relief, and peacekeeping. We need a defense policy based not on military might but on wisdom, compassion, and diplomacy. As the New Democratic Party of Canada (1988) put it,

Canadian security depends upon a stable international order that recognizes and respects Canadian sovereignty and territory, rather than on Canada's ability to defend itself militarily. Thus, Canada's primary responsibility in its own defence is to contribute to the development of a just international order. The role of the United Nations is central to this process. (p. 50)

REFERENCES

Adamichin, A. (1987). Working session no. 1. In United Nations Department for Disarmament Affairs, *Symposium on global security for the twenty-first century* (pp. 41-50). New York: United Nations.

Adeniji, O. (1987). Working session no. 3. In United Nations Department for Disarmament Affairs, *Symposium on global security for the twenty-first century* (pp. 99-112). New York: United Nations.

Anderton, J. P. (1986). Nuclear freedom in one country—How and why: A case study of the development of a nuclear-free policy in New Zealand. In T. L. Perry & J. G. Foulks (Eds.), *End the arms race: Fund human needs* (pp. 185-195). West Vancouver, BC: Gordon Soules.

Blackburn, D. (1987). *Canadian sovereignty, security and defence: A New Democratic response to the Defence White Paper.* Ottawa: New Democratic Party.

Caldicott, H. (1986). Commit yourself to saving the earth. In T. L. Perry & J. G. Foulks (Eds.), *End the arms race: Fund human needs* (pp. 311-320). West Vancouver, BC: Gordon Soules.

Canada, Department of National Defence. (1987). *Challenge and commitment: A defence policy for Canada* (White Paper on Defence). Ottawa: Minister of Supply and Services.

Carroll, E. J. (1986). A new concept for security in the nuclear age. In T. L. Perry & J. G. Foulks (Eds.), *End the arms race: Fund human needs* (pp. 29-36). West Vancouver, BC: Gordon Soules.

Cassese, A. (1987). Closing session. In United Nations Department for Disarmament Affairs, *Symposium on global security for the twenty-first century* (pp. 143-150). New York: United Nations.

Corradini, A. (1987). The quest for real security. In United Nations Department for Disarmament Affairs, *Symposium on global security for the twenty-first century* (pp. 151-163). New York: United Nations.

Creighton, P. (1987). Cold war heat. *The Ploughshares Monitor, 8,* pp. 4-6.

Davies, L., & Marchant, G. (1986). The special role of municipalities in working for peace. In T. L. Perry & J. G. Foulks (Eds.), *End the arms race: Fund human needs* (pp. 235-244). West Vancouver, BC: Gordon Soules.

DeRoo, R. J. (1986). Our war economy and conversion for peace. In T. L. Perry & J. G. Foulks (Eds.), *End the arms race: Fund human needs* (pp. 81-91). West Vancouver, BC: Gordon Soules.

Dyer, G. (1988, March 5). Nuclear submarines and our Canadian politics. *The Mercury,* p. 4.

El-Shafei, O. (1987). Working session no. 3. In United Nations Department for Disarmament Affairs, *Symposium on global security for the twenty-first century* (pp. 113-120). New York: United Nations.

Epps, K. (1987a). Canadian military industry update. *The Ploughshares Monitor, 8,* pp. 10-12.

Epps, K. (1987b). More military work on Canadian campuses. *The Ploughshares Monitor, 8,* pp. 8, 16.

Epstein, W. (1987). Is Canada joining the arms race? *The Ploughshares Monitor, 8,* pp. 6-7.

Galbraith, J. K. (1986). The military power: Tension as a servant; arms control as an illusion. In T. L. Perry & J. G. Foulks (Eds.), *End the arms race: Fund human needs* (pp. 103-110). West Vancouver, BC: Gordon Soules.

Garcia-Robles, A. (1987). Working session no. 2. In United Nations Department for Disarmament Affairs, *Symposium on global security for the twenty-first century* (pp. 81-90). New York: United Nations.

Gaundun, K. (1987). NWFZ: The Canadian scene. *Peace Magazine, 3,* pp. 11.

Government of Canada, Minister of Finance. (1978). *Public Accounts of Canada.* Ottawa: Minister of Supply and Service.

Government of Canada, Minister of Finance. (1982). *Public Accounts of Canada.* Ottawa: Minister of Supply and Service.

Government of Canada, Minister of Finance. (1986). *Public Accounts of Canada.* Ottawa: Minister of Supply and Service.

Government of Canada, Minister of Finance. (1988). *Public Accounts of Canada.* Ottawa: Minister of Supply and Service.

Greene, O., Percival, I., & Ridge, I. (1985). *Nuclear winter: The evidence and the risks.* Cambridge, UK: Polity Press.

Gumbleton, T. (1986). The arms race protects the power and wealth of the privileged. In T. L. Perry & J. G. Foulks (Eds.), *End the arms race: Fund human needs* (pp. 129-36). West Vancouver, BC: Gordon Soules.

Kelly, P. (1986). New forms of power: The Green Feminist view. In T. L. Perry & J. G. Foulks (Eds.), *End the arms race: Fund human needs* (pp. 207-225). West Vancouver, BC: Gordon Soules.

Lambert, S. (1987). The Canadian peace pledge campaign. *Peace Magazine, 3,* p. 24.

Melman, S. (1984). Peace, employment and the economics of permanent war. *Project Ploughshares Working Paper 84-85,* pp. 1-7.

Michalos, A. C. (1980a). *North American social report: Vol. 1. Foundations, population and health.* Dordrecht, the Netherlands: D. Reidel.

Michalos, A. C. (1980b). *North American social report: Vol. 2. Crime, justice and politics.* Dordrecht, the Netherlands: D. Reidel.

Michalos, A. C. (1981a). *North American social report: Vol. 3. Science, education and recreation.* Dordrecht, the Netherlands: D. Reidel.

Michalos, A. C. (1981b). *North American social report: Vol. 4. Environment, transportation and housing.* Dordrecht, the Netherlands: D. Reidel.

Michalos, A. C. (1982). *North American social report: Vol. 5. Economics, religion and morality.* Dordrecht, the Netherlands: D. Reidel.

Miller, J. (1986). The arms race and suffering in the Third World: One problem. In T. L. Perry & J. G. Foulks (Eds.), *End the arms race: Fund human needs* (pp. 125-127). West Vancouver, BC: Gordon Soules.

Nadis, S. (1988). After the boycott. *Science for the People, 20,* 21-26.

New Democratic Party of Canada. (1988). *Canada's stake in common security.* Ottawa: Author.

North-South Institute. (1988). Fighting different wars: Canadians speak out on foreign policy. *Review '87/Outlook '88,* 1-13.

Pentz, M. (1986). To prevent nuclear war and promote nuclear disarmament: It's time for a new look. In T. L. Perry & J. G. Foulks (Eds.), *End the arms race: Fund human needs* (pp. 271-295). West Vancouver, BC: Gordon Soules.

Perry, T. L. (1986). What the arms race is doing to people in the Third World. In T. L. Perry & J. G. Foulks (Eds.), *End the arms race: Fund human needs* (pp. 167-177). West Vancouver, BC: Gordon Soules.

Prince, M. J. (1986). The Mulroney agenda: A right turn for Ottawa? In M. J. Prince (Ed.), *How Ottawa spends; 1986-87: Tracking the Tories* (pp. 1-60). Toronto: Methuen.

Rasgotra, M. (1987). Working session no. 3. In United Nations Department for Disarmament Affairs, *Symposium on global security for the twenty-first century* (pp. 129-139). New York: United Nations.

Regehr, E. (1975). *Making a killing: Canada's arms industry.* Toronto: McClelland & Stewart.

Regehr, E. (1987). *Arms Canada: The deadly business of military exports.* Toronto: James Lorimer.

Robinson, B. (1987a). Canada's White Paper doesn't add up. *The Ploughshares Monitor, 8,* p. 9.

Robinson, B. (1987b). Is NATO hopelessly outnumbered? *The Ploughshares Monitor, 8,* pp. 10-13.

Sanger, C. (1982). *Safe and sound: Disarmament and development in the eighties.* Ottawa: Deneau.

Sivard, R. L. (1986). *World military and social expenditures 1986.* Washington, DC: World Priorities.

Sivard, R. L. (1987). *World military and social expenditures 1987-8.* Washington, DC: World Priorities.

Statistics Canada. (1976). *Federal government finances.* Ottawa: Minister of Supply and Services.

Statistics Canada. (1979). *Federal government finances.* Ottawa: Minister of Supply and Services.

Statistics Canada. (1982). *Federal government finances.* Ottawa: Minister of Supply and Services.

Statistics Canada. (1985). *Federal government finances.* Ottawa: Minister of Supply and Services.

Statistics Canada. (1987a). *Canada year book 1988.* Ottawa: Minister of Supply and Services.

Statistics Canada. (1987b). *Federal government finance 1985.* Ottawa: Minister of Supply and Services.

Treddenick, J. M. (1984). *The arms race and military Keynesianism* (Report No. 3). Kingston: Royal Military College of Canada, Center for Studies in Defence Resources Management.

Treddenick, J. M. (1985). The arms race and military Keynesianism. *Canadian Public Policy—Analyse de Politiques, 11,* 77-91.

Treddenick, J. M. (1986). *The military Keynesianism debate* (Report No. 9). Kingston: Royal Military College of Canada, Center for Studies in Defence Resources Management.

Treddenick, J. M. (1987). *The economic significance of the Canadian defence industrial base* (Report No. 15). Kingston: Royal Military College of Canada, Center for Studies in Defence Resources Management.

Tsipis, K. (1986). Technical and operational considerations of space-based defensive systems. In T. L. Perry & J. G. Foulks (Eds.), *End the arms race: Fund human needs* (pp. 37-46). West Vancouver, BC: Gordon Soules.

UNESCO. (1989). *Yearbook on peace and conflict studies 1987.* New York: Greenwood.

United Nations, Department for Disarmament Affairs. (1985). *Unilateral nuclear disarmament measures.* New York: United Nations.

United Nations, Department for Disarmament Affairs. (1987). *Symposium on global security for the twenty-first century.* New York: United Nations.

United Nations, Expert Group on the Relationship between Disarmament and Development. (1981). *Disarmament and development* (The Thorsson Report). New York: United Nations.

United Nations, Panel of Eminent Personalities in the Field of Disarmament and Development. (1986). *Disarmament and development.* New York: United Nations.

Wallace-Deering, K. (1986). The economics of war and peace. In T. L. Perry & J. G. Foulks (Eds.), *End the arms race: Fund human needs* (pp. 75-80). West Vancouver, BC: Gordon Soules.

Watkins, M. (1984). Roundtable discussion. *Project Ploughshares Working Paper 84-85,* pp. 11-18.

Werlin, D. L. (1986). Conversion to peaceful production. In T. L. Perry & J. G. Foulks (Eds.), *End the arms race: Fund human needs* (pp. 93-102). West Vancouver, BC: Gordon Soules.

Wilson, L. M. (1986). Blessed are the peacemakers. In T. L. Perry & J. G. Foulks (Eds.), *End the arms race: Fund human needs* (pp. 137-145). West Vancouver, BC: Gordon Soules.

Index

About the Author

Alex C. Michalos has four university degrees, a B.A., M.A., B.D., and Ph.D. He taught philosophy and social sciences at the University of Guelph before joining the Faculty of Management and Administration at the University of Northern British Columbia. He was elected to the Royal Society of Canada in 1993.

He has published 16 books, 50 articles, and 160 reviews. Most of his scholarly work, consulting, and teaching has been concerned with improving the quality of life through applications of science and technology, and improving science and technology by recognizing them as human creations whose ultimate justification lies in their capacity to improve the quality of life.

His first four books (1969-1978) involve the integration of mathematical logic and the formal theories of probability and statistics with human values to be used in practical decision making, the application of probability theory to the problem of determining the acceptability of scientific theories, and a general theory of rational and moral decision making.

His five-volume treatise, *North American Social Report: A Comparative Study of the Quality of Life in Canada and the USA from 1964 to 1974* (1980-1982), received the Secretary of State's Award for Excellence in interdisciplinary studies in the area of Canadian Studies. It is the most extensive and intensive attempt to integrate the results of scientific research in sociology, economics, psychology, geography, politics, and environmental science to provide a quantitative measure of the quality of life.

His Science for Peace volume on *Militarism and the Quality of Life* (1989) argued that some scientific research and development was counterproductive from the point of view of improving the quality of life, making it necessary for researchers, first, but finally for all citizens to consider ways to obtain an optimum mix of appropriate research and development.

His four-volume *Global Report on Student Well-Being* (1991-1993) gives the results of a survey of more than 18,000 university students in 39 countries. It is the biggest international survey of students ever undertaken and involves the most extensive testing of a social scientific theory across national boundaries. The theory, which was invented by Michalos, is called Multiple Discrepancies Theory. It provides a new foundation for research in technology and risk assessment, microeconomics, exchange and decision theories, and moral consequentialist theories.

His 50 published scholarly articles include studies of rational and moral decision making; values in science and in science education; values in the sociological, historical, and philosophical study of science and technology; a design for a science court to adjudicate controversial public issues in technology and science; the role of facts and values in technology and risk assessment; the quantitative study of the growth and quality of science and technology; feminism and the quality of life; the taxation of wealth; and the impact of public goods on human migration.

He founded and still edits two scholarly journals, *Social Indicators Research* (an international and interdisciplinary journal for quality-of-life measurement) and the *Journal of Business Ethics*. He has also served on the editorial boards of the *Journal of Medicine and Philosophy, Research on Philosophy and Technology, Theory and Decision, International Journal of Value-Based Management,* and *Optimum* (the journal of public sector management).

He is a past President of the International Society for Philosophy and Technology (1983-1985), a past member of the Board of Governors of the Philosophy of Science Association (1978-1982), and the current Chair of the Working Group on Social Indicators of the International Sociological Association.

He has been a management consultant to the Department of Veterans' Affairs; Department of Secretary of State; Statistics Canada; Correctional Services of Canada; Science Council of Canada; Department of Industry, Trade and Commerce; Regional Planning Board of Hamilton-Wentworth (Ontario); Solicitor General of Nova Scotia; United Nations Educational, Scientific and Cultural Organization (UNESCO, Paris); the Organization for Economic Cooperation and Development (OECD, Paris); the Royal Commission on Electoral Reform and Party Financing; the Ontario Fair Tax Commission; and government agencies of Norway, Sweden, Germany, Japan, Italy, and the United States.